Advances in Teacher Education

Volume 1

Advances in Teacher Education

Editors:

Lilian G. Katz and James D. Raths
University of Illinois
Champaign, IL

Editorial Board

Advances in Teacher Education Volume 1

Editors:

Lilian G. Katz and James D. Raths

University of Illinois at Urbana-Champaign

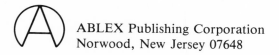

ABLEX Publishing Corporation
Norwood, New Jersey 07648

ISBN: 0-89391-185-2
ISSN: 0748-0067

ABLEX Publishing Corporation
355 Chestnut Street
Norwood, New Jersey 07648

Contents

Introduction

One of the characteristics of teacher education is that while the titles of many books, articles, and research presentations suggest that the field is burgeoning, very few persons identify with it. Perhaps because of influences that arose from as far away as Europe and as long ago as 200 or 300 years, most persons in teacher education identify more readily with a "discipline" than with teacher education. Ask professors to name the field in which they attend national conventions, subscribe to journals, or submit research reports, and the answers that are likely to be forthcoming are English education, mathematics education, social studies education, early childhood education, reading education, science education, secondary education, and the like.

The teacher education research endeavor is beset with other problems. The major problem is perhaps the view of critics, kibitzers and other observers who feel that the only central concern in teacher education is determining what it is that teacher educators should teach and teacher candidates should learn. Of course, everyone's field looks simple from the outside, and none more so than teacher education. And yet those in the field know that there are many, many avenues of inquiry which deserve attention beyond that of merely defining what it is that should be taught. This series, *Advances in Teacher Education,* is dedicated to the illumination of the problems that we face.

The papers which comprise this first volume contribute to the field in fairly distinct ways. The first three chapters address the question, "Why prepare teachers at universities?" There are still some people who see teachers as technicians, and not very precise ones at that, who could easily be prepared in a normal school or a community college. Harry Broudy defends the intellectual base of teacher education and suggests the appropriateness of its being carried out in university settings. The age old dilemma of professional training vs. professional education is addressed in two companion papers authored by Miriam Ben-Peretz and Margaret Buchmann. As evidence of the currency of this dispute and its cross-professional relevance, it is interesting to note that for many years a major eastern U.S. university refused to "hood" medical students at graduation time since the "hood" is the symbol of attaining a research degree; the faculty at this distinguished university recognized that medical students are trained and not educated. In teacher education, the dilemma of training candidates to cope with today's problems and teaching them how to deal with as yet unanticipated problems still causes furor. Some light is cast on this issue by suggesting the importance of the subject-matter components of teacher-education programs and by urging that teacher candidates be invited to extend their ability to solve new problems, not to apply recipes thought to be efficacious to the current ones.

A second issue addresses the way in which candidates acquire appropriate behaviors, skills, attitudes, and dispositions for effective teaching. Donald M. Medley's contribution, acknowledged as 1982's outstanding article in teacher education by the American Association of Colleges of Teacher Education (AACTE), sets out a distinction between *competency* and *competence* that is helpful in understanding what teacher educators are trying to do, and their limitations. David Gliessman seems to accept the notion that behavior can be changed and speaks to the question of what practices are useful in changing it. R. P. Tisher's contribution looks at less systemic influences on the behavior of teachers, namely the process of induction into the profession, and suggests ways that teachers and teacher educators might take advantage of the opportunities this process affords to improve teaching practice.

In a third section, Professor Heather Carter addresses the question, "Who are the teacher edcuators?" Her preliminary work is effective in better understanding the mentality that teacher educators bring to their tasks and the frustration they feel in carrying them out.

A fourth segment of this volume focuses on the evaluation issues in teacher education. Marleen Pugach describes current trends and issues in the evaluation of candidates from admission through certification. Tom Fox tells about evaluating a particular teacher education program that accentuates the issues and the realistic day-to-day problems that evaluators face, including the difficulty of working together as a team in carrying out program evaluation.

The volume is crowned by the final chapter, an eloquent call for an extended period of preparation for teachers. No other profession in the United States provides for entry level status of candidates after only four years of preparation. George Denemark and Nutter explain why current practice is unreasonable and why more time is needed to properly implement the ideas that are expressed in the first nine chapters of this volume.

This series is dedicated to giving teacher education a broader, more respectable visibility by highlighting the scholarship that is taking place. Already, the editors are busy soliciting manuscripts for succeeding volumes of *Advances in Teacher Education*. One of the dilemmas of scholarship is that, on the one hand, we want to prize our own personal experiences and learn from them. It is unusual for people not to attempt to make sense of the events, the responses, and the experiences that they undergo. On the other hand, our experiences are often sheltered or interpreted through the lenses of our intuitive theories which can be blinding. We need to continually reconsider our experiences in the light of data and the ideas provided by high quality scholarship. It is our belief that the chapters in this volume will contribute to this end.

Lilian Katz
James Raths
Urbana, 1984

1

The University and the Preparation of Teachers*

H. S. Broudy
University of Illinois at Champaign-Urbana

It would be difficult to imagine a university without teachers and students, so that, in a broad sense, the preparation of teachers is about as old as the idea of a university itself. The medieval university was authorized to grant licenses to teach; the examination for the doctoral degree included a demonstration by candidates that they could carry on a disputation and otherwise comport themselves as members of the guild of teachers. The candidates readied themselves for the final test by what today would be called practice teaching, imitating the instructional methods of their masters.

In the modern university, the scholar is expected to become a teacher without learning to teach; "scholar" and "teacher" are regarded as synonymous terms. Dissident students in the late 1960s and early 1970s challenged this assumption with rude remarks about professors' unwillingness and inability to teach (complaints that were not uncommon even in the medieval universities).

The principle of university teaching—do unto others what has been done unto you—works fairly well when the student is mature and disposed to become an apprentice in scholarship, at least as a major in the field. It has never worked with very young pupils or those reluctant to study—at any age. With such tutees, teaching had to be artful and, as educationists ever since the Sophists have hoped, an art as well. Hence, pedagogy, as a field of study, has a long history. In our country, Horace Mann more than a century ago institutionalized pedagogy in normal schools. In time they become

---

* Centennial Visiting Professor Address, Texas A & M University, January 22, 1976.

four-year collegiate institutions, while on university campuses colleges, schools, and departments of education became common.

University schools of education have attempted both to prepare teachers and to carry on the study of education after the fashion of other professional schools, with their disciplinary study, theory about the problems of practice, and the testing of theory by experiments. They have never quite succeeded in being fully accepted by the professoriate in the established professional schools; they were not intellectual enough for the disciplinarians and not sufficiently research oriented for engineering and medical-school faculties. But insofar as schools of education trained classroom teachers, they attracted large numbers of students to low-cost curricula. They had a strong financial clout in the arena of academic finance.

Many of us wonder why schools of education have not emerged from their ambiguous situation, while schools of engineering and agriculture succeeded beyond the fondest expectations of the advocates of the land-grant colleges. My view is that colleges of education have not been fully committed to a genuinely professional preservice program of teacher preparation. The *performance-based* or *competency-based teacher training* movement supports my opinion, not only because it has strong financial and political support, but also because it is the most recent effort to reduce the training of teachers to a technical or at best a craft level. That this is tolerated in a modern university priding itself on high intellectual and professional standards is itself an intriguing problem.

Is the answer to be found in the fact that acquiring a teaching certificate is for most university students—unlike students at other types of institutions—not the primary reason for attendance? Is it that the teaching certificate is a low cost, undemanding bonus incidental to acquiring the AB or BS degree? The questions that have been raised about Performance-based Teacher Education (PBTE) have relevance for the future role of the university in the preparation of teachers. Competency-based Teacher Education (CBTE) is a response to a general indictment of the public schools. It accuses the schools of failure to achieve their goals and places the blame for the failure first on the teacher and ultimately on the institutions preparing teachers. CBTE attempts to make teacher preparation and certification agencies responsible for competence.

PBTE/CBTE

It may seem puzzling that anyone with a sound heart and tolerably clear head would dissent from the current enthusiasm for competency-based programs of teacher training and other educational personnel. It is no wonder that arguments against CBTE proposals are dismissed as misunderstanding, defensiveness of the status quo, and fear lest colleges of education be shown up for their ineffectiveness in preparing teachers who, in turn, allegedly have caused the public schools to become "disaster areas." A conclusion, interestingly enough, that is not borne out by recent Gallup polls. Nor is it any wonder that the dissenters are not numerous; not too many institutions are inclined to buck the U.S. Office of Education, AACTE, state legislatures, and eminent professors of education. And yet there are some vocal dissenters and many more quiet ones who have doubts about the theoretical bases for the movement, its practicability, and its effects on the future of professional education for school personnel.

Inasmuch as nobody, as far as I know, favors incompetency-based teacher education programs, CBTE advocates must have a special meaning of competence in mind. Is it a set of special research-based criteria of competence not available or not utilized by conventional programs? But research has neither uncovered such criteria nor provided evidence that CBTE programs achieve their objectives any better than other approaches. Nor has research diminished the number of teaching models, strategies, and approaches that are competing for ideological allegiance and financial support.

It is not general competence that distinguishes CBTE, but rather how teaching competence is to be identified, achieved, and tested. CBTE proposes to define competence in terms of prespecified performances stated as segments of overt behavior; it argues that practicing the performance directly is more efficient than achieving it indirectly through the conventional courses. Finally, it tests competence by having the prospective teacher perform the desired performance. The main force of competence training, therefore, lies in that it contrasts an overt performance with the conventional program's promise of performance. Accordingly, the key to the CBTE rationale is an inventory of performances that count as the criteria for the presence or absence of competence. Some such inventories contain as few as 50 items; some are measured by the foot, but in general the more items the better.

Now it is possible to have a course-based program consisting of a set of courses and a set of performances and a performance test, and this indeed is what many advocates of CBTE *seem* to propose; but two factors make it unlikely that this is the form such programs will take. One is the common-sense notion that, if performance is to be the test of competence, the best way of passing the test is to practice the performance; the other is that in the programs recommended for CBTE the key activity seems to be the compiling of lists of performances into which the teaching act can be sliced, moduled, and practiced.

Some Theoretical Considerations

When competence is translated into test performances, it is important that they be stated in behavioral terms; skills that are manifested in overt behavior are the least questionable tests of competence. It has never been denied that, insofar as teaching or supervision are skills or composed of skill components, they can be reduced to identifiable, observable behavior sequences, although there is some doubt whether putting all the bits together is itself a skill or a higher cognitive process. If all that PBTE means is that the teaching skill has a performance component, there is little room for controversy.

Controversy arises at the point where teaching as the unified act of a person exercising a skill is equated with the overt behaviors to which it has been reduced. Are judgment, organization of responses, choice of teaching strategies, and other teaching decisions reducible to overt performances? Do promoters of CBTS/PBTE really mean to exclude all objectives not so reducible, or do they mean by performance something broader than publicly observable, overt behavior?

It is difficult to find a general answer in the numerous lists of objectives and competences, and the performance kits that are flooding the market. Some objectives are as broad as "ability to conduct a meaningful discussion," and some as narrow as "ability to adjust an opaque projector." The broader the objective, the more difficult it is to capture its character in purely behavioral terms. Further, the broader the objective, the greater the variety of behaviors and tactics that can be used to reach it, so that no single behavioral test represents it unambiguously.

There is much to be said for making instructional outcomes as precise as possible and to measure these outcomes as accurately as possible. But the converse is not true, that only that which has been specified and measured has been learned—even at the end of an instructional episode. It certainly runs counter to common sense to believe that life outcomes of schooling can be specified in advance and tested on demand and that, if they are not, they are not worth achieving.

Some Professional Considerations

The theoretical difficulties with CBTE, insofar as it equates competence with the performance of prespecified behaviors, are almost directly translatable into professional difficulties. These are of two sorts: one deals with the kind of preparation a professional program has to provide and whether it ought to be offered at a university; another is the type of person who is admitted to the professional program and the status of professionals in terms of remuneration, prestige, etc. I shall concentrate on the first difficulty.

There is a difference between a professional school program (of law, architecture, engineering, argiculture) and one that is strictly technical (court stenographer, lathe operator, repairer of farm machinery). The difference consists in the range of problems practitioners are expected to deal with and the way they deal with them. With respect to teachers, the professional duties include not only the skills of instruction and classroom management, but also the knowledge which enables diagnosis, decision making, and judgment—in short, contextual knowledge. By contrast, craftsmen or technicians are restricted to specific operations, and their decisions are confined to judging whether a given situation requires the application of a particular rule.

Occupational training tends to be performance based; professional education uses performance to illustrate general principles. The professional schol is designed to teach the student theory; subsequent practice as an intern or on the job is supposed to supply the familiarity with the problems of professional practice and the perfection of special skills to cope with them. Most preservice programs of teacher education follow this general design, but there is great pressure to move these programs in the direction of occupational training; in some states, there is a movement to provide training in the field, rather than in schools of any kind. Perhaps the best example of performance based occupational training is apprenticeship. Apprentices imitate the master with whom they work on the job. Professional education is almost never an apprenticeship (which may follow the receiving of the degree).

How far a program can claim to be professional depends on the cognitive demands it makes on the prospective practitioner. Any overt act—especially if it is broken down into small segments—can be performed to some acceptable criterion of correctness by imitation, practice, and correction. This can be accomplished without the practitioner understanding why the performance is appropriate. In other words, theory—which alone provides explanation and understanding—is not necessary for correct performance. Or to put it differently, although there may be a rationale of correct performance, the individual performer *need* not be aware of it and, contrariwise, knowledge of it does not guarantee a correct performance.

If teaching can be reduced to a set of imitable performances, two training methods are immediate candidates to supplant conventional programs containing large segments of theory, principles, and the like. One is the apprentice program, which is not feasible; the other is a technician type of training in which practice of procedures according to rules constitutes the bulk of instruction. The advantages of this latter program are not insignificant: First, it would downgrade the scholastic aptitude requirements for entry in the program, because scholastic aptitude is pretty much aptitude for theory; second, the program could be carried on in postsecondary institutions other than four-year colleges; and, finally, as paraprofessionals, teachers would not command or expect a "professional" salary.

For the technician route, there is little doubt that the PBTE program has great advantages. It will not take long for shrewd students and administrators to note that a two-year course in a community college can turn out paraprofessionals, and that the university can be bypassed altogether. For the professional route, one must be ready to invest heavily in context-building knowledge—both scientific and humanistic—if teachers are to justify their claim for a voice in curriculum design and autonomy in pedagogical decision. The broader the range of responsibility, the less practice guided by predetermined rules can be mechanically applied; the responsibility is justified by superior knowledge and perspective, by understanding the *why* of the rules. CBTE/PBTE cannot theoretically manage this contextual knowledge without surrendering its basic rationale.

Practical Difficulties

Let us assume, for the sake of argument, that the theoretical and professional objections are ill-founded or answered. Consider the tests of (a) writing behavioral objectives, (b) translating them into performances, (c) testing or monitoring the performer, (d) evaluating the program training the performer, and (e) evaluating and accrediting the institution offering the program purporting to train the performer.

1. The writing of objectives is onerous. It takes time and endless editing by committees, because objectives are supposed to represent a consensus. Furthermore, objectives can be stated at many levels of generality and in any number of dimensions: knowledge, skills, attitudes, character traits, social roles, ideologies. This is not surprising inasmuch as the school amiably adopts as obligations all the distresses of humanity and society.

2. Clearly the translation of objectives into behavioral language is even more exacting and time consuming, especially when the outcomes contain dispositional terms such as "ability to do X" or such cognitive operations as understanding, explaining, judging, or appreciating. No less sticky is finding performance equivalents of "paying attention," "being considerate," and a whole slew of attitudes covered by the word "relating." Furthermore, since motives, intentions, and perceptions of meaning are notoriously subjective and inaccessible to external observation, the task of describing external observable behaviors that are reliable indicators of them is something like isolating and naming the behaviors that will betray the intent of spouses to deceive each other.

Thus even if in principle it were possible to translate all educational objectives into criterion performances, it would still be a job that nobody with anything better to do would willingly undertake. That it is, nevertheless, being done is an indication that there are people in the school business who do not think they have anything better to do or have no choice in the matter.

3. Suppose that the objectives have been written, the performances defined and bundled into modules. Let it be assumed, further, that the apparatus to permit students to do what is expected of them is ready and in place. The next step is to check each student on each performance. Did he/she do a, b, c, . . . or not? Somebody, somewhere in the system, must certify this for every performance and for every student. This is no mean logistical feat but one that, one hopes, will be brought off conscientiously, because all the claims to efficiency and credibility of CBTE depend on it.

Clearly either the teacher-preparation faculty or someone else will have to make the test. If the faculty does so and certifies the performance, then its work will take on great importance, because this will be the foundation for the evaluation of the program and the institution as well as of the certification of the student. The degree of trust to be placed in professors of education is gratifyingly impressive, especially in view of the distrust of grades given by the very same faculty members. Presumably observing performances, by requiring less judgment than the awarding of grades, makes faculty more trustworthy.

If, on the contrary, the professor's word is not to be trusted, then the several layers of bureaucracy will themselves have to monitor every student in every performance or some highly representative sample of them. But unless there is more reason to trust the integrity of bureaucrats than than of faculty, they too will have to be checked for their competence and integrity.

Without being overly cynical, we can expect that instead of all this checking and testing we may settle for a monitorial illusion. In other words, documents testifying to competence will be accepted at their face value much as grades now are. From my conversations with legislators, certification officials, et al., this seems to be all they really want—a document assuring complaining constituents that monitoring has been attested to, not necessarily that it has been done or done conscientiously and competently.

On theoretical, professional, and practical grounds, there still are reasons for dissent from the CBTE movement if it really means what it claims in behalf of "performance" and "competence." With those proponents who are using these terms as honorific slogans for polemical and political purposes, there is little point in dissenting or agreeing.

THE ROLE OF THE UNIVERSITY

What a university chooses to do is decided by its governing authorities, and these authorities can offer technician training if they choose to do so. Yet the heavy investment of a good university in scholarship both in the disciplines and in its professional schools would seem to indicate that it should concentrate its resources on genuinely professional preservice and postgraduate teacher-education programs. Such programs should demand the same sort of cognitive ability and career commitment that are now expected of students in engineering, law, agriculture, architecture, and other well-established callings.

There is an important difference, however, between the intellectual base for the teaching professional and for the prospective engineer, physician, agricultural expert, or lawyer. These professions have their theory base in generalizations derived from empirical science or highly codified bodies of principles and precedents that are accepted by the members of the guild. This is not the case in education. In this field, the important empirical generalizations are very few. Education has to rely on a great variety of disciplines to provide contexts and perspectives for the human encounter we call teaching. For every item that we teach *to* the pupil, there are dozens of ideas, images, concepts, categories *with* which we teach but do not teach *to* anybody.

Unfortunately, the nature of building is not clear, although the lack of facility in context building and context apprehension is quickly discernible. For one thing, the context-building resources furnished by the study of psychology, history, philosophy, and the arts operate tacitly more often than explicitly. Like good manners, they work best when one no longer has to pay attention to them. For another, the disciplines as learned in school are transformed in time into structure or schemata while many of the details are forgotten, so that tests of retention are not indicative of the presence of these interpretive structures. Yet a lack of such structures is far harder to remedy than a lack of specific items of knowledge or skill.

It is a sad circumstance that only in an educational depression, when there is a real or imagined surplus of teachers, can the university experiment with a genuinely professional program. For some of the reasons already mentioned, a low-cost, intellectually undemanding teacher certification program is an attractive option for the university. The unexpressed hope that somehow being intelligent enough to acquire the AB or BS degree will make up for very meager professional training has been proved wrong. Although the public schools are not the disasters proclaimed by their critics, the problems confronting the classroom teacher have proved to be more than many of them can manage with the training provided by the ordinary certification, preservice program.

This is perhaps the time to devote some of the unique resources of the university to shaping a genuinely professional unity of theory and practice that has eluded American educationists for more than 100 years.

2

Curriculum Theory and Practice in Teacher-Education Programs

Miriam Ben-Peretz
University of Haifa

How should curricular issues be dealt with in teacher education? The basic approach put forth in this chapter is that "teacher education cannot simply transmit solutions that others have devised. The more fundamental task is to develop the teacher's capacity for informed problem solving" (Feiman, 1979, p. 63). Informed problem solving is perceived here in the context of curriculum implementation by teachers whose role is to shape curricula to the needs of their own teaching situations rather than accept solutions proposed by curriculum developers who function outside of the school. For many teachers, preservice training consists largely of separate theoretical and practical programs which do not involve prospective teachers in "research and development as consumers, participants, partners or planners" (Brown & McIntyre, 1982, p. 50). These practices do not adequately prepare students for their professional life. The field of curriculum is proposed as an appropriate area for involving teachers, in pre- and inservice programs, because it may well develop their capacities for problem solving in their daily task of curriculum implementation and lesson planning.

This chapter argues for a more central role for curriculum theory and practice in curriculum development in teacher-education programs. The nature of curricular expertise required by teachers in their everyday professional activities is analysed and implications for teacher education are noted.

One of the enduring problems of teacher education pertains to the nature of expertise required by teachers in order to act as professionals. Lortie (1975) describes the complexity of the teaching craft which is defined as a tenuous, uncertain affair calling for a combination of subject knowledge, planning abilities, and interpersonal skills. Yet, Lortie's review of schooling reveals that "teaching does not require as much preparation as some professions, crafts, or other skilled fields. Teaching is relatively high on general schooling and somewhat low on specialized schooling" (p. 60).

Teachers themselves are highly critical of the professional preparation they received (National Education Association [NEA], 1967; Lortie, 1975). Thus, a majority of teachers participating in the NEA study claimed that they had too little preparation in the practical aspects of teaching, including the use of instructional materials. The professors who teach "how to teach" are said to be too remote from classroom reality and offer student teachers little help for their daily planning and execution of instruction.

Accepting the notion that a professional group possesses shared knowledge not available to laymen, it is disturbing to note that teachers "do not claim to be common partakers in a shared body of specialized knowledge" (Lortie, 1975, p. 80). In other professions, such as law and medicine, practical experience is systematically codified and becomes part of the shared professional knowledge which allows new generations to pick up where earlier ones left off. According to Lortie, teachers are not inclined to see themselves as sharing in a common "memory"; they tend to fall back upon individual recollections and solutions to their professional problems.

In such a situation, teachers may be lacking some of the expertise demanded by school reforms, such as the establishment of comprehensive schools or the implementation of innovative curricula. According to P. H. Taylor (1978) and Hacker (1975), innovations have become an integral aspect of the teaching profession. McLaughlin and Marsh (1978), reporting on the Rand Change Agent Study (Berman & McLaughlin, 1977), maintain that successful implementation of an educational innovation, such as an innovative curriculum, depends on the active involvement of teachers as decision makers. Teachers play a leading role in curriculum implementation (Connelly, 1972; Connelly & Ben-Peretz, 1980; Fox, 1977; Hacker, 1975; Schulz, 1981). It is even claimed that: "in a sense, teachers and administrators need to reinvent the wheel each time curriculum change is brought to or generated within the school" (Czajkowski & Patterson, 1980, p. 172).

Given these prevailing conditions a number of questions arise:

- For what functions and in what contexts do teachers require curriculum expertise?
- In what ways is the curricular expertise of a teacher different from the expertise of curriculum developers?
- What are the components of curriculum expertise, theory and practice, which can or should be incorporated in teacher education programs?
- What are the roles of inservice teacher education in helping teachers with curriculum issues?

TEACHERS' CURRICULAR FUNCTIONS

In order to explicate the special nature of curricular expertise required of teachers, some of the relevant functions of teachers and the special contexts in which they may be asked to demonstrate curricular competencies must be examined.

Teachers are considered to be central figures in curriculum implementation whether old or new. They may fulfill this role in a variety of ways. Teachers may be viewed as neutral implementors, transmitters of curricular "messages," such as required content and designed learning experiences, who achieve predetermined goals through "teacher-proof" materials. Another view recognizes the considerable influence teachers have on the implementation process and assumes teachers to be full partners in the process of curriculum development as "user-developers" (Connelly, 1972). Teachers are expected to adapt and mold curriculum materials to the requirements of their specific educational situation. According to this view, the curriculum potential of any given set of materials encompasses developer interpretations as well as possible uses that might be revealed by external analysts or implementors. "If we look upon materials as the end product of a creative process, then any single interpretation yields only a partial picture of the whole" (Ben-Peretz, 1975). The various approaches to teachers' functions in curriculum implementation, based on a review by Connelly and Ben-Peretz (1980), are summarized in Figure No. 1.

The ideas of curriculum developers about goals, appropriate content, and instructional strategies, designated X, are translated by them into curricular materials such as guides or text books, changing somewhat in this process, and therefore designed as X'. Teachers who use these materials may serve as agents who implement these ideas as faithfully as possible. Because of the nature of changing classroom situations, X' is transformed into X''. Whenever teachers are treated by policymakers as passive consumers of external innovations, it is considered ideal if $X = X' = X''$. This is the reason for developing "teacher-proof" curricula. Even if teachers are expected to make sure that chosen curriculum materials are implemented without change, it is deemed necessary to educate them specifically for this task.

The ability to grasp the full meaning of curriculum materials is a prerequisite for their professional use in classrooms. This ability has to be developed in pre- and inservice teacher-education programs. The view of teachers as active decision-makers, who have an important impact on the implementation of curricular ideas, require the necessary background in instruction and curriculum matters. Manolakes (1980) views curriculum modifications, and the matching of them to specific groups of children, as the central professional activity of teachers. This calls for specific training

FIGURE 1   Approaches to Teachers' Functions in Curriculum Implementation

Teacher-proof Curricula	Teachers as active Implementors	Teachers as Partners in Development
X ↓ X' ↓	X ↓ X' ↓	X ↓ X' ↓
Materials designed to minimize teacher influence on programs.	Teacher assumed to have impact on implementation of curricular ideas. Implementation-oriented strategies aimed at helping teachers understand curricular innovations.	Teachers assumed to be full partners in development as user-developers. Teacher inquiry oriented toward discovery of curriculum potential, change, and transformation of materials, devising of new alternatives, and decision making.
↓ X''	↓ X''	↙ ↓ ↘ y X'' z

Legend: X —developers' curricular ideas
X'—translation of ideas into curriculum materials
X''—implementation of curricular ideas in classroom
y, z—alternative version of curricular ideas

in areas such as knowledge about learners, existing curricula, and different ways of carrying out instructions. The third approach, viewing teachers as partners in development who discover and realize the potential of the curriculum and who may transform materials and devise new alternatives, calls for special abilities of autonomous adaptive planning (Fullan and Pomfret, 1977).

In a variety of situations, the work of central professional centers for curriculum development is complemented by the activities of teachers acting as local developers (Ben-Peretz, 1980; Gray, 1974; Sabar et al., 1982). Teachers may function as "grass-roots" developers, preparing small curriculum units for use in their classrooms, responding to special needs or interests of students. S. Eden (1979) suggests a model for cooperation between external projects and teachers. Curriculum guidelines and materials are produced by the professional project and additional materials are produced by teacher teams. These additional materials focus on local circumstances, such as historical, geographical, or biological phenomena, that cannot be treated adequately in centrally prepared materials. Teachers participating in curriculum development activities need special training which can be provided through inservice programs.

As part of their everyday activities, teachers plan their courses and lessons (Clark & Yinger, 1977; P. H. Taylor, 1970). These activities require abilities and sound judgment in the selection of preferred instructional activities (Yinger & Clark, 1982). Lesson planning is one of the professional challenges facing teachers and may be discussed in terms of the principle of *congruity* (Katz, 1977). Katz uses this principle in relation to teaching, maintaining that the way teachers are taught should be congruent, in many basic aspects, with the way they are supposed to teach children. Analogously, the question of congruity is raised in the context of curriculum. Is there or should there be congruency between the planning of curricula by curriculum developers, for the use of teachers, and the planning of courses and lessons by teachers for their classrooms? Connelly (1972) analyzes the major sources of incongruence as follows: Though both curriculum developers and teachers have a shared goal in their planning—the embodiment of an image of humankind and society—their short term goals differ. The short term goal of curriculum developers is developing materials, focusing on content and structure. The short term goals of teachers planning their lessons is a specific classroom situation. They start with an image of that classroom focusing on pupils and appropriate learning activities. Curriculum developers often use an "if—then methodology", testing the possible consequences of adopting various ways for expressing their intentions in a set of materials. Teachers, on the other hand, have to decide what is best, under specific one-time circumstances.

In the light of these differences, it seems that teachers who do not participate in curriculum development projects, but plan for their own classes, need different training than external curriculum developers. Because teachers start to plan their lessons from the beginning of their professional lives, the necessary training has to be part of the preservice programs.

Teachers play an important role in determining the overt as well as the "hidden curriculum", namely, the social implications and meanings that are conveyed through use of specific curriculum materials, in actual classrooms. Jean Anyon (1981) examined data on school knowledge collected in a case study of five elementary schools in contrasting social settings. She concluded "That while there were similarities in curriculum topics and materials there were also subtle as well as dramatic differences in the curriculum and the curriculum in use among the schools" (p. 4). What counts as knowledge in the various schools differs and conveys divergent meaning to learners. This phenomenon may have far reaching social implications and may contribute to processes of conservation or transformation in society. Teachers who are not aware of these possibilities lack an important component for their reflections, deliberations, and actions in the classroom. Therefore, analysis of the different aspects of the hidden curriculum may be considered an important component of pre- and inservice teacher education.

CURRICULAR EXPERTISE REQUIRED OF TEACHERS

Teachers functioning in different roles with respect to curriculum are called upon to use curricular expertise. What is the nature of this expertise and in what way does it differ from the expertise of curriculum developers?

Schwab (1973) suggests that members of a curriculum development team are scholars drawn from five areas of experience: subject matter, learners, milieu, teachers, and curriculum making. Consideration and coordination of what Schwab calls the four "commonplaces" of education—learner, teacher, milieu, and subject matter—is indispensable for curriculum development. It is the task of the curriculum expert to monitor the process of development and coordinate the contributions of the participants. Teachers who act as curriculum developers, whether in a central development project or in a local situation, do not usually represent these areas of experience as scholars. On the other hand, they may possess valuable knowledge about the classroom setting (learners and milieu), as well as insights into the needs and interests of teachers.

In a curriculum development project carried out by teachers, the coordinator assists the teachers in their task. The coordinator, or curriculum specialist, directs the team and establishes contact with different specialists (Ben-Peretz, 1980; Sabar, Silberstein, & Shafriri, 1982). The principle of congruity is to a certain extent appropriate here. The same basic topics have to be treated and the process of development is similar. Yet, most teachers do not participate in developmental projects, though these may be highly conducive to their professional growth. Therefore, we shall limit our discussion to the curricular expertise needed by curriculum implementors and lesson planners, whose decisions and actions determine to a large extent the classroom curriculum. Figure 2 presents the different areas of expertise required by curriculum developers and by teachers.

Curriculum development teams have to possess scholarly knowledge of the subject matter under consideration; teachers implementing the curriculum have to share this knowledge to a certain extent, but beyond that they have to understand how this knowledge might be presented to learners. Central questions that teachers have to answer are: What is the approach, to the nature of inquiry in the curriculum? What information, concepts, or general principles are emphasized in the materials? How do the curriculum materials convey the relationship between everyday life and the subject matter being taught? How do the materials express possible links with other disciplines?

For instance, teachers who are aware of a curricular orientation that views modes of scientific inquiry as closely related to the basic assumptions guiding specific investigations, rather than viewing inquiry as the adoption of a universal method of scientific investigation, can judge whether their own view of science is compatible with this approach. Thus teachers' choice

FIGURE 2   Areas of Curricular Expertise Required of Curriculum Developers and Teachers.

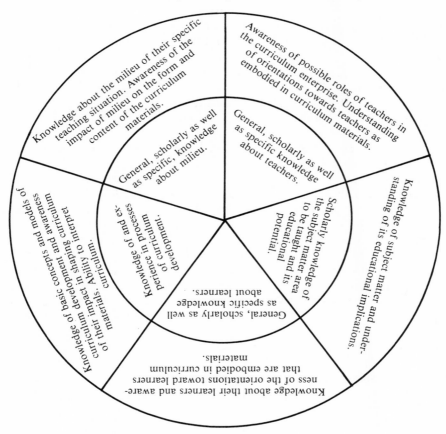

Legend: Inner circle: Curriculum Developers
             Outer circle: Teachers

of curriculum materials would be facilitated and the implementation process would become more meaningful. Clear understanding of the centrality of certain concepts in a curricular unit would aid teachers' instructional planning, and could lead to a decision to establish these concepts as a "core" which has to be mastered by all students. Teachers searching for explicit ties between different disciplines or between everyday life and the curriculum, and find that the curriculum lacks such ties, may decide to complement the materials through their own planning.

Knowledge of learners' potentialities, interests, aspirations, and background has to be incorporated in the curriculum-development process.

Teachers need to be aware of the orientations toward learners in the curriculum materials. Examples of pertinent issues are:

- What perceptions of learners and their involvement in the learning process are expressed in the materials?
- What opportunities for learner development are included in the curriculum?
- What is the focus of instruction, the individual or the group?
- What learning styles are anticipated by the materials?

Different answers to these questions could lead to different courses of action in the classroom. Learners may be perceived as passive acquirers of knowledge whose role is to absorb and retain information. Conversely, learners may be viewed as active and autonomous participants, who seek answers to their questions in ways they devise themselves. If, for instance, teachers reject the first orientation, although it is prevailing in the curriculum, they may be able to modify the learning experiences suggested in the materials.

Curriculum materials may be rich in providing opportunities for developing cognitive abilities such as deductive reasoning. On the other hand, they may lack opportunities for affective involvement of learners, such as promotion of feelings of empathy. A science curriculum, for example, might fail to raise the issue of the need to conserve the environment. Teachers may decide to allocate time in class differently according to their knowledge and understanding of specific learner needs, if they are fully aware of the educational potential embodied in the curriculum they use.

Curriculum analysis may show that the focus of instruction is the group, namely, educational objectives and learning experiences are the same for all learners. On the other hand, a curriculum may be rich in learning alternatives. Anticipation of learning styles is another feature of curriculum. Hunt (1974), for instance, differentiates between different degrees of structures of the learning experience which are optimal for various learners. Curriculum materials may impose more or less rigid structuring; it is important for teachers to be aware of this, in order to achieve an appropriate match between their students' learning styles and the curriculum.

The milieu or the social environment (school and community) is a third body of experience which should be presented in the curriculum-making groups. Teachers have to identify the impact of the milieu on the content and form of the curriculum, and to anticipate implications for curriculum implementation. Relevant themes are:

- What are the possible interactions between society and the discipline being taught, the curriculum's development, and its impact on society?

- Do the materials reflect a response to perceived social needs?
- In what ways do the materials relate to classroom structure?

Curriculum materials may respond to perceived social needs and ideologies. Examples are curricula in environmental education or the presentation of the "creation" story as an alternative to evolution theory. Teachers' sensitivity to the social implications of curriculum development may make them better and more deliberate curriculum "consumers".

Understanding teachers, their background, education, personalities, interests, and preferences is also important in the curriculum-development process. Teachers have to be aware of their possible roles in the curriculum and to identify the orientation toward them in the materials. Important issues include:

- How are developers' deliberations and choices communicated to teachers?
- How much teacher autonomy is implied by the materials?
- What role is the teacher supposed to play in the process of instruction as determined by the curriculum?
- Do the materials reflect considerations of teacher needs, attitudes, and values?
- Do the materials reflect an awareness of necessary prerequisites and anticipated difficulties in curriculum implementation?

Teachers who are uninformed about the reasoning behind curriculum development will have difficulty in implementing and adapting the curriculum to their teaching situation. Teachers' guidebooks may communicate to them reasons for choosing specific curriculum content. For instance. some choices are based on assumptions about the potential for raising learners' motivation. Teachers who are made aware of considerations like these are in a better position to decide whether, indeed, the selected content should be taught in their classes or replaced by other topics. Lack of knowledge about the curriculum developers' rationale may lead to a blind acceptance of materials, even if they prove to be inappropriate for learners. Curriculum materials may restrict teachers' autonomy through detailed specification of objectives and instructional methods, or they may support teachers' initiatives. These materials may impose certain instructional roles on teachers, such as the role of aiding and assisting learners. Teachers may not be conscious of this orientation and may completely distort the instructional process as implied by the curriculum.

One of the most important areas in curriculum development is consideration of teachers' needs and priorities. It is sometimes vital for teachers to be aware of inherent difficulties in implementing certain curricula, of possible incompatibilities between their own set of values and the implicit or explicit values embodied in the curriculum. Different kinds of interpersonal relationships may be implied by the curriculum. Thus, the teachers' guide may call for a partnership between teachers and learners which is based on the notion of equality. This notion may be alien to the teacher and lead either to rejection or to an honest attempt at implementing this approach in spite of its strangeness.

Teachers are aided when they understand how different modes of development shape the form and substance of available materials. Examples of some themes are:

- Are the materials rigidly structured or modular?
- Are the materials content or process oriented?
- What conceptions of curriculum evaluation guided the developers?

These areas are the components of curricular expertise needed by teachers who implement centrally developed curricula. Teachers act as curriculum interpreters, based on their understanding of the ways in which decisions of curriculum developers are embodied in curriculum materials. Therefore, teacher education has to deal explicitly with the issues of curriculum interpretation. The planning of lessons by teachers, based on their personal interpretations of available curriculum materials, may be viewed as encompassing the following competencies:

- Selecting and sequencing of instructional activities proposed in curriculum materials.
- Modifying instructional activities to adapt them to the specific educational situation.
- Creating varied instructional activities beyond those specified in a given set of curriculum materials.

INCORPORATION OF CURRICULAR EXPERTISE IN TEACHER-EDUCATION PROGRAMS

Unless the required curricular expertise and competencies become an integral part of teacher education programs, it is unlikely that teachers will acquire them.

Teacher educators may note this deficiency. Silberstein (1982) reports on a survey of teacher educators focusing on their teaching of curricular issues. Among 57 teacher educators, who participated in special staff development sessions on curriculum development, 67 percent stated that they lacked appropriate resources for teaching curriculum development. The total number of lessons allotted to this topic was small; 22 percent did not teach the subject at all, 44 percent devoted to it between 1–5 lessons, 30 per-

cent 6–10 lessons, and only 4 percent assigned more than 11 lessons to curricular issues.

Ben-Peretz and Tamir (1981) found that teachers have a high level of concern for the "subject matter" aspect of curriculum materials, whereas questions related to the "teacher" were considered as least important. It appears that teachers are reluctant to ask questions focused on this aspect. One possible explanation for these findings is that teachers expect curriculum materials to focus on content and/or students, and accept this as a legitimate and defensible orientation. On the other hand, they do not expect curriculum materials to deal with the mode of interaction between themselves and the materials. In the light of growing awareness that active involvement of teachers is crucial for the successful introduction of innovations into the educational system, it seems that teachers' views about their role in curriculum implementation should become a focus of attention.

What then, are possible bodies of knowledge and experience that will provide the basis for reflective, problem-solving oriented curriculum implementation and lesson planning? The previous section has outlined required understanding in five curricular areas: subject matter; learner, milieu, teacher; possible curriculum formats. The following elements in teacher education are presented as comprising a basis for teacher-education programs:

- Awareness of theoretical "choice points" in curriculum development.
- Abilities of curriculum analysis.
- Participation in curriculum-development experiences.
- Reflection on curriculum-implementation studies.
- Cooperation and collaborative skills in working with colleagues.

These elements constitute an enquiry-oriented teacher-education program aimed at teacher growth in required curricular expertise.

Awareness of Theoretical "Choice Points"

Deliberate choices made by curriculum developers determine the nature of their product, namely, curriculum materials which are available to teachers. Developers' choices may be viewed as relating to the five areas already mentioned: subject matter, learner, milieu, teacher, and curriculum format. According to Connelly (1972) "a choice point refers to a philosophical, psychological, sociological or methodological issue that underlies particular curriculum development" (p. 172). Developers decide which of a number of possible alternatives to adopt at each "decision crossroad" (Ben-Peretz & Silberstein, 1982).

Awareness of these choice points and sufficient theoretical knowledge to grasp the meaning and possible consequences of the alternatives is necessary for teachers whether using externally developed curriculum materials or developing their own curriculum. Connelly and Dienes prepared special instructional materials, *Choice and Deliberation* (1971), for teacher education and teacher educators. These booklets present teachers with selected readings in the relevant disciplines. Analytic discussions with teachers which are based on these readings aim at developing awareness of theoretical choice points.

An example of a Masters of Education program in which teachers are educated in the assumptions, principles, and methods by which new curricula are developed is referred to by Connelly and Ben-Peretz (1980). The goals of the program were:

- To develop skills in reading curriculum literature, through careful analysis of texts using, for instance, the framework of Schwab's (1973) idea of "commonplaces": subject matter, learner, milieu, and teacher.
- To develop critical skills in assessing and using curriculum research for schools. For example, an experienced math teacher may be asked to examine the implementation of new math programs in elementary schools.
- To develop skills in curriculum problem solving. For example, a school supervisor may use a case-study analysis method to examine barriers to autonomous curriculum development by teachers. Study results may be used to establish a project of curriculum development involving teachers (Connelly, 1980).

Abilities of Curriculum Analysis

Awareness of theoretical choice points provides the initial background for interpretation of curriculum materials. Curriculum analysis is the tool for studying decisions that are embodied in the materials. It is defined by Eraut et al. (1975) as an organized set of questions designed for general application to curriculum materials with the aim of elucidating their most important characteristics.

In order to analyse curriculum materials, frames of reference are needed which serve as sources for categories of analysis. A distinction can be made between *internal* and *external* frames of reference (Ben-Peretz, 1981). Internal frames of references originate from the rationale of the curriculum developers. An example of the use of such an internal analytical scheme is the work of Adar and Fox (1978), who analysed the content of a history curriculum based on the rationale of the developers. Examples of their categories are: use of historical documents; actualization; value clarification. Theoretical perspectives guiding the development of categories of curriculum analysis constitute external frames of reference. Examples of such external schemes are Stevens and Morrissett (1968) or Eash (1971–1972). Eash's categories include: objectives; organization of materials; methodology; evaluation. These categories are based on Tyler's model (1949) of curriculum development.

Different frames of reference, leading to a variety of analytical schemes, yield diverse aspects of the complexity and richness of any set of curriculum materials. Teacher-education programs could use curriculum analysis as a regular component of methods courses, as well as of general courses on curriculum development. Through curriculum analysis, it is possible to reveal the educational potential of the materials, their possible contributions to learners, and their inherent limitations. Examples of teacher-education programs incorporating curriculum analysis are the STEP program (Haysom & Sutton, 1974) and the Teacher Education for Curriculum Implementation program (Ben-Peretz & Lifman, 1978). In both programs student teachers engage in curriculum analysis using a variety of analytical schemes. They are provided with instruments and criteria for lesson planning based on available curriculum materials. Awareness of the different possible interpretations of curriculum materials may guide their flexible and imaginative use in a variety of teaching situations. The *matching wheel,* an instrument used in the Ben-Peretz/Lifman program, serves as an example. Student teachers are presented with a circle divided into sections; each section represents a major objective of the curriculum being analyzed. Thus, the matching wheel serves as an internal analytical scheme. One task of analysis is to match components of curriculum materials, such as parts of a text or work sheets, to their appropriate objectives. This matching is based on the perception of the potential of curriculum components to serve the attainment of these objectives. The matching wheel can be used to analyze curricula with external frames of reference, if, for instance, its sections represent categories stemming from other sources and not from curriculum developers. The matching wheel and other procedures of curriculum interpretation were extentively used with pre- and inservice populations. Participants noted the enhancement of their understanding of the nature of available curricula and their potential uses in classrooms.

Participation in Curriculum-Development Experiences

Teachers' involvement in curriculum development may be viewed as a means toward enhancement of professional autonomy, fostering the reflective stance that is important for participation in innovations and curriculum reform (Brown & McIntyre, 1982; Connelly & Ben-Peretz, 1980; Gray, 1974; W. Taylor, 1978). This approach is person-oriented rather than material-oriented. The expected outcome and benefits of the curriculum planning process are mainly in the realm of teachers' professional development. Professional development of teachers is perceived in terms of greater sensitivity to these needs. Expertise in curriculum analysis yields a more complex and comprehensive understanding of curriculum materials and, therefore, may be viewed as material-oriented. On the other hand, participation in curriculum development provides student teachers or teachers with opportunities for experiencing decision making at the various crossroads of development: choice of content; choice of instructional strategies; and decisions about scope and sequence. These experiences involve interactions among participants and may be viewed, therefore, as person-oriented.

Involvement in curriculum-development projects may even be one means of preventing and remediating "teacher staleness" (Smith, 1978). An example of incorporating curriculum-development experience in teacher education is the graduate studies practicum described by Connelly and Ben-Peretz (1980). In one instance, graduate studies practicum students, all of whom were practicing teachers, worked for a full year with a geography curriculum committee. Participants learned about the resolution of curricular problems and thus gained insight into the nature of the curriculum enterprise.

Reflection on Curriculum Implementation Studies

The literature on curriculum implementation is growing rapidly (Fullan & Pomfret, 1977; McLaughlin & Marsh, 1978; Reid & Walker, 1975). An important element in a teacher-education program would consist of examination of those studies. Teachers would gain insight into the problems that arise in curriculum implementation. Moreover, they would become aware of the different assumptions and principles guiding enquiry into implementation. Teachers should be able to distinguish between curriculum-evaluation questions and implementation questions and to understand the relationship between them (Fullan, 1981). In their practical situations, they may experience failure in using certain curriculum materials though they are convinced of the inherent value of these materials. Sensitivity to the many factors involved in the implementation process may be helpful in clarifying the possible reasons for failure.

Cooperative and Collaborative Skills

W. Taylor (1978) emphasizes the demand for greater teacher autonomy and curricular responsibility that characterizes much of the international educational rhetoric. Cooperation among teachers is considered to be a prerequisite for school-based curriculum reform and decision making. Teacher education should give greater attention to the development of cooperative and collaborative skills for a variety of reasons, among them the introduction of novel teaching styles such as team teaching and open classrooms. In the reform of teacher education, emphasis has to be given to developing teachers' ability to cooperate with pupils, colleagues, and community groups.

Taylor notes that these tendencies are reflected in the emphasis on T-group techniques, group activities that are designed to promote personal growth through interaction in a supporting environment, and on study of the sociodynamics of social interaction in teacher education. Such activities may well serve teachers in their future involvement in curricular activities, such as team work in adapting curriculum to local needs. Conversely it may be argued that participation in joint curriculum-analysis activities, small development projects, and group discussions related to curricular choice points during teacher education, may contribute to the development of co-operative skills which are required for a wide range of teacher-professional functions.

INSERVICE TEACHER EDUCATION AND CURRICULAR ISSUES

The previous section dealt with a variety of learning experiences which could help teachers acquire curricular expertise. This section will treat differences between pre- and inservice programs regarding curricular issues. During preservice training, student teachers may find curricular studies too far removed from the anticipated daily confrontation with students, problems of classroom management, and the requirement to cover certain subject areas. It is maintained that two theoretical and two more practical areas of study would be appropriate at the preservice stage.

In the theoretical realm, knowledge of curriculum terminology, curricular concepts, and processes would give student teachers a sense of some of the professional aspects of teaching, thus promoting an awareness of "a shared body of specialized knowledge" (Lortie, 1975, p. 80). Insights into the history of curriculum development would help student teachers to understand the nature of educational change. In the practical realm, student teachers would be involved in curriculum interpretation exercises and in instructional planning based on their personal interpretations. These learning experiences would serve to enhance their sense of confidence in their ability to practice teaching.

Inservice teacher-education programs would benefit from the following theoretical and practical elements based on the previous experience of teachers:

- Examination of curriculum-implementation studies would help teachers clarify their own attempts at curriculum implementation.
- Exploration of curriculum, the transmission of knowledge, appropriate instructional styles, and the nature of students, and sharing

these insights with colleagues, could provide a basis for assessing and restructuring their teaching.

- Participation in curriculum-development experiences, matching content and instructional strategies to concrete learner images, would heighten sensitivity to curricular problems and alternative solutions.
- Awareness of frameworks, methods, and tools of self-assessment would enable teachers to improve their curricular abilities.

SUMMARY

Theoretical and practical curricular knowledge is required for teachers to fulfill their curricular functions in education. Those functions may be carried out in the context of implementation of external curricula or of local curriculum development. Teacher educators have to consider curriculum theory and practice as part of the body of knowledge to be incorporated in teacher-education programs.

This approach raises certain questions. How much can a teacher modify a curriculum to suit a particular type of student body without causing serious distortion of the curriculum? How can one help teachers to identify their needs which may cause them to distort a curriculum, rather than accomodate it to the needs of their pupils?

The notion of the *curriculum envelope* is helpful in examining the first problem. Bridgham (1971) suggested that we view new curricula as "trajectories through pedagogic space, they are properly defined not by single lines in that space but rather by envelopes containing an infinite set of allowed solutions to the problems envisaged by the curriculum designers." (Bridgham, 1971, p. 64). As long as teachers' modification efforts are confined within the curriculum envelope they are not distorting it. Boundaries of curriculum envelopes are determined by the general characteristics of the curriculum, namely, its main attributes which were deliberately chosen by the developers. These general characteristics may relate to the specific content chosen by curriculum developers or to instructional strategies recommended by them. Thus, a biology curriculum may be characterized by emphasizing principles of homeostasis or by adopting an enquiry approach. Teachers' ability to discriminate between "trajectories" inside and outside the envelope can be developed through curriculum analysis (Silberstein, 1978).

Teachers who are aware of the distinct features of a curriculum, and of its potential applications within its envelope, may decide to restrict their modifications to these limits. On the other hand, teachers may decide to go beyond the boundaries of a curriculum if they consider this appropriate for students or consistent with their own needs. Thus, a biology curriculum may be characterized by experimentation with live animals. Teachers who find that they are unable to perform such experiments would change their instruction accordingly. This change would be justifiable if teachers were aware of their breaking away from the curriculum envelope and the reasons for it. Participation in simulation exercises, focusing on deliberations and decisions related to curriculum implementation, may help teachers to identify their own needs as well as those of their students. If we accept that teachers are autonomous professionals and may act as user-developers in curriculum implementation, and not just as neutral transmitters, the consideration of teachers' needs becomes a legitimate component in teacher-education programs and in the practice of teaching.

REFERENCES

Adar, L., & Fox, S. (May 1978). *An analysis of the use and content of a history curriculum.* Jerusalem, Israel: The Hebrew University, School of Education (in Hebrew).

Anyon, J. (1981). Social class and school knowledge. *Curriculum Inquiry, 11* (1), 2–42.

Ben-Peretz, M. (1975). The concept of curriculum potential. *Curriculum Theory Network, 5* (2), 151–159.

Ben-Peretz, M. (1980). Teachers' role in curriculum development: An alternative approach. *Canadian Journal of Education, 5* (2), 52–62.

Ben-Peretz, M., & Lifman, M. (1978). *Teacher education for curriculum implementation,* Jerusalem, Israel: Ministry of Education (in Hebrew).

Ben-Peretz, M., & Tamir, P. (1981). What teachers want to know about curriculum materials. *Journal of Curriculum Studies, 13* (1), 45–53.

Ben-Peretz, M. & Silberstein, M. (1982). A curriculum development case study in biology: two levels of interpretation. *The European Journal of Science Education, 4* (4) 377–389.

Ben-Peretz, M. (1981). Curriculum analysis as a tool of evaluation. In A. Levy and D. Nevo (Eds.) *Evaluation roles in education,* London, Gordon and Breach.

Berman, P., & McLaughlin, M. W. (1977). *Federal programs supporting educational change, Vol. VII: Factors affecting implementation and continuation* (R-1589/7 HEW), Santa Monica, CA: Rand Corporation.

Bridgham, K. G. (1971). Comments on some thoughts on science curriculum development. In E. W. Eisner (ed.), *Confronting curriculum reform.* Boston, MA: Little Brown.

Brown, S., & McIntyre, D. (1982). Influences upon teachers' attitudes to different types of innovation: A study of Scottish integrated science. *Curriculum Inquiry, 12* (1), 35–51.

Clark, C. M., & Yinger, R. J. (1977). Research on teacher thinking. *Curriculum Inquiry, 7* (2), 279–304.

Connelly, F. M. (1972). The functions of curriculum development. *Interchange, 2/3,* 161–177.

Connelly, F. M. (ed.) (1980). *Foundations of curriculum development: Syllabus of readings.* OISE, Department of Curriculum, Informal publication.

Connelly, F. M., & Ben-Peretz, M. (1980). Teachers' role in using and doing of curriculum development. *Journal of Curriculum Studies, 12* (21), 95–107.

Connelly, F. M., & Dienes, B. (1971). *Choice and deliberation: A practitioner's perspective of curriculum development.* Toronto, Canada: Ontario Institute for Studies in Education.

Czajkowski, T. J., & Patterson, J. L. (1980). Curriculum change and the school. In A. W. Foshay (Ed.), *Considered action for curriculum improvement.* Alexandria, VA: ASCD.

Eash, M. W. (1971–1972). Developing an instrument for assessing instructional materials. *Curriculum Theory Network, 8/9,* 59–69.

Eden, S. (1979). Implementatiaon of innovations in education: A case study in curriculum planning. *Studies in Educational Evaluation,* Monograph No. 2, 1–160.

Eraut, M. R., Goud, L., & Smith, G. (1975). *The analysis of curriculum materials* (Occasional paper 2). University of Sussex.

Feiman, S. (1979). Technique and inquiry in teacher education: A curricular case study. *Curriculum Inquiry, 9* (1), 63–79.

Fox, S. (1977). The scholar, the educator and the curriculum of the Jewish school. In S. Fox & G. Rosenfield (Eds.), *From the scholar to the classroom.* New York: Melton Research Center for Jewish Education, the Jewish Theological Seminary of America.

Fullan, M. (1981). The relationship between implementation and evaluation. In A. Lewy & D. Nevo (Eds.), *Evaluation roles in education.* New York: Gordon and Breach.

Fullan, M., & Pomfret, A. (1977). Research on curriculum and instruction implementation. *Review of Educational Research, 47* (2), 335–397.

Gray, K. R. (1974). What can teachers contribute to curriculum development. *Journal of Curriculum Studies, 6* (2), 120–132.

Hacker, W. (1975). *Curriculumplanung und Lehrerrolle.* Weissheim und Basel, Switzerland: Beltz Verlag.

Haysom, J., & Sutton, C. (1974). *The science teacher education project.* New York: McGraw-Hill.

Hunt, D. E. (1974). Learning styles and teaching strategies. *Behavioral and Social Science Teachers, 2* (1), 22–34.

Katz, L. G. (1977). *Talks with teachers.* Washington, DC: National Association for the Education of Young Children.

Lortie, D. C. (1975). *Schoolteacher: A sociological study.* Chicago, IL: The University of Chicago Press.

Manolakes, T. (1980). *A content filter for professional education in the preparation of elementary school teachers.* Discussion Paper, College of Education, University of Illinois, Champaign-Urbana.

McLaughlin, M. W., & Marsh, D. D. (1978). Staff development and school change. *Teachers College Record, 80* (1), 69–94.

National Education Association. (1974). *The American public-school teacher* Washington DC: Author. (Research Report 1967-R4).

Reid, W. A., & Walker, D. F. (Eds.). (1975). *Case studies in curriculum change: Great Britain and the United States.* London: Routledge & Kegan Paul.

Sabar, N., Silberstein, M., & Shafriri, N. (1982). Needed: Curriculum coordinators for teachers developing learning materials: A systematic analysis of coordinators characteristics for better planned training. *Curriculum Inquiry, 12* (1), 53–67.

Schulz, W. (1981). *Unterrichtsplanung,* Munchen, Germany: Urban and Schwarzenberg.

Schwab, J. J. (1973). The practical: Translation into curriculum'', *School Review, 81,* 501–522.

Silberstein, M. (July–August 1978). *Training teachers to implement general characteristics of the curriculum.* Paper presented at the Bat Sheva Seminar on Curriculum Implementation and its Relationship to Curriculum Development in Science. Rehovot and Jerusalem, Israel.

Silberstein, M. (1982). *Teaching curricular issues in teacher education programs in Israel—A survey of teacher education colleges.* Research Report. Jerusalem, Israel: Ministry of Education and Culture (in Hebrew).

Smith, L. M. (1978). Science education in the Alte Schools: A kind of case study. In R. Stake & J. Easley (Eds.), *Case Studies in Science Education.* Washington, DC: National Science Foundation.

Stevens, W. S., & Morrissett, J. (1968). A system for analyzing social science curricula. *EPIE Forum, 1*(4-5), 10–15.

Taylor, P. H. (1970). *How teachers plan their courses.* Slough, England: National Foundation for Educational Research.

Taylor, W. (1978). *Research and reform in teacher education.* Slough, England: National Foundation for Educational Research.

Tyler, R. W. (1949). *Basic principles of curriculum and instruction.* Chicago, IL: University of Chicago Press.

Yinger, R. J., & Clark, C. M. (1982). *Understanding teachers' judgments about instruction: The task, the method and the meaning.* Paper presented at the annual meeting of the American Educational Research Association, New York.

3

The Priority of Knowledge and Understanding in Teaching*

Margret Buchmann
Michigan State University

WHO CARES FOR CONTENT?

At the beginning of one of my courses, I often discuss with the class of future teachers Schwab's (1978) *commonplaces of education.* After arguing for the coordination of teacher, learner, content, and milieu (or environment) in educational theory, practice, and policy, I give students the task of rank-ordering these commonplaces. If rank-ordering is sensible at all, which one would you put first? For what reasons? Based on what assumptions? This exercise leads to group work in which thoughts, arguments, and evidence about the importance of the four commonplaces are discussed.

When I first ventured into teacher education, I assumed that four groups would sort themselves out by student loyalty to each of the common-places, and that each commonplace would get a fair share of the votes. Now I know better. In a class of about 30 students, content sometimes musters no partisan at all, milieu two, teacher three to six. The other votes go to the fourth commonplace of education, student. Groups of about equal size

* Sections of this chapter appeared in an earlier article, "The Flight Away From Content in Teacher Education and Teaching." *Journal of Curriculum Studies, 14*(1982), 61–68. The author wishes to thank Sharon Feiman-Nemser, John R. Schwille, and Ian Westbury for their criticisms and comments. I have drawn much profit from Robert E. Floden's suggestions, especially in writing the last part of the chapter.

Preparation of this chapter was supported in part by the Institute for Research on Teaching, College of Education, Michigan State University. The Institute for Research on Teaching is funded primarily by the Teaching Division of the National Institute of Education, U.S. Department of Education. The opinions expressed in this publication do not necessarily reflect the position, policy, or endorsement of the National Institute of Education.

have then to be formed by persuasion and coercion. After the group presentations, the class takes a second poll. There is always some shifting of votes away from student to teacher and milieu, but very few or no votes fall to content.

A recent book sponsored by the National Society For the Study of Education, *Improving Educational Standards and Productivity: The Research Basis for Policy* (Walberg, 1982), covers people, processes, and contexts involved in education. There is a chapter on extracurricular activities. But the book remains silent on the content of education. In the 1983 call for papers for the meeting of the American Association of Colleges For Teacher Education, "Essential Knowledge for Beginning Educators," topics include the evaluation of learning and teacher evaluation, instructional planning and management, and the influence of context. Content knowledge is not listed. Who cares for content?[1] This is a disturbing question.

WHY SHOULD WE CARE?

All professionals use knowledge. In teaching, knowledge enters into professional work in a unique fashion: Knowledge is what teaching is about. For teachers to do justice to this intrinsic connection, they need to have content knowledge. To acquire, for example, delivery skills is pointless unless teachers know something they can deliver. Yet curriculum practices and development in many schools and colleges of education can be interpreted as a flight away from content. Curricula include life skills such as interpersonal communication. Preservice work for teachers emphasizes teaching strategies and skills. These skills may be useful, but they do not add to the content knowledge that is required for teaching. In fact, while no degree of mastery of teaching skills can overcome lack of content knowledge, given content knowledge, we have something that we can teach.

The flight away from content in education is a move to the periphery: away from what is essential to what is of lesser importance. In this chapter,

---

[1] There are exceptions. For instance, the Content Determinants Project, Institute for Research on Teaching, Michigan State University, investigates institutional and social influences on teachers' content decisions in elementary school mathematics (See, for example, Freeman et al., 1983; Floden et al., 1981; Schwille et al., 1983). Currently this team of researchers is conducting studies at the state, district, school, and classroom level to find out how state and district policies influence content taught, as opposed to the influences of teacher convictions and the opinions of other teachers.

At the same university, a program for teacher preparation, begun by Jere Confrey and now led by Perry Lanier, has been approved at the pilot level. The program begins with a course combining study of children's understanding of subject matter with study of the epistemological foundations of four focal subject matters. The tentative foundation of subject-matter knowledge is a theme continuing through the program. The student teaching component of the program is supervised by faculty with expertise in the particular academic content areas.

I offer considerations which aim at advancing content to at least a position of equal rank among the commonplaces of education. My argument is hierarchical. After discussing content knowledge as a logical precondition for teaching, I examine the yields of different levels and kinds of content knowledge for the work that teachers do.

CONTENT KNOWLEDGE AS A PRECONDITION FOR TEACHING

Green (1971) analyzes the activities of teaching in a way that allows one to detect and describe this move to the periphery. Under his first category of activities of teaching, *logical acts,* Green includes activities such as explaining, concluding, demonstrating, and giving reasons. These logical acts relate to the element of reasoning in the practice of teaching. His second category, *strategic acts,* includes disciplining, evaluating, motivating, and planning. These activities have to do with the direction and encouragement of students and the organization of lessons and classroom life. Teachers also collect milk money, patrol halls, keep records and consult with parents and specialists; he calls these *institutional acts.*

Green admits that the categories of logical, strategic, and institutional acts are imprecise. One can easily come up with additions to his lists of teacher activities, and it may be difficult to place some aspects of the work of teachers under these three headings. What is important and helpful about Green's categories is that they roughly describe what teachers do, while marking out clearly the activities without which teaching can still occur. The institutional activities of teachers "are in no way required by the nature of teaching itself. *There is no inconsistency in the claim that teaching may go on even when the institutional acts of teaching are not going on"* (p. 5, emphasis in the original). Socrates did not collect milk money. That, however, did not make him less of a teacher.

Strategic and logical acts, on the other hand, are required by the nature of teaching. Teachers who never explain or demonstrate anything, who neither answer questions nor question answers, may be engaged in some useful activity, but they do not teach. Classroom life that shows no evidence of teacher planning in instruction, where rules for behavior create no order, and where teacher interest in pupil learning is not discernible would leave one puzzled. Where neither the logical nor the strategic acts of teaching occur, it is unlikely that teaching is going on.

I interpret Green's categories as going from the central to the peripheral, institutional acts being farthest off-center. To return to what is closer to the center means to focus on the logical and strategic activities of teaching. These activities, however, presuppose a content on which they can be exercised. Second, and more importantly, the logical and strategic activities of teaching presuppose subject matter knowledge on the part of teachers.

The following question by a student illustrates this point. As a teacher reported in a study by Lampert (1981):

> A ten year old boy asked his fourth grade teacher: "Does Dataman have eyes?" He was wondering about his hand-held computer game that looks like a robot. "If not, how does he know if my answers are right?" (p. 1)

The teacher felt that this question was silly; she judged the boy as not very smart and worried whether he could learn what she would teach over the course of the year. Then, in what Lampert calls the role of teacher "as a provider of right answers," she told the child that Dataman was "programmed." However, in discussing the incident with other teachers she conceded that "she did not really know exactly how the machine works."

Unless they already know what being programmed means, to tell children that Dataman is programmed will not result in an increase of knowledge and understanding. However, without understanding the inward workings of Dataman, the teacher cannot answer student questions in a fashion that promotes learning.

Part of the meaning of teaching is an understanding of what is to be taught. It would be odd to expect a teacher to plan a lesson on, for instance, writing reports in science and to evaluate related student assignments, if that teacher is ignorant about writing and science, and does not understand what student progress in writing science reports might mean. Through a case study of curriculum change, McKinney and Westbury (1975) show just what kind of planning—with what kinds of results—is to be expected where content knowledge is lacking. The work on the science curriculum guide for grades 7–12 in the Gary, Indiana school system took two years; here is what it resulted in:

> The committee members did the easiest thing they could do. They simply copied the chapter topics into the major areas column of the guide for each course from the primary textbook for that course (p. 28).

Given lack of teacher preparation and resources, there was no significant outcome of the work of the science curriculum committee. Nothing changed until 1960, when the Gary science supervisor attended a Physical Sciences Study Committee Institute. He was enthusiastic about their physics program, "but felt that before teachers should use it, they...should attend an appropriate institute" (McKinney & Westbury, 1975, p. 29). Tuition and materials were free and teachers attended with eagerness. After this substantive exposure, science education in the Gary schools started to change.

Immanual Kant argues in the *Critique of Pure Reason* that it is a sign of wisdom to avoid unreasonable questions and find the ones that are reasonable to ask. To this purpose, it is sometimes necessary to start with a statement of the obvious, namely, that teacher activities essential to teaching point beyond themselves to some content to be taught—and known—by the teacher.[2] The relations between the logical and strategic activities of teaching and content knowledge follow almost by definition. Remote hypotheses —for example, that student achievement depends on at which one of the necessary and invariant developmental stages the teacher happens to be, on the teacher's mastery of taxonomies of educational objectives, or on the formation of personal teaching (or, for that matter, learning) styles—may appeal to the initiates of various ideological camps. But these hypotheses are often mistaken, misleading, and unnecessary. A problem with overlooking the obvious is that in the attempt to understand and remedy a puzzling or unsatisfactory state of affairs, such as a lack of student learning, centrifugal tendencies are liable to be strengthened, thus creating more puzzlement and dissatisfaction.

When student achievement is disappointing, it is useful to recall that teaching is conditional upon the presence of educational content in teacher activities, and that essential activities of teaching are conditional upon the content knowledge of teachers. If command of content is insufficient, teacher education has to address lacks in content knowledge. In this sense, content has priority in teacher education and teaching.

> If anything is to be regarded as a specific preparation for teaching, priority must be given to a thorough grounding in something to teach. There are other things which a teacher must know well—about children, for instance, and the social conditions which shape their lives. But social workers, therapists, and juvenile employment officers must also know about these things. A teacher, in so far as he is concerned with teaching and not just therapy, "socialization," or advice about careers, must have mastered something which he can impart to others. Without this he would be like an actor who was exquisitely sensitive to the reactions of an audience, a master of gesture and of subtle inflections of voice, but who omitted to do one thing—to learn his words. (Peters, 1977, p. 151)

In the next section, I elaborate on the relationship of knowledge that is abundant and assured to logical and strategic activities of teaching.

---

[2] In education, the obvious tends to be stated in less than homely ways. Consider, as a pertinent example, the "curriculum deficiency hypotheses": "Indeed, one of the more clearcut results of the IEA studies is that the presence or absence of a topic in the curriculum is generally a crucial factor in determining whether students will 'know' it on a test" (Inkeles, 1977, p. 163).

A FIRM GRASP OF CONTENT

Dewey (1904/1965) argues that teachers at their best are observers and directors of the mental life of learners. The detachment presupposed in this role implies a shift of focus from the teacher to learners, and what they are doing, imagining, and thinking. As Dewey says, this point is of particular importance for teaching in the early grades, where the processes of learning subject matter are being learned. On the part of the teacher it requires an understanding of mental life, a firm grasp of content, and conceptions of the student and the relationship between teacher and student that revolve around content and learning. Contemporary British philosophers share this point of view (see Hirst, 1974; Oakeshott, 1972; Peters, 1978); and Wilson (1975) has given it the following clear expression.

> To be interested in education is to view him [the student] primarily as a *learner:* to have in mind the process and benefits of learning and understanding...themselves, rather than other goods...and to view him under other descriptions only insofar as these descriptions are importantly relevant to him as a learner. (p. 44)

Knowledge of Learners Requires Knowledge of Content

When students seem to miss the point or are confused, the remedy is seldom just a provision of right answers. Students' understandings and misunderstandings have to be traced, fathomed, and responded to by the teacher to promote learning. Content knowledge helps the teacher to see a point from the perspective of the learner and to recognize the internal logic of student questions and answers. Responding to the concepts and mental activities of learners can be a process of considerable intricacy. It involves sidestepping and second-guessing; the resulting conversational exchanges can appear odd. Davis (1980) analyzes a pedagogical dialogue observed by Page that seems to come straight from the Mad Hatter's tea party:

> (1) The teacher asks a question, (2) the student mistakenly answers a *different* question, (3) the teacher...identifies the question the student had in mind and *asks t h a t question,* (4) the student does *not* answer the question just asked, but instead *revises* the answer to the *first* question. (p. 178)

This exchange is quite common and useful when students confuse addition and multiplication; it does not seem as strange and elaborate in this context.

Teacher: How much is four times four?
Student: Eight

Teacher: How much is four plus four?
Student: Oh! It should be sixteen. (p. 178)

Teachers' responses to student error require a firm grasp of pertinent concepts and relations. In this instance, we can assume it. In other instances, this is not so, and—under the surface of orderly instructional exchanges or progression on workbook assignments—the mental reality of classroom life may be that of the Mad Hatter's tea party.

In a classic study of a sixth grade student, "Benny," Erlwanger (1973) showed that the creation and use of a complicated set of idiosyncratic concepts and rules is consistent with the appearance of student learning. Benny's mathematical world is strange and a bit frightening. Learning mathematics is "a 'wild good chase' in which he is chasing particular answers" (p. 16). And the rules of mathematics, though invented, work like magic "because the answers one gets from applying these rules can be expressed in different ways, 'which we think they're different but really they're the same'" (p. 18). Benny progressed as one of the best pupils through programmed exercises in adding fractions and multiplying decimals; he typically got his answers right. But in his habits of learning and views of subject matter, arbitrary rules rather than reasons were dominant. Nevertheless, Benny's system of rules—inflexible and wrongheaded—was certified as achievement by the teacher.

Evidence on student conceptions and misconceptions is accruing for different subject areas and age levels (Novick & Nussbaum, 1978; Nussbaum, 1979; Tamir, Gal-Choppin, & Nussinovitz, 1981). Whether one calls these cognitive structures *frames,* as Davis does, or *schemata,* in the language of cognitive science, Anderson's (1977) observations hold and have implications for teaching and teacher preparation:

> The schemata by which students assimilate their lessons may not be the ones certified by some discipline or other. This fact can easily escape detection since the student will often be able to repeat segments of the text and lecture even though he/she understands them in terms of an incorrect, incomplete, or inconsistent framework. Indeed, students may develop specialized frameworks for maintaining the particular identity of lesson material in order to cope with the demand for veridical reproduction. (p. 429)

Erlwanger as well as Lampert (1982) point out that what is involved in pedagogical responses to children's thinking is more than a change of teacher behavior. Both authors stress that teachers' attention to the child as a thinker requires a change in role conception. The teacher as a "provider of right answers" changes into a person intent on understanding and directing the mental life of students. Erlwanger, in particular, would like this mental life to be of a kind that enables the learner to participate, with others, in the experience of mathematics as a particular form of the life of the mind.

Knowledge Legitimates Teacher Authority

The term *creative spelling* is sometimes used to describe deviations from accepted usage. No doubt many spelling errors show creative minds at work. However, the point of teaching, especially in the elementary grades, is not the cult of idiosyncrasy, but the induction into frames of reference with standards for what is appropriate, true, and right. The common stock of reason contains, for instance, historical lore, elementary arithmetic, and the Golden Rule, as well as the basics of grammar and spelling. It is equally removed from idiosyncratic rules and untutored beliefs and the alternative, specialized conceptions of theorists. Even at this level, the life of reason is in an important sense impersonal; it is intersubjectively rather than subjectively validated. An expansion of the common stock of reason and conceptual change within it come when individuals know what they are doing and are not arbitrary in their deviations.

Partnership in understanding presupposes mutual respect and a real interest in the thought processes of others. However, in the classroom, teachers are in authority. They determine what is to count as an appropriate assumption and which answers or rules are to be discounted as wrong. Thus they have not only social control, but epistemic control as well. Unfortunately, teachers act with authority, whether or not they are in authority on subject matter. It is unlikely that youngsters will be able to distinguish between social and epistemic control—or, if they do, that they can act on this distinction—even where the latter is exercised, not by right, but by power (see Freeman, 1981).

The merger between social and epistemic authority in schools makes knowledge to the best of the teacher's capacity a requirement with moral dimensions. I have discussed pedagogical responses to student error. But student inventiveness that is not wrongheaded must not be penalized simply because it deviates from the teacher's way of arriving at a solution, or the results and procedures laid out in the textbook. Where teacher authority is legitimate and exercised to benefit the student as a learner, it rests on a thorough grounding in something to teach.

Dewey (1904/1965) held that the "delicate and far-reaching matter of intellectual responsibility" (p. 147) is too frequently ignored by the teaching profession. This concern bears restatement. The teacher's experience, thoughtfully explored, can yield knowledge and insight that can help in teaching and understanding children's thinking. However, no amount of reflection, observation of students, general information, and personal experience can overcome lack of knowledge in areas such as mathematics and chemistry. On the other hand, content knowledge delimits the significance of management concerns and affects the very occurrence of management problems.

With Adequate Content Knowledge, Management Problems May Vanish

Knowing something allows us to teach it; and knowing a subject thoroughly means to be mentally organized and well prepared to teach it in a general way. Getting ready to teach a lesson means to think about what teacher and students will be doing—in substance, grouping, sequence, and so forth. And having students do things in reasonable order will relate to instructional tasks. If the teacher presses forward to new content or responds with care to student understanding, teacher and students will be busy enough with teaching and learning. Under normal circumstances, management is nested in instruction and requires no separate techniques.

The occurrence and severity of management problems depend on what the teacher believes to be the point of classroom life and that belief, in turn, is often shaped by the amount and assurance of teachers' content knowledge. Sheer lack of content knowledge will be a powerful factor in predisposing teachers toward a process view of classroom life, while thorough knowledge in itself may tip the conceptual scale in favor of student learning. If learning is seen as the practical end of teacher and student activities, student questions and remarks that show engagement, bewilderment, and thoughtfulness will be taken by the teacher as instructional occasions. When we look at the child as a learner, there is no independent value in order, prompt obedience, and taking turns. But if process is a primary concern, teachable moments may go unrecognized or be tackled as challenges to teacher authority. Of course, appropriate conceptions of classroom life alone won't do the job. Their realization depends on teachers' substantive capacity to act on them—on content knowledge that is deep and abundant.

E. L. Smith and Charles Anderson (1981) have found that procedure is a key category as teachers interpret curriculum guides in science. The 18 fifth-grade teachers they studied constructed "story lines" from textbooks: "For many teachers this story line is primarily procedural in nature: a chapter is thought of as a sequence of pages to be read or activities to be done" (p. 17). The learning goals of activities often become invisible when activities are edited and re-arranged to accomodate procedural considerations. Linda Anderson and her collaborators (1981) identified a similar phenomenon in the thinking of first-graders about school work. Thirty-two students were observed as they completed their seatwork assignments. These children understood their work in terms of content coverage rather than learning. On the spot interviews document this phenomenon; what follows are excerpts:

Researcher: Tell me about this work you're doing (as student is working in math workbook.)
Student: This is my math. I'm almost done with a unit! Only two more pages. (Said with excitement...)
Researcher: What was this unit about?
Student: Well, when it's done I get to take it home.
Researcher: What were you learning about when you did this unit?
Student: (Brief pause, slightly puzzled expression) Oh, I learned how to work hard.

The following exchange occurred with several students:

Researcher: What are you learning about when you do this page?
Student: (Shrugs) I don't know.
Researcher: Why did the teacher give you this page to do?
Student: This is just our work (said as if the question seemed very odd.) (L. Anderson, 1981, pp. 8-9)

The researchers report that teacher presentations to these first-graders focused primarily on procedure and rarely touched on the content-related aspects of assignments. Their hypothesis, namely that students' perceptions of the point of their work may be related to the information they receive from teachers, is supported by the findings of E. L. Smith and Charles Anderson regarding teachers' procedural reconstruction of science texts.

During instruction, the surface responses of teachers who have learning as opposed to process views of classroom life may look similar. But it is likely that the direction of thoughts during and after teaching will be affected by differences in the conception of the point of teacher and student work. For, while lack of subject matter preparation or a concern for the robustness of a lesson may make teacher responses to teachable moments minimal under both conceptions, a process or management view of teaching will give the teacher a sense of success and accomplishment where interruptions—whatever their source and potential—have been contained or suppressed in the flow of activities. However, teachers who have a view of classroom life that centers on student learning will be more likely to see where their actions fall short of promoting such learning, and less likely to develop a sense of success and accomplishment that may be deceptive.[3]

---

[3] These observations are supported by research on elementary level mathematics lessons (Shroyer, 1981) and by findings from studies (Peterson, Marx, & Clark, 1978; Zahorik, 1970)

Where teacher thinking during instruction is problem-oriented (see Morine-Dershimer, 1979), decisions that take instructional difficulties into account are often postponed. They may not be made in flight, but then they are not made *by flight* either.

Given that teacher views of classroom life authoritatively influence students' beliefs about its purpose, it can furthermore be argued that student behavior which does not fit teacher conceptions is not only liable to pass teachers by, but less likely to occur in the first place. The effects of such conceptual and behavioral traps may be particularly unfortunate for low achievers. Linda Anderson (1981) analyzed the strategies of low achieving students as they completed difficult assignments; she believes that the following conditions detract from content learning and the development of skills in learning to learn:

> First, low achievers (or anyone, but it happens most frequently to them) are given work that is not easy enough for them to do quickly, automatically, and with a clear sense of whether they are correct. Second, these assignments are given in a setting where working independently and finishing in the time allotted is valued and encouraged by the teacher. Our present hypothesis is that when these two conditions are frequent, students do not learn to ask whether their work makes sense to them. However, they develop other strategies that allow them to get the answer and get finished. (p. 11)

Low achievers are more likely than high achievers to find themselves with assignments that are difficult for them and less likely to expect their work to make sense. But the rewards for developing strategies in getting work done are clear, with predictable effects on student learning.

Two different claims have been made so far in this chapter. First, content knowledge has some payoffs for the logical and strategic activities of teaching, while training people in the moves of teaching does not teach them its content. Second, knowledge and understanding are distinctive points of teacher and student work. If the first claim is conceded, the route to teaching strategies and management skills through content knowledge is reasonable because it is economical. Given the limited time available for the education of teachers, this point is important. If the second claim is granted, the route through content is desirable because it maintains, maybe restores, the

---

that link teachers' planning to subsequent instruction. Shroyer found that, of the three teachers she studied, the teacher who was most concerned about promoting pupil understanding exploited the most teachable moments, and the teacher who was most bound to lesson plans and to obtaining correct answers to preset questions did the most avoiding. The larger studies of teacher planning indicate that teachers who planned thoroughly but perhaps overly rigidly were less sensitive to pupil needs and less likely to encourage or develop pupils' ideas than teachers who were less rigid or more comprehensive in their planning.

proper attention of teachers and teacher educators to educational content and student learning. Oakeshott (1972) lists teaching as encompassing many activities, to highlight this relationship.

> Thus, teaching is a variegated activity which may include hinting, suggesting, urging, coaxing, encouraging, guiding, pointing out, conversing, instructing, informing, narrating, lecturing, demonstrating, exercising, testing, examining, critizing, correcting, tutoring, drilling and so on—everything, indeed, which does not belie the engagement to impart an understanding. (pp. 25-26)

In what follows, I will advance a third claim. It links knowledge about knowledge to a particular form of classroom life and of pedagogical knowledge.

LETTING GO OF CERTAINTY

Why does thunder follow lightning? Why does Johnny always hit Mary? Teachers who attempt to answer such questions in ways that are satisfactory to themselves, while being clear and understandable to students, benefit greatly from scholarship (Scheffler, 1968). Not only does scholarship lend depth and clarity to their answers, but it also reveals that groups of phenomena can be understood and perceived in different ways. If not always appropriate as a source of instructional content, learned uncertainty is a pedagogical asset. It helps the teacher to look and to listen in a simple and direct fashion, without an epistemic arrogance for which the history of science gives no warrants.

The knowledge which allows teachers to come up with answers compelling to themselves is the knowledge that opens the door to uncertainty. It makes a relationship of equal respect between teacher and learner possible. Hawkins (1974) cites an example:

> One of the nicest stories of this kind that I know comes from a young physicist friend who was very learned...My wife was asking him to explain something to her about two coupled pendulums. He said, "Well, now, you can see that there's a conversion of...Well, there's really a conservation of angle here." She looked up at him. "Well, you see, in the transfer of energy from one pendulum to the other there is..." and so on and so on. And she said, "No, I don't mean that. I want you to notice this and tell me what's happening." Finally, he looked at the pendulums and he saw what she was asking. He looked at *it,* and he looked at *her,* and he grinned and said, "Well, I know the right words but I don't understand it either." This confession, wrung from a potential teacher, I've always valued very much. It proves that we're all in *it* together. (p. 62)

Teachers and learners can meet on the common ground of uncertainty. But uncertainty comes in learned and untutored versions. In the *Republic,* Socrates leads—with a good deal of guile—a group of adults to a common, reasoned understanding of the ideal structure of society. But Socrates' truest teaching comes at the end, when he teases the people who have become his followers by (almost) saying: "Yes, it is thus. But is it so?"

In teaching, the aim is "to give the child reason" (Duckworth, 1981). As I see it, this means to treat youngsters as persons with minds and to be determined to teach them. In respecting the mental integrity and force of children, one honors their quest for understanding. And their understandings need not be about matters that are innocuous, vapid, and trivial.[4] Banalities "about the home, then the friendly postman and trashman, then the community...[are] a poor way to compete with the child's own dramas and mysteries" (Bruner, 1968, p. 160; see also Bettelheim & Zelan, 1982). Thus Lewis Thomas (1982), the chairman of the board of the Scientists' Institute for Public Information, suggests:

> that the introductory courses in science, at all levels from grade school through college, be radically revised...At the outset, before any of the fundamentals, teach the still imponderable puzzles of cosmology. Describe as clearly as possible, for the youngest minds, that there are some things going on in the universe that lie still beyond comprehension, and make it plain how little is known.
>
> Do not teach that biology is a useful and perhaps profitable science... Teach instead that there are structures squirming inside each or our cells that provide all the energy for living. Essentially foreign creatures, these lineal descendants of bacteria were brought in for symbiotic living a billion or so years ago. Teach them we do not have the ghost of an idea how they got there, where they came from. (p. 91)

---

[4] In a recent multidimensional content analysis of 34 basals from eight major publishing companies (second, fourth and fifth grade), Schmidt, et al. (1983) have found that 42 percent of all the selections coded were without content that reflects the traditional subject areas of the elementary school curriculum. Of those selections with subject matter content, about a third covered language skills. On the dimension of process, the how of practical and mental functioning, 70 percent of all selections were content-free. Knowledge about living and acting rightly, or ethos content, was absent in 88 percent of all basal selections. Only four percent of all selections in these representative American texts were found to have content on all three dimensions of subject matter, function, and ethos.

The application of Thorndike's word lists in the composition of texts for young readers has very likely contributed to their vacuousness. Thorndike himself warned against the confusion of frequency with importance (see Clifford, 1978). Important words in learning to read and write are often neither bland nor typical (Paley, 1981).

Teachers interact with students as the first and often only representatives of the life of the mind. The empirical fact that different sorts of content are taught at different levels of schooling—learning about uncertainty and the conceptual foundations of knowledge occurs primarily at the doctoral level—amounts to a radical equity problem in the distribution of educational opportunities (Bernstein, 1975; Meyer, 1980).

Respect for Student Integrity

From the point of view of theory of knowledge, there is a weak and a strong version of the principle of respect for student integrity (Petrie, 1981). The strong version attributes, in principle, equal merit to all knowledge claims; Niels Bohr was "just fond" of his opinions about atoms. However, as Petrie points out, "it might be urged that most if not all of the time, the reasons contained in the disciplines are simply better than the student's reasons" (p. 29). The weaker version of the principle of respect for student integrity that is argued here requires that students, like anyone else, should be treated and regarded as the potential source of thoughts and behavior that makes sense. This equality of respect does not commit the teacher to a relativistic stance that reduces what is true or right to whatever youngsters happen to believe in, thus depriving them of the benefits of accumulated knowledge and good sense (see Kohlberg & Mayer, 1972).

Lack of factual or conceptual control over subject matter can lead the teacher to an unconscious application or a conscious endorsement of the troublesome strong version of the principle of student integrity. B. O. Smith (1972) gives an example. During a biology lesson, the question came up how "thoroughbred" could be defined:

> One of the pupils insisted that *his* decision was true and that all the others were false; "A thoroughbred race horse is a flat race horse originating in England," he said. After some discussion, an observer in the room asked if the following would be acceptable, "a flat race horse originating in England we choose to call a thoroughbred." The pupil replied, "No, you do not *choose* to call him a thoroughbred. That is what he is." (p. 128)

Students confused definitions with facts; they identified statements about words with statements about the world. The teacher did not know the meaning of definition and did not correct this misconception.

Mistaking definitions and classification schemes as simple statements of facts has repercussions in social perception. Terms such as *angora rabbit* and *thoroughbred racehorse* are logically equivalent to terms that designate people as members of groups that are seen as different in society. Bias in matters of class, sex, culture, or race is impossible to combat unless people understand the conventional and valuative aspects of terms such as *girl* and *boy* or *poverty-stricken* and *advantaged*. Such words do not just describe what is the case, they make a case that implies hypotheses and prescriptions about what members of different social groups are like and what they typically do. As the history of science and the theory of knowledge show, even statements about the world describe facts *as we know them,* and are open to revision on the basis of new evidence and alternative ways of seeing things.

Flexible Control of Subject Matter

Where knowledge is well understood it will not be confused with the comforts of settled opinion. Knowledge about how and why a set of propositions comes to be called knowledge encourages the willingness to be surprised by new evidence (Scheffler, 1977). The history and theory of knowledge can shape teachers' dispositions so that thoughts and beliefs are entertained seriously, but as hypotheses held lightly. The mobility of teacher conceptions—more than their logic, clarity, and, to a certain extent, their truth—is a safeguard of thought that is free to live up to the commitments of teaching (Brophy & Good, 1974). It is here that subject matter experts pure and simple and teachers part company. For, although mobility as a habit of mind is central to the work of both, the point of this mobility marks out different enterprises (Gustin, 1982; Wilson, 1975). And though communication is central to what scientists as well as classroom teachers are doing, their principal audiences can be distinguished; scientists address a universal audience, often remote in time and place, while teachers face a particular, concrete group.

Scientists, mathematicians, and poets strive toward integration and simplicity in working with symbols so that they can approximate more closely what is true and beautiful. Teachers strive toward clarity in order to increase knowledge and understanding in students. A great part of the difficulty rests with mastery of subject matter. But another part lies in the difficulty of understanding and communicating with other minds—minds of people divided from the teacher, certainly by age, and often by sex, race, culture, and language (Soltis, 1981). In his classic book on teaching, Highet (1966) clarifies what teachers have to think about if their aim is to give students reason:

> You must think, not what you know, but what they do not know; not what you find hard, but what they will find hard; then, after putting yourself inside their minds, obstinate or puzzled, groping or mistaken as they are, explain what they need to learn. (p. 280)

The pursuit of student achievement often results in simplification given "the sense of 'pruning' or 'stepping down to a lower level'" (Kirsch, 1976). Teaching that does not dilute or distort knowledge from the disciplines while reaching a variety of students requires a wide and theoretically differentiated knowledge of subject matter. This flexible understanding can provide multiple entry points for students who differ in outlook and capacities (see Hawkins, 1974; for physics, Karplus, 1980; for geometry, Vollrath, 1976).

In learning, individual growth sometimes mirrors the growth of knowledge: what individuals learn may repeat episodes of growth and conceptual change in the common stock of reason. As research on subject-matter specific student conceptions has shown (Novick & Nussbaum, 1978; Nussbaum, 1979; Tamir, Gal-Choppin, & Nussinovitz, 1981), students are divided and creative in their beliefs about the nature of matter (e.g., continuous versus particulate), the earth as a cosmic body (e.g., flat versus spherical), or the principle of life (e.g., animism versus biological attributes such as nutrition and reproduction), to give a few examples. History does not of course necessarily or completely repeat itself. But the evolution of scientific understanding in general and the history of the disciplines provide the teacher with a collection of examples of conceptual change:

> By looking *both* at individuals' cognitive schemes and how they have developed *and* at the development of intellectual disciplines we may be able to see the crucial points of conceptual change, compare them and see how they might justifiably be made congruent. (Petrie, 1976, p. 129)

In teaching, requirements for the depth and breadth of content knowledge shade into moral imperatives.

Telling the Story of Knowledge

Telling the story of knowledge is to give an account of how knowledge comes into being; it is to reveal the ways and means of coming to knowledge which lie concealed in the end result. Telling a story is associated with a powerful pedagogy; it means to include the dimensions of time and change and, with that, of variation and choice. The story of knowledge shows to both teachers and students that great scholars in other ages have thought in ways that we now dismiss, too readily, as childish. Thus astronomers have written a curriculum for children organized historically around themes like *Charting the Universe* and *The Universe in Motion;* the latter theme

> centers on accounting for common observations like the daily apparent motion of the sun, moon, and stars, and most particularly the apparent motion of the planets. We embark in considerable detail about geocentric and heliocentric models of the solar system and point out that in the seventeenth century the finest observational astronomers, like Tycho, preferred the geocentric model. A few, with exactly the same data at the same time, preferred the heliocentric. (Atkin, 1981, pp. 6–7)

The point is not so much the parallelism between the growth and change of knowledge in a domain of enquiry and conceptual change in children, but the fact that data alone cannot tell a story.

No one lives in reality. People think and act by perceptions and intentions that construe and reach beyond the immediately given. Schooled imagination is disciplined imagination. But schools can be places where the discipline of thought can be liberating. Initiation into the history and theory of knowledge helps teachers and students to see the human mind at work, shaping itself and the conditions of its existence. This knowledge brings with it the understanding that freedom is one part of the human condition, while the other part is determination. Every student has the right to be initiated into what is baffling about the social and natural world: the sunset, the ocean, family life, and the social organization of labor. Epistemology, ethics, and pedagogy converge in content.

SUMMARY

In this hierarchical argument, I have examined the place of content knowledge in teaching, such as it logically is, and such as it could and should be. Content knowledge is a logical precondition for the activities of teaching; without it, teacher activities such as asking questions or planning lessons cannot proceed. This reminder about the meaning of the term teaching does not set minimal or desirable levels of content knowledge. It simply clarifies the intrinsic connection between content knowledge and teaching as a distinctive form of professional work.

When we consider under what conditions a teacher can legitimately be the intellectual leader of a group, we find that a firm grasp of content and abundant knowledge are required. Deficiencies in the depth and assurance of teachers' content knowledge can act as conceptual and behavioral traps that lead teachers and students away from education to outward forms of achievement, confusion, preoccupation with process, and management concerns.

Research studies on teaching suggest that teachers' orientation toward process affects students' opportunities to learn directly, through teacher behavior and indirectly, through shaping student conceptions of the nature of schoolwork. There is some evidence that this orientation may come by default, i.e., that it stems from lack of content knowledge. But an orientation toward process as opposed to content can also be an expression of teacher beliefs (Carew & Lightfoot, 1979). A straightforward concern for responsible action requires that future teachers should be aware of the historical and personal sources of their beliefs, and of the empirical and conceptual consequences for students.

If we do not want to miss the practical and ethical mark of teaching, teachers' intellectual responsibility has to be taken seriously. But for teachers, factual and conceptual control of content is not enough. The firm grasp of subject matter has to be relaxed to allow for its pedagogical or "fluid" control, that is, "the extent to which the teacher holds knowledge flexibly and easily, incorporating new or conflicting information, tolerating dissonance and ambiguity, and keeping the door open to alternative points of view" (Joyce & Harootunian, 1967, p. 40).

Given the pedagogical requirement for flexible control of subject matter, knowledge of epistemology and history of science is a specific preparation for teaching. Content knowledge of this kind and at this level deepens understanding of knowledge and subject matter, encourages the mobility of teacher conceptions, and yields pedagogical knowledge in the shape of multiple and fluid conceptions. It also contributes to a form of classroom life in which all participants are seen and treated as the potential source of thoughts and actions that makes sense. Thus, as the stringency of content knowledge requirements is increased, the yields of content knowledge for teaching are increased and diversified: content knowledge lends substance, strength, and rightness to the activities of teaching.

It is no good having teachers who are ill-informed. Few people will disagree with this. But to act on this simple insight, it is necessary to look dispassionately at beliefs and institutional realities that dilute or crowd out content in teacher education.

The fascination of educators with things and techniques is troublesome, no less so than unexamined beliefs in learning by doing and the unrealistic goals that seem to come with the territory. The philosophy and social sciences of education compass much that is dry theory and energetic folly. Thus I submit three pleas for discussion.

1. No more learning by doing. Student or practice teaching should either be dispensed with as a frill (and an often uneducative one at that), or be institutionalized in earnest after graduation. In this case, subject matter experts should supervise all beginning teachers, regardless of levels of schooling. The obvious model is the training of physicians with its emphasis on knowledge and appropriate action in the face of uncertainty (Coser, 1979; Fox, 1957). Use all time allotted to conventional forms of classroom induction for the study of the history and conceptual foundations of a specialized academic subject.

2. No more "soap operas" in learning to teach. It is not evident that university curricula ought to reflect the problems of new professionals or be geared toward their psychological adjustment. In taking on the teacher role, transitional problems are normal and should not be made much of. People who have fantasies about their effects as a teacher, or who cannot settle down to do their work with the necessary persistence and attack, should not become teachers. Instead of interpersonal skills and parent-teacher relations, teach about the subject-matter specific conceptions and misconceptions of learners.

3. More inspirational education. The teacher's calling has dignity. It requires a good mind and heart and a sense of obligation. The teacher's work gives people access to the life of the mind. Don't be afraid to tell future teachers so. Instead of so-called educational theories and the foundations of education, let them study the lives of people who took teaching seriously.

None of this is surprising. But for the requisite mix of sophistication and common sense, we will have to draw on sources outside of schools and colleges of education.

REFERENCES

Anderson, L. (1981). *Student responses to seatwork: Implications for the study of students' cognitive processing* (Research Series #102). East Lansing, MI: Institute for Research on Teaching, Michigan State University.

Anderson, R. C. (1977). The notion of schemata and the educational enterprise: General discussion of the conference. In R. C. Anderson, R. J. Spiro, & W. E. Montague (Eds.), *Schooling and the acquisition of knowledge*. Hillsdale, NJ: Lawrence Erlbaum Associates.

Atkin, J. B. (1981). *The nature of astronomy: Implications for teaching children.* Paper presented at the annual convention of the American Educational Research Association, Los Angeles, CA.

Bernstein, B. (1975). *Class, codes and control* (Vol. 3). London: Routledge & Kegan Paul.

Bettelheim, B., & Zelan, K. (1982). *On learning to read: The child's fascination with meaning.* New York: Alfred A. Knopf.

Brophy, J. E., & Good, T. L. (1974). *Teacher-student relationships: Causes and consequences.* New York: Holt, Rinehart and Winston.

Bruner, J. S. (1968). *Toward a theory of instruction.* New York: W. W. Norton & Co.

Carew, J. V., & Lightfoot, S. L. (1979). *Beyond bias.* Cambridge, MA: Harvard University Press.

Clifford, G. J. (1978). Words for schools: The applications in education of the vocabulary researches of Edward L. Thorndike. In P. Suppes (Ed.), *Impact of research on education: Some case studies.* Washington, DC: National Academy of Education.

Coser, R. L. (1979). *Training in ambiguity: Learning through doing in a mental hospital.* New York: The Free Press.

Davis, R. B. (1980). The postulation of certain specific, explicit, commonly-shared frames. *Journal of Mathematical Behavior, 3*(1), 167–201.

Dearden, R. F., Hirst, P. H., & Peters, R. S. (Eds.). (1972). *Education and the development of reason.* London: Routledge & Kegan Paul.

Dewey, J. (1904/1965). The relation of theory to practice in education. In M. Borrowman (Ed.), *Teacher education in America: A documentary history.* New York: Teachers College Press.

Duckworth, E. (1981). *Understanding children's understanding.* Paper presented at the Ontario Institute for Studies in Education, Ontario, Canada.

Erlwanger, S. H. (1973). Benny's conception of rules and answers in IPI mathematics. *Journal of Children's Mathematical Behavior, 1*(2), 177–196.

Floden, R., Porter, A., Schmidt, W., Freeman, D., & Schwille, J. (1981). Responses to curriculum pressures: A policy capturing study of teacher decisions about content. *Journal of Educational Psychology, 73,* 129–141.

Fox, R. C. (1957). Training for uncertainty. In R. K. Marton, G. G. Reader, & P. L. Kendall (Eds.), *The student physician: Introductory studies in the sociology of medical education.* Cambridge, MA: Harvard University Press.

Freeman, D. J., Kuhs, T. M., Porter, A. C., Knappen, L. B., Floden, R. E., Schmidt, W. H., & Schwille, J. R. (1983). The fourth-grade mathematics curriculum as inferred from textbooks and tests. *Elementary School Journal, 83,* 501–513.

Freeman, H. (1981). Authority, power, and knowledge: Politics and epistemology in the "new" sociology of education. *Philosophy of Education 1980: Proceedings of the thirty-sixth annual meeting of the Philosophy of Education Society, Illinois State University.*

Green, T. F. (1971). *The activities of teaching.* New York: McGraw-Hill.

Gustin, W. (1982). *Critical moments in the teaching of mathematics: What makes teaching difficult?* Unpublished doctoral dissertation, Michigan State University.

Hawkins, D. (1973). *Finding the maximum surface area in education.* Paper presented at the Conference on Open Education, Education Development Center, Newton Massachusetts. It appeared in *New Ways, 1*(1).

Hawkins, D. (1974). *The informed vision: Essays on learning and human nature.* New York: Agathon Press.

Highet, G. (1966). *The art of teaching.* New York: Alfred A. Knopf.

Hirst, P. H. (1974). *Knowledge and the curriculum: A collection of philosophical papers.* London: Routledge & Kegan Paul.

Inkeles, A. (1977). The international evaluation of educational achievement. *Proceedings of the National Academy of Education, 4,* 163.

Joyce, B. R., & Harootunian, B. (1967). *The structure of teaching.* Chicago, IL: Science Research Associates, 1967.

Karplus, R. (1980). *Educational aspects of the structure of physics.* Paper presented at the annual convention of the American Educational Research Association, Boston, MA.

Kohlberg, L., & Mayer, R. (1972). Development as the aim of education. *Harvard Educational Review, 42,* 449–496.

Kirsch, A. (1976). Aspects of simplification in mathematics teaching. In *Proceedings of the third international congress on mathematical education.* Karlsruhe Federal Republic of Germany: International Congress for Mathematics Education, 1976.

Lampert, M. (1982). *Learning about thinking from the perspective of the classroom teacher: A case study of collaboration with practitioners in educational research.* Cambridge, MA: Division for Study and Research in Education, Massachusetts Institute of Technology.

McKinney, W. Lynn, & Westbury, I. (1975). Stability and change: The public schools of Gary, Indiana, 1940–1970. In W. A. Reid & D. F. Walker (Eds.), *Case studies in curriculum change: Great Britain and the United States.* London: Routledge & Kegan Paul.

Meyer, J. W. (1980). Levels of the educational system and schooling effects. In C. E Bidwell & D. M. Windham (Eds.), *The analysis of educational productivity (Vol. II: Issues in macroanalysis). Cambridge, MA: Ballinger Publishing Co.*

Morine-Dershimer, G. (1979). *Teacher plan and classroom reality: The South Bay study* (Research Series #60). East Lansing, MI: Institute for Research on Teaching, Michigan State University.

Novick, S., & Nussbaum, J. (1978). Junior high school pupils' understanding of the particulate nature of matter: An interview study. *Science Education, 62*(3), 273–281.

Nussbaum, J. (1979). Children's conceptions of the earth as a cosmic body: A cross age study. *Science Education, 63*(1), 83–93.

Oakeshott, M. (1972). Education: The engagement and its frustration. In R. F. Dearden, P. H. Hirst & R. S. Peters (Eds.), *Education and the development of reason.* London: Routledge & Kegan Paul.

Paley, V. G. (1981). *Wally's stories.* Cambridge, MA: Harvard University Press.

Peters, R. S. (1977). *Education and the education of teachers.* London: Routledge & Kegan Paul.

Peters, R. S. (1978). *Ethics and education.* London: George Allen & Unwin.

Peterson, P. L., Marx, R., & Clark, C. M. (1978). Teacher planning, teacher behavior, and student achievement. *American Educational Research Journal, 15*(3), 417–432.

Petrie, H. G. (1976). Evolutionary rationality: Or can learning theory survive in the jungle of conceptual change? In *Philosophy of Education,* Normal, IL: Philosophy of Education Society.

Petrie, H. G. (1981). *The dilemma of enquiry and learning.* Chicago, IL: University of Chicago Press.

Scheffler, I. (1968). University scholarship and the education of teachers. *Teachers College Record, 70*(1), 77–87.

Scheffler, I. (1977). In praise of cognitive emotions. *Teachers College Record, 79*(2), 167–185.

Schmidt, W. H., Caul, J., Byers, J. L., & Buchmann, M. (1983). Content of basal text selections: Implications for comprehension instruction. In G. G. Duffy, L. Roehlers & J. Mason (Eds.), *Comprehension instruction: Perspectives and suggestions.* New York: Longman.

Schwab, J. J. (1978). The practical: Translation into curriculum. In I. Westbury & N. Wilkof (Eds.), *Science, curriculum and liberal education.* Chicago, IL: University of Chicago Press.

Schwille, J., Porter, A., Belli, G., Floden, R., Freeman, D., Knappen, L., Kuhs, T., & Schmidt. W. (1983). Teachers as policy brokers in the content of elementary school mathematics. In L. Shulman & G. Sykes (Eds.), *Handbook on teaching and policy.*

Shroyer, J. C. (1981). *Critical moments in the teaching of mathematics: What makes teaching difficult?* Unpublished doctoral dissertation, Michigan State University.

Smith, B. O. (1972). *Teachers for the real world.* Washington, DC: The American Association of Colleges for Teachers Education.

Smith, E. L., & Anderson, C. (1981). Elementary school science. In *Progress Report for the period from July 1, 1980–September 30, 1981.* East Lansing, MI: Institute for Research on Teaching, Michigan State University.

Soltis, J. F. (1981). Education and the concept of knowledge. In *Philosophy and education: 80th yearbook of the National Society for the Study of Education.* Chicago, IL: University of Chicago Press.

Tamir, P., Gal-Choppin, R., & Nussinovitz, R. (1981). How do intermediate and junor high school students conceptualize living and nonliving? *Journal of Research in Science Teaching, 18*(3), 241–248.

Thomas, L. (1982, March 14). The art of teaching science. *New York Times Magazine,* 123–126.

Vollrath, J. H. (1976). The place of geometry in mathematics teaching: An analysis of recent developments. *National Studies in Mathematics, 7,* 431–442.

Walberg, H. J. (1982). *Improving educational standards and productivity: The research basis for policy.* Berkeley, CA: McCutchan Publishing Corp.

Wilson, J. (1975). *Educational theory and the preparation of teachers.* Windsor, England: National Foundation for Educational Research Publishing Co.

Zahorik, J. A. (1970). The effect of planning on teaching. *The Elementary School Journal,* 143–151.

4

Teacher Competency Testing and the Teacher Educator*

Donald M. Medley
University of Virginia

INTRODUCTION

Teacher education faces a crisis of confidence today. Unless teacher educators can convince the public—and themselves—that professional teacher education is necessary to the future of public education, and can make immediate visible progress toward the transformation of present-day teacher-education programs into genuine professional programs, teacher education will cease to exist.

Critics of teacher education do not hesitate to assert that teaching is not a profession, that there is no mystique, no body of knowledge, skills, and professional values necessary to effective teaching on which teacher-education curriculum may be based, analogous to those which characterize medicine, law, and other learned professions. These critics maintain that there are no differences between graduates of our programs and graduates of liberal-arts colleges which make our graduates any more effective teach-

---

* This chapter draws on 25 years of reading, research and reflection; as a result it is impossible to give credit to all of the many colleagues whose findings or ideas I have appropriated and presented as though they were my own. Discussions with Robert B. Howsam during the early phases of its preparation were particularly valuable and influential. The original impetus to write it came from Karl Massanari. The support of the School of Education and the Bureau of Educational Research at the University of Virginia, which made the whole thing possible, is also gratefully acknowledged. Last but not least, the secretarial assistance of Mary Rolfe made the process of preparation almost a pleasure.

Reprinted with permission from the Association of Teacher Educators and the Bureau of Educational Research; copyright (c) 1982.

ers. Teacher educators today are powerless to refute this charge, are unable to demonstrate any differences between graduates of teacher-education programs and liberal-arts college graduates in knowledge, skills, or professional values.

The major reason why we are in this predicament is because we do not have the instrumentation we need to detect such differences (if, indeed, there are any). The procedures we use to assess the competence of teachers are too insensitive to the differences to detect them or to convince anyone but ourselves that they exist. The only approaches available are paper-and-pencil tests and performance ratings. The paper-and-pencil tests are too irrelevant and the rating scales are too subjective to be either reliable or valid. We are forced to admit that we ourselves cannot reliably measure the competencies that are supposed to distinguish the competent, professionally trained teacher from the incompetent or the untrained. When the graduates of our own program say that nothing they learned from us was relevant, we have no way of refuting them, because we cannot measure what they are supposed to have learned from us, much less demonstrate that by learning it they have become better teachers.

The teacher-education institutions of this country have two functions to perform: a training function and a gatekeeping function. The training function requires that they make students competent practitioners of the teaching profession. The gatekeeping function requires that they graduate only those students who actually become competent practitioners.

In the past, by far the greater share of the resources and efforts of program faculties has been devoted to fulfilling the training function. Meanwhile, the gatekeeping function has been largely neglected, which has inspired the crisis of confidence that we face. When the public accuses us of graduating too many incompetent teachers, they may be correct: we cannot tell because we cannot measure and therefore do not know which of our graduates are competent. There is no evidence that either scores on our tests or the ratings we make of our students have any correlation with teacher effectiveness.

The analysis of the problem of assessing the competency of an individual teacher that will be presented here is designed to demonstrate that the present lack of a valid procedure for assessing teacher competence reflects not an absence of means but a failure to use them; we can develop ways to discriminate competent teachers from incompetent ones if we will only commit enough resources and effort to the task. I submit that we must do so, and do so soon, or we may be out of business in a few years.

The solution that I suggest is offered primarily to demonstrate that the problem can be solved, and only secondarily to suggest what I consider the best strategy for solving it.

Definitions and Assumptions

The first step in analyzing the problem is to accept—at least for the moment
—some assumptions and definitions. I have assumed, first of all, that teaching is, or must become, a profession, as has been so eloquently argued by
the Bicentennial Commission on Education for the Profession of Teaching
of the American Association of Colleges for Teacher Education (Howsam,
Corrigan, Denemark, & Nash, 1976). Since the central task of the practitioner of any profession is professional problem solving, I have further
assumed that problem-solving skill is the central ability that we must assess.
This assumption has had considerable impact both on the way in which I
will enter the domain to be assessed, and on the strategy I shall propose for
measuring it.

I have assumed, third, that the teaching profession (like any other)
must bear the responsibility itself for the competence of its members, and
that this responsibility can best be discharged by the training arm of the profession, that is, by the professional schools. As a consequence, the specific
procedures I will propose are ones best implemented in the teacher-education institutions.

Some definitions. There are four terms often treated as synonymous:
teacher effectiveness, teacher performance, teacher competence, and *teacher
competency.* It seems to me that these terms will be much more useful if
clear (though somewhat arbitrary) distinctions in their meanings are made
and carefully preserved. I propose the following definitions:

1. *Teacher competency* will be defined here as any single knowledge,
skill, or professional value which (1) a teacher may be said to possess, and
(2) the possession of which is believed to be relevant to the successful practice of teaching. The level of complexity at which a competency is defined is
arbitrary and depends on the use to be made of the term. The ability to
thread a 16mm projector has been proposed as one such competency. The
ability to adapt media to current instructional goals has been proposed as
another. The general ability to solve professional problems may be regarded
as a competency. Although these examples vary widely in complexity, all
may be useful for certain purposes and may therefore be legitimately referred to as competencies.

The individual competency (however defined) is no more than a convenient unit to use in discussing teacher education or teacher evaluation.
The oft-heard phrases "competency assessment" and "competency testing"
themselves imply that what is assessed or tested are competencies. The term
"Competency-Based Teacher Education" refers to teacher education organized in terms of specified competencies. The objectives of such a program
take the form of a list of competencies which each graduate will possess.

Our definition of competency implies two properties that need emphasis. One of them is that competencies must be defined in terms of *process,* or what the teacher does, not in terms of *product,* or the effect on others of what the teacher does. "The ability to communicate effectively" is not a competency because the term *effectively* has to do with outcomes. The possession of some set of communication skills necessary to effective communication is a competency, however. As we shall see, this point is important because it implies that any competency must be assessed directly in terms of what a teacher knows, does, or believes; but it may be assessed only indirectly in terms of what the teacher can get a pupil to know, do, or believe. It also means that when we teach a competency to a teacher we are trying to change the teacher in some way, not some pupil that may be encountered in the future. It is only when competencies are defined in this way that competency assessment becomes feasible.

Second, we speak of competencies in terms of *mastery.* In defining competency-based teacher education, Elam (1971) did not speak of the amount of any one competency a teacher has but only whether he or she has reached a point referred to as mastery. If (s)he has, the teacher is said to possess that competency; if (s)he has not, the teacher is said to lack that competency.

2. *Teacher Competence,* on the other hand, is conceived of as a matter of degree. Some teachers are more competent than others; teachers grow in competence with training and experience. Minimum competence is the lowest level of competence at which a teacher can practice the teacher profession safely—i.e., without undue risk of harming a child.

Teacher Competence is defined in terms of repertoire; how competent a teacher is depends on the repertoire of competencies he or she possesses. Because of the arbitrariness of the level at which individual competencies may be defined, there is some flexibility in the way that a particular level of competence may be specified. It is perfectly possible to say that teachers are "competent to teach" if they have mastered one central competency: if they can solve the professional problems that teachers encounter. Such a definition is correct enough, but it is not very useful, either for designing a program to produce competent teachers or for designing a competency test with which to identify them. Clearly, *competence* must be defined differently to meet the demands of each situation, in terms of competencies that are specified at whatever level of detail we need in order to achieve our purpose.

The major contribution that the competency-based teacher education movement made to the profession was the propagation of this way of defining competence. The idea was not new; it was clearly stated and used by Joyce and Harootunian (1967). Until this concept was generally adopted, teacher competence was generally regarded as some sort of a unitary trait in terms of which teachers could be ranked uniquely. The nature of this dimension was mysterious; indeed, it had almost a mystical quality to it. Any specification of the nature of teacher competence, proposed as a basis for measuring it, was almost certain to be dismissed as inadequate. The whole, we were told, was greater than the sum of its parts. This view made it almost impossible to measure teacher competence, to validate measures in use, or even to design programs for developing competence.

The situation is very different if we define the whole of teacher competence as the sum of a set of competencies that are its parts. To define a set of competencies that everyone will accept as an adequate definition of competence is, of course, impossible. But it is not necessary. As we learned from competency-based teacher education, what is necessary is that we be explicit and frank. Once we have done so, we can design programs to train competent teachers; we can construct instruments to measure how competent teachers are, and we can find out whether "competent" teachers are also effective.

3. *Teacher Performance* refers to what the teacher does on the job rather than to what he or she can do (that is, how competent he or she is); it is, therefore, specific to the job situation. Unlike teacher competence, which is a characteristic the teacher can take along to a new situation, teacher performance may be expected to differ in different situations. The quality of a performance depends, of course, on the competence of the teacher; but it also depends on the context in which the teacher works. We speak of how well a teacher performs; of how competent a teacher is; and of which competencies the teacher possesses.

4. *Teacher effectiveness* refers to the effect that the teacher's performance has on pupils. It is the bottom line. Like teacher performance, teacher effectiveness depends in large part on the context in which the teacher performs. In addition, it depends on the responses pupils make—on what pupils do. Just as equally competent teachers perform differently in different situations, so identical performances would not be expected to have identical effects in different situations. Teacher competence is related to teacher effectiveness only by way of its effect on teacher performance.

It is useful to distinguish two kinds of effects that teachers have on pupils which call for different assessment strategies. One kind of effect is manifest in the behavior of the pupils in the classroom that results in pupil learning. The other kind of effect is manifest in pupil behavior after the learning has taken place—in those changes in pupils' abilities, knowledge, or attitudes usually referred to as the "outcomes" of instruction. Both kinds of effects must be measured in terms of pupil behavior, but they are quite different.

Teacher effectiveness differs from competence or performance, then, in that it cannot be measured in terms of the behavior of the teacher, in whole or in part. By definition, effectiveness must be assessed in terms of the behavior of pupils, or, more precisely, in terms of changes in their behavior.

Dynamics of Teacher Evaluation

These distinctions may be clarified by inspection of the flowchart in Figure 1. Along the horitontal line I have indicated five points in a teacher's career at which the teacher might be evaluated, five potential assessment points we might use. At one time or another, or for one purpose or another, attempts have been made to evaluate teachers at each of these points. Since very different characteristics can be assessed at each point, which point teachers should be assessed at depends very much on the purpose for which the assessment is made; making the assessment at the point appropriate to the purpose for which it will be used is critically important. Much of the confusion that surrounds the problem of teacher evaluation results from failure to observe this obvious principle.

The first point at which teachers can be assessed is when they enter teacher education as students (or in some other way become identified with the teaching profession). Some of the characteristics that can be measured at that time will persist unchanged and will eventually have an impact on the pupils that students encounter after they become teachers. Other characteristics will interact with training experiences to determine how competent teachers become—that is, what competencies they acquire in training, and so eventually have an impact on the pupils the teachers encounter. If there are competencies that teachers are expected to possess on entry to teacher education (rather than to acquire with training), they should be assessed at this point. To wait to assess such a characteristic until the students complete training and then deny them certification is indefensible.

The second assessment point follows the teachers' training experience, but normally precedes their admission into the practice of teaching. This is the point at which competence may be assessed most directly, independently of any specific job situation. As the diagram indicates, competence interacts with contextual variables and teacher motivation to determine teacher performance. Since teacher performance affects pupil learning experiences and outcomes, teacher competence also has an impact on them, but as only one of several factors that affect them and determine teacher effectiveness—factors external to the teacher and not under her or his control.

The third assessment point is based on the actual behavior of the teachers while they are teaching. Notice that, in all, four distinct types of influences have been identified as affecting teacher performance: (a) pre-existing teacher characteristics, (b) the training experiences the teacher has had, (c) the situational context in which the teacher works, and (d) teacher motivation (how the teacher feels about her or his job on a particular day).

The fourth assessment point identified in the diagram is labeled *pupil learning experiences.* The idea of evaluating teachers on the basis of the quality of the learning experiences they provide for the pupils is an attractive one, since it is based on how well teachers perform their central function (Fisher et al., 1980; Medley, R. S. Soar, & R. M. Soar, 1975). This is

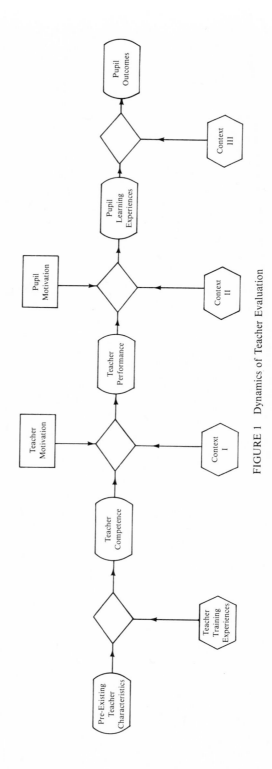

FIGURE 1 Dynamics of Teacher Evaluation

the first assessment point at which we have proposed to base our evaluation of teachers, not on their own behaviors, but on those of their pupils; the first point at which direct competency assessment becomes impossible. What we can assess directly is one type of teacher effectiveness.

Note that the learning experiences a pupil has are affected, directly or indirectly, by no fewer than six different influences, including two contextual variables—Type I (which affect teacher performance) and Type II (which do not, but affect the way pupils respond to teacher performance)— and pupil motivation as well as teacher motivation. Pupil motivation here refers to what the pupil brings to the situation; pupils, like other human beings, have good days and bad days. The effectiveness of a teacher will vary from one to the other.

The final assessment point is the point at which outcomes are measured—that is, pupil knowledge, abilities, and/or attitudes after instruction has ended. Outcomes of instruction are assessed by comparing the status of pupils before and after instruction on appropriate tests and other measures. The part of these outcomes attributable to the teacher (teacher effectiveness) may be assessed only by isolating the many factors that affect these outcomes. These other factors include all of those mentioned as affecting pupil-learning experiences plus a third kind of context variable which interacts with pupil-learning experiences to determine how much the pupil will learn from them. The important thing to realize is that when we want to assess teacher competence, factors of all seven types function as sources of errors of measurement.

One major point that Figure 1 makes about contextual variables is that more of them affect evaluations of teacher effectiveness than affect evaluations of teacher performance, but that none of them affect direct assessments of teacher competence. As a result, it is much more difficult to obtain information about teacher competence from either than by direct assessment of teacher competence itself. Indeed, it is all but impossible to do so, especially from teacher effectiveness.

Teacher competence can be assessed directly only at the first or second of the five points; it must be inferred indirectly from assessments made at later points. The accuracy of such inferences depends, of course, on our ability to measure and take into account the effects of all of the contextual factors. We do not at present know how to identify these other influences separately, much less to assess their effects. Therefore, it would seem clear that the best, if not the only way to assess teacher competency is directly, that is, at the second point.

It might seem obvious from all this that competency should be assessed directly at the second point; but to judge from general practice, the fact must not be as obvious to everyone. Indirect assessment of competence, that is, assessment at other points, is the rule rather than the exception. The general assumption seems to be that the closer to pupil outcomes the evaluation is made, the more valid it is. Whether the assumption is justified depends on what you are trying to measure: competence, performance, or effectiveness? Since the only one of the three that is a characteristic of the individual teacher is competence, it seems clear that evaluation of teachers must be based on assessment of competence, not of performance or effectiveness.

At lease one state has enacted legislation requiring an annual assessment of the competence of every public-school teacher every year. It also requires any teacher whose competence falls below a certain level to undergo remedial training as a condition for continued certification. This particular law also prescribes how the competence of the teacher is to be assessed. The assessment is to be based partly on the teacher's *performance* and partly on the teacher's *effectiveness* (estimated from pupil outcome measures). No provision is made to assess and take into account any of the other factors that affect these two measures. Any deficiency in performance or effectiveness is automatically attributed to a lack of competence—by law. This is a striking instance of what happens when the terms competence, performance, and effectiveness are confused.

Another state has, after several years of study of the problem, implemented what they call "competency based teacher certification." In this scheme, teachers are certified on the basis of ratings of their performance on the job. Once again, any deficit in performance is interpreted as a deficit in teacher competence. We would, of course, describe this as a system of "performance-based teacher certification."

All over the country school administrators and supervisors routinely rate teacher performance and interpret the ratings as measures of teacher competence; in most cases performance ratings are used to diagnose incompetence and to prescribe remedial training, without allowance for or (apparently) awareness of the other potent influences which remedial training cannot possibly affect. How much effort and money is wasted on in-service training designed to help teachers develop competencies they already possess under the mistaken notion that some defect in performance can be corrected by such training? The least we can do is make sure that a teacher does in fact lack a competency before forcing her or him to undergo training designed to develop it.

The rest of this chapter will be devoted to a discussion of how we can do just this. We will first examine in more detail the problems involved in attempts to infer competence from measures of performance and effectiveness, and then discuss those involved in attempts to assess competence directly.

THE INDIRECT ASSESSMENT OF TEACHER COMPETENCE

Inferring Competence from Outcomes

To the lay person, the obvious way to evaluate a teacher is by measuring how much pupils learn from the teacher. There are plenty of precedents in other occupations. The salesman who does not sell is fired; the salesman who sells the most gets promoted or is given a trip to Hawaii. The television repairman is not entitled to be paid until he makes your set work again. Shouldn't teachers be discharged as incompetent unless their pupils achieve up to standard? It is, incidentally, not just the lay public who think this way; there are reputable—even eminent—professional educators who take the same position (Popham, 1971; Millman, 1972). Does it make sense?

To say that teacher competence should be assessed on the basis of pupil learning makes sense only if you regard the work of the teacher as subprofessional, as comparable to that of the salesman or the television repairman. If you regard the teacher as a professional, as one whose role is comparable to that of the physician or the attorney, it does not make sense. One of the essential characteristics of the practitioners of any profession is that they are not expected, are not even permitted, to guarantee results. No physician guarantees that all patients will recover (much less that they will never die); no lawyer promises to win every case; no dentist guarantees that you will never lose a tooth. Professional ethics demand that the professional accept any case, however hopeless; professionals offer their services, their best efforts—not results. It is recognized that professionals offer services whose outcomes cannot be guaranteed; that they deal with problems which have no known solution as well as with ones that have known solutions, accept hopeless cases as well as the hopeful ones. Subprofessionals may (and should) be asked to deal only with problems they can solve. If my television set is beyond repair, I expect the technician to say so and not to try to fix it. Instead, I scrap the set. If my father has terminal cancer, I expect the physician to do whatever he can for him anyhow. I may secretly hope for a miracle—which just might happen. I do not scrap my father, and the physician does not refuse to treat him. If my father dies, I still pay the physician's fee.

The widespread demand from the lay public that teachers be held accountable for the results they obtain—for the amount that their pupils learn —reflects, then, a serious misconception of the nature of the teacher's task. Until the misconception is corrected the demand will continue. The public accepts the fact that some diseases cannot be cured because medical science, being imperfect, knows no way to cure them; but the public does not accept the fact that some children cannot learn some things because pedagogical science, being imperfect, knows no way to teach them!

Measurement problems. The inadequacies of the science of pedagogy are not the only factors which prevent teachers from producing the achievement gains that society sets for their pupils. We can see from Figure 1 that there are multiple factors not controlled by the teacher which affect pupil outcomes either directly (Context III) or indirectly (Context I, Context II). It is these factors that are of concern to us because if we decide to assess teacher competence on the basis of pupil outcomes, we must take into account all of these factors, so that the part of the outcomes due to the teacher's competence—or lack of it—can be isolated and measured.

But it is not possible to take all such variables into account; first, because we do not know enough about them to measure them all, and second, because it would cost far too much to do so even if we could. We would need first to predict how much each of the teacher's pupils would learn if the teacher were able to realize each pupil's full potential, and then compare the pupil's actual learning with this potential in order to assess how effective the teacher was with that child.

The best we can do is to approximate this by measuring some of the context variables, including the previous achievement of each pupil, and from these measurements predict, by some form of regression analysis, how much that pupil might be expected to learn from the average teacher. If pupils learn more than was predicted, the excess is credited to the teacher; if they learn less, that is blamed on the teacher.

Experience with this method indicates that such measures are too unreliable, as well as too low in validity, to be adequate to our purpose. When we try to infer how competent a teacher is from how much one class of pupils learns from her or him, we are assuming that a similar measure based on another, similar class of pupils would be just as good a measure. Since teacher competence is a characteristic of the teacher, not of the class, both measures should yield similar scores; and any variations in scores of the same teacher from class to class must be regarded as errors of measurement. Such errors, of course, reduce the reliability of the scores. How unreliable can these scores be and still be usable?

It is generally agreed that in order to be suitable for evaluating individuals, a meausre should have a reliability coefficient of at least .90. A number of studies have been made of the reliability of the kind of teacher effectiveness scores we have been discussing (Brophy, 1973; Rosenshine, 1970; Veldman & Brophy, 1974). The results consistently indicate that the reliability lies somewhere between .30 and .40; which indicates that teacher effectiveness as measured varies a great deal from one situation to another. So much so that we must conclude that a measure of teacher effectiveness is a very unreliable indicator of teacher competence.

It would, of course, be possible to increase this reliability by measuring the effectiveness of each teacher with two or more classes of pupils and using the mean score. This would involve testing in different sections in the case of a secondary school teacher, or in successive years in the case of an elementary teacher. Using the Spearman-Brown formula, I estimate that in order to obtain a mean score with a reliability of .9 or more, one would have to test each teacher's effectiveness in at least 14 classes. In the case of an elementary school teacher, this means it would take at least 14 years to find out whether a teacher was competent or not.

The fact that differences in learning in different classes taught by the same teacher are so great gives some idea of the potency of contextual factors; particularly when one realizes that most of the data cited above involved two or more classes in the same school, so that differences between schools and communities were not taken into account. It is clear, then, that there are many kinds of differences between classes that we have not yet learned to measure.

There is one other serious threat to the validity of measures of teacher effectiveness based on pupil outcomes. This is the fact that no satisfactory measuring devices are available for measuring some of the most important outcomes that education is supposed to achieve. If things like inquiry skills, love of learning, regard for the rights of others and for the environment are regarded as important goals of teaching along with the basic skills of reading, writing, and so on, it is important that pupils' progress toward both outcomes should enter into any measure of teacher effectiveness.

When one's advancement, or even one's livelihood, depends on how well one does on any specific test or other assessment device, it is only natural to devote a major part of one's effort to doing whatever is necessary to earn a high score, and less effort or none to activities that are not rewarded. If a teacher's future depends on pupil gains on a reading test and/or an arithmetic test, whatever the teacher can do that will increase pupils' scores on those tests will be done. The effect of the Regents' Examinations on the teaching in high schools in the state of New York is notorious and not generally admired. A similar effect can be expected whenever pupils' test-score gains are used to assess teacher effectiveness. Pupil gains on those tests will go up. Any other kind of learning will go down.

In the short run, this would change the pattern of pupil learning in the district, the city, and the state in which the tests are used. In the long run, it would tend to eliminate teachers with any competencies other than those needed to raise pupils' test scores, and so lower the overall competence of teachers instead of raising it.

The teaching test. A particularly dangerous variation of this idea called a "teaching test" has been advocated by a few misguided educators (Popham, 1971; Millman, 1972). This scheme attempts to measure how effective a teacher is by having her or him teach a special brief unit to a group of pupils over a period usually no longer than a few hours. A special test is administered before and after the unit, and the amount of gain shown by the average pupil is taken as a measure of how effective or competent the teacher is.

Because the time allotted is so brief, the teacher cannot be expected to bring about any changes in pupils that take time to effect, that is, any of the more important kinds of learning. What he or she can do is raise scores on tests that measure only concepts that can be absorbed quickly by most pupils—such as facts. The kinds of outcomes measures are, then, representative of only a small part of those a teacher is expected to achieve, a part limited to those things that pupils can learn (and presumably forget) very quickly. Progress in learning to read—or to get along with others—would be much too slow to detect in the few hours involved in these tests.

If such a test were used to certify teachers, or to select them for some other purpose, the average quality of teachers certified would plummet rapidly, and the quality of education would follow closely behind it.

We have noted that the results a teacher obtains with one class in a year correlate .40 or less with those the same teacher achieves with another class in the same period. How high can the correlation be between what a teacher achieves with one class in a year and how much the same teacher achieves with another in a few hours? The validity of a teaching test can be no higher than this value.

Concluding remarks. Our analysis of the potential usefulness of teacher effectiveness measures based on pupil learning as measures of teacher competence has indicated that they have neither enough reliability nor validity to be recommended. There is one other reason which limits their usefulness. Their use implies the assumption that teacher competence is a unitary trait, an assumption discredited long ago. They do not provide any diagnostic information, any indication as to which competencies teachers possess and which they need to acquire before they can be said to be competent; a limitation which sharply limits their usefulness.

Inferring Teacher Competence from Use of Pupil Time

The idea of evaluating teacher competence on the basis of the amount and quality of the learning experiences they provide for pupils in their classroom is almost as attractive as that of evaluating teachers on the basis of how much pupils learn from them, if not more so. It is certainly more reasonable to hold teachers accountable for the learning experiences they provide in their classrooms than for the learning that results. Providing such experiences is the role of the teacher in the same sense as the role of the pupil is to learn from them. Outcomes relate more directly to what pupils do than to what teachers do. Since the only way the teacher can affect outcomes is by affecting the learning activities of pupils, we should be able to find out more about the competence of the teacher by looking at the activities (s)he provides than by looking at the outcomes.

So far as I know, this approach is as yet largely untried, although pupil learning experiences were a focus of research in teacher effectiveness in the Beginning Teacher Evaluation Study in California; and their use as a basis for teacher evaluation has at least been discussed elsewhere (Fisher et al., 1980; Medley, R. S. Soar, & R. M. Soar, 1975). We have as yet only begun to understand what the nature of these experiences should be, and objective and reliable methods of assessing these experiences have yet to be developed and tested. When and if they are, they may be very useful in assessing teacher performance in a particular situation, by providing accessible measures that are unaffected by context factors of Type III.

But even if measures of overall competency could be derived from those performance measures, they would still be of limited practical value because they would provide no indication of which competencies the teachers possessed and which they lacked—no diagnostic information.

Since teacher competence is defined in terms of what the teacher knows, believes, and can do, it would seem to make more sense to evaluate teacher competence by looking at what the teacher does, rather than at what the pupils do—that is, by observing teacher performance rather than observing pupil behavior or measuring pupil learning. Let us therefore consider teacher performance as a source of information about teacher competence.

Inferring Teacher Competence from Teacher Performance

Teacher performance is at present by far the most widely used basis for teacher evaluation. Teacher performance is usually assessed for one of two purposes: one is to support personnel decisions, decisions related to certification, selection, promotion and so on; the other is as a basis for planning efforts to increase teacher competence by preservice or inservice training. Use for the first purpose assumes that performance evaluations are predictive of or related to teacher effectiveness—that the higher the evaluation of a teacher's performance, the more effective the teacher may be assumed to be. Use for the second purpose assumes that such evaluations contain accurate information about teacher competencies, about which competencies the teacher possesses and which need to be acquired through additional training. As we shall see, neither assumption is quite as plausible as it may seem at first glance.

Performance-based teacher certification. Ratings of teacher performance in the classroom are widely regarded in the profession as the most desirable measures on which to base the decision whether or not a candidate should be certified as competent to teach. It is usually proposed that only a temporary or probationary certificate should be issued to the beginning teacher, and that it be replaced with a permanent one only after the teacher has taught for (say) three years and received a satisfactory rating or recommendation from her or his employer. This is another effect of the general view of the teacher as a subprofessional employee rather than as a professional practitioner, particularly unfortunate and harmful because it comes from within the profession.

The main objective of teacher certification (like that in any profession) is to protect the clients—in this case the children in the schools—from practitioners who are incompetent. The proposed scheme is questionable, then, since it allows incompetent practitioners to practice for three years before they are identified. Since teachers with less than three years experience form a large proportion of all teachers, this scheme defeats its own purpose to a considerable extent by admitting a substantial number of incompetent teachers into practice. No one suggests that any other professionals such as physicians, should practice for three years under a probationary license before their competence is assessed; no one wants an incompetent physician practicing for even three short years. I doubt that it is any easier to assess a physician's competence before (s)he is admitted to practice than it is to assess that of a teacher; if the medical profession accepts full responsibility for the competence of beginning medical practitioners can the teacher profession do less? If the profession cannot accept this responsibility it does not deserve to be regarded as a profession. To transfer this responsibility to supervisors in the schools would be defensible only if we could assume that all supervisors in the state were competent to make valid assessments of competence; and, worse yet, that they could do so using any rating scale they choose, basing the rating on one or two brief observations of the teacher's performance, if that.

The practice of evaluating teacher competence with ratings based on observations of the teacher's behavior while teaching is so well established, so generally accepted, that to question the practice smacks of heresy. I know of no religious faith whose believers have more confidence in it than educators have in this extraordinary notion that they can recognize competent teaching when they see it, a delusion shared equally by every lay person. I have yet to meet anyone, inside or outside the profession, who does not have a strong impression of the overall competence of any teacher (s)he has ever had. Ask the next person you meet to name that teacher and, whether that person has some claim to expertise or not, whether (s)he is an educator or a lay person, the answer will be swift, definite, and confident.

Since around 1915, experts have been using rating scales to assist them in arriving at valid, considered opinions about teacher competence (Boyce, 1915); most such scales provide for separate ratings of various characteristics supposed to contribute to the overall competence of the teachers which can then be combined into a single overall rating. A rater using one of the most sophisticated of the hundreds of rating scales that have been used is expected to be sensitive to 25 or more different teacher characteristics during an observation, and to rate a teacher on each and every one of them after a half-hour or so of observation is over. (Barr, 1930; Ryans, 1960;

Johnson, Elliott, & Capie, 1980). It is not clear whether the individual ratings contribute more to the rating of overall competence or whether the overall impression of competence contributes more to the individual ratings. Whichever it may be, there is no evidence I can find that teachers rated high on such instruments are the least bit more effective than teachers rated low. Very few studies have been made of this problem (apparently researchers are as susceptible to this notion as anyone else). Those few I have been able to find are unanimous in indicating that as predictors of teacher effectiveness, supervisory ratings have no validity whatsoever (Medley & Mitzel, 1959). There is no factual basis for this belief, then.

I have already drawn an analogy to the medical profession; let me extend it. How valid would you expect a rating of a physician's effectiveness to be if it were based on a half hour of observation of behavior with a patient? Remember that the observation (like those made of teachers) is to be made at a time chosen at random, and without any knowledge on the rater's part of what is wrong with any patient(s) the physician happens to treat during the visit, or of what the physician's diagnosis may be. And suppose, further, that the rating is made by whichever one of several hundred medical administrators in the state happens to know the physician best.

Suppose, further, that whether or not the physician was to be allowed to continue to practice depended on such a rating (or perhaps on the average or more than one rating, the number being left to the option of the rater) made after the physician has been practicing medicine for three years. Does this sound like the ideal way to license physicians? Does it even sound like a reasonable approach? Does it sound any better than the present system which requires the physician to pass a board examination before being allowed to begin to practice? On what basis could we say that it makes any more sense to certify teachers in such a fashion than physicians? Not only is there no factual evidence that the approach is valid; there is no logical basis for expecting that it should be.

What do performance ratings really measure? Whenever I reflect on this analogy I find myself wondering how the use of ratings of teacher performance became so popular in the first place; and has managed to survive virtually unchanged for over 65 years. The only way that I can account for it has to do with face validity. The fact is that the teachers who get high ratings look to the supervisors who make the ratings like better teachers than the teachers who get low ratings, as might be expected through a phenomenon similar to the self-fulfilling prophecy. And those same teachers usually look better to other people besides the raters, too—to other teachers, to administrators, to parents. When two or more raters rate the same teacher, their ratings tend to agree on how competent (s)he is even when both of them are probably wrong!

This is, of course, a most important question for a teacher to answer. The ability to impress everyone favorably, to make everyone think one is competent is much more important to success in the profession than any other teacher characteristic, including being competent. Since such evidence as exists indicates that the two are unrelated, the way to success in teaching lies in the direction of learning to look competent rather than learing to be competent.

Whatever characteristic it is that makes a teacher look competent seems to be stable, since how a teacher is rated is relatively unaffected by when the rater observes her or him, or who the rater is. If what a rater sees during a visit affects the rating that the teacher gets, then, there must be something about the way a teacher performs that is constant over various activities and times, something to which all raters respond similarly. This stable element has been given many names. It has been called *teaching style, classroom climate,* and *learning environment,* for example. But what does it look like? What are the raters responding to?

The process-product research has used low-inference instruments instead of ratings in an observational strategy essentially the same as that used by raters; that is, based on visits scheduled in random fashion, without regard to what the teacher is trying to accomplish during any one visit. Any behavioral pattern found to correlate with teacher effectiveness in this research must therefore be stable over random visits made by different observers.

It has become increasingly clear from recent reviews of this research that such stable behavior patterns exist, and that some aspects of the teaching style, classroom climate, or learning environment in the classroom can be identified. It has also become clear that some of these aspects are correlated with teacher effectiveness measured in pupil gains.

The failure of ratings to correlate with teacher effectiveness when low-inference measures do correlate seems to confirm the suspicion that whatever stable elements of classroom climate impress raters favorably must be irrelevant to teacher effectiveness. In other words, the raters must have an erroneous notion of what an effective teacher looks like.

It is time we accepted this unpleasant fact, the fact that you and I and the school administrator and the parent, even though we all agree on who is the best teacher, are all wrong. If the day ever arrives when one of the proposed schemes for certifying teachers on the basis of ratings of teacher performance goes into effect, so that someone's opinion determines who will and who will not be certified, two predictions can be made. It will cost more to certify teachers than it does today, and the average effectiveness of those certified will be no better than it is today.

Are low-inference measures of performance the answer? We have noted that the results of the process-product research indicate that if we use low-inference observation schedules instead of rating scales to assess teacher performance, we can (to a degree) distinguish effective teachers from ineffective ones. Then why not base certification upon such measures? If we certified teachers only after they had demonstrated the ability to create and maintain a classroom learning environment favorable to pupil learning, then those certified would be bound to be more competent than those not certified. In order to make the test fair, we might not assess teachers until they have had three years of practice in creating such an environment. Or, if we are worried about protecting children from incompetent teachers, we might evaluate teachers' performance in the first class they teach.

This plan has merit—more than any yet considered. But there are problems. It is likely to be rather expensive because it requires the use of specially trained observers who must visit classrooms all over the state, and must visit each one several times. How well teachers perform depends not only on how competent they are, but also on context factors that vary from class to class and school to school (the kind of pupils, facilities, and the amount and kind of support they receive from the school system, parents, and the community. It will be necessary to measure and take account of these variables, at additional cost, so that the part of the performance that is due to the competence of the teacher can be isolated. If this is not done, and done successfully, whether or not teachers are admitted to the practice of the profession may depend so much on what kind of a job they happen to get in their first year that new teachers would be foolish to accept positions in difficult situations, such as inner-city classrooms. Moreover, teachers certified on the basis of successful performance under favorable conditions might be quite incompetent to teach under less favorable ones. On the whole, this approach is probably not practicable because of cost and other problems (Clark & Marker, 1975).

But the most serious difficulty with this approach is a different kind of a problem: the measure of competence obtained is inadequate. At best it can only measure these teachers' ability to establish and maintain a classroom environment favorable to learning. It cannot yield measurements of other important competencies that the teachers use only under certain conditions or at certain times. The sample of performance competencies that teachers are likely to display during a single half-hour visit is neither large enough nor sufficiently representative of the full range of competencies they may possess to yield an adequate measure of the teachers' full repertoires.

In addition there are other kinds of competencies, competencies defined in terms of knowledge, of value positions, of perceptual abilities, of skill in decision-making, and so on, that the observer cannot infer from such an observation, or even a large number of them, because the observer does not have access to the information needed to make the inference.

Unless we are willing to use teaching style or classroom climate as the sole criterion for deciding whether a teacher is competent or not, and make more than one or two visits per teacher, we cannot make valid certification decisions on the basis of assessments of teacher performance on the job either in the form of ratings or of low-inference measures. This is not to say that such assessments may not have other legitimate uses; but as a means of measuring teacher competence they are inadequate.

Concluding remarks. At the beginning of our examination of performance assessment we identified two assumptions widely and uncritically made about performance ratings: (a) that they are valid-predictors of teacher effectiveness and (b) that they are viable ways of assessing teacher competence. We have seen that there is no evidence that either assumption is true; but that the face validity of such ratings is so great that their use is almost certain to continue to frustrate efforts to improve teaching by improving teacher selection. We have also seen that although the first of the two assumptions is tenable (to a degree) when low-inference instruments are used in place of rating scales, the second is not. We will have to employ other means to develop the valid, reliable, and objective measurements of the competence of individual teachers that we need. And it appears that these means must be based on the direct assessment of the competencies that make up teacher competence.

DIRECT ASSESSMENT OF COMPETENCE

Role of the Teacher-Education Institution

According to our definition, competencies must be defined and measured in terms of process, not product—that is, in terms of what teachers do, how they behave, rather than in terms either of what they get pupils to do in class or of what happens to pupils' achievement, abilities, or attitudes. We have defined competence in this way, not because outcomes are not important (they are, of course, far more important than what the teacher does), but because any impact that teacher education, teacher selection, and retention may have on the quality of education must be mediated by a change in what teachers do while they are teaching. Any improvement in the effectiveness of a teacher is the result of some change in the teacher's behavior, a change which usually results from the acquisition of a new competency.

The objectives of a teacher-education program, then, must be specified in terms of the changes in teacher behavior that the program is supposed to bring about in teachers trained in it; or, to use the terminology of this discussion, the objectives of a teacher-education program may be specified in terms of the competencies teachers trained in the program are expected to acquire. The objectives of any instrument or other device used for teacher evaluation may likewise be specified in terms of the competencies that the instrument requires the teacher to demonstrate. The term *competency test,* or *competency examination* is, then, an entirely appropriate term to apply to such an instrument.

It seems quite reasonable to require a student teacher to earn a certain score on a competency test; that is, to demonstrate mastery of a certain number of competencies, or to demonstrate a specified level of competence, before passing a course, graduating from a program, or receiving a teaching certificate. Such command of competencies, or competence to teach, is what teachers need in order to practice their profession safely (i.e., without undue risk of harming pupils).

The agency of government responsible for protecting citizens from incompetent practitioners can demand as a condition for admission to practice that each candidate demonstrate mastery of a specific set of competencies—of knowledges, abilities, and value positions—believed to be necessary to safe practice. The ultimate responsibility of the agency is, of course, for the effects that schooling has on pupils; this portion of the agency's responsibility has to do with teachers' qualifications which are seen as one important factor determining those effects. There are other equally important factors—physical facilities, for example—for which the agency is also responsible, for which the teacher cannot be held responsible.

The teacher-education program is concerned with teacher competence. (Other programs in the school, college, or department of education may be concerned with other factors: the training of administrators and other support personnel are examples.) In the operation of a teacher-education program, there will be many occasions that will involve assessments of students' acquisition of competencies; such occasions may be more frequent as well as more visible in so-called competency-based programs, but they occur in all teacher-education programs.

The task of assessing the competence of individual candidates and deciding whether they are competent enought to be certified is usually delegated to the institution that has trained the candidates. One alternative is for the responsible government agency to assess the competence of candidates; another is for the agency to hire someone else to do it. There was a time when the common practice was for a civil servant to examine each student's credentials and make the decision whether the candidate was competent to teach. This has generally been superseded by the approved-program approach, in which the institution that prepares the student rather than the civil servant assesses the student's competence and recommends certification or rejection. How the institution reaches this decision is usually left to the institution's discretion. Program approval is based on assessment of institutions or programs by the responsible agency, rather than of individual candidates, based on periodic site visits designed to evaluate the program on process criteria.

This approach assigns the responsibility for the critically important decision about the individual candidate to the agency best qualified to make it wisely (although that agency—the program faculty—can hardly be regarded as disinterested). The faculty of the program have each candidate under supervision for from two to four years, during which they have considerable opportunity for formative as well as summative evaluation. In the last analysis, then, it is the teacher-education faculty that makes the decisions that must be made about a student's competence until the student is actually allowed to enter the practice of teaching.

If the public is correct in asserting that too many incompetent teachers are practicing today, the blame rests squarely on the teacher-education faculty, then. The teacher-education institution has two important functions to perform: one is the training function and the other is the gatekeeping function. It is difficult to argue whether either is more important than the other; but there is no question which receives more emphasis, to which more time and effort is devoted. Program faculties see themselves primarily as teaching faculties: the gatekeeping function receives scant attention indeed.

If a faculty decided to put more emphasis on teacher evaluation, on the gatekeeping function, the question arises: How would it do so? Do we know enough about competency assessment so that if enough resources were committed to the task it could be accomplished?

My answer to this question will occupy the rest of this chapter, which will present an analysis of the problem that, although incomplete, should suffice to indicate that we do have the knowledge, skills, and technical resources to do the job. Whether or not we are willing to reallocate the limited resources available from training to assessment is the question. If indeed the professional education institutions of this country accept the two responsibilities as equally important, such a reallocation must take place. Right now I would estimate that no more than 5 percent of available resources are committed to the second function; in any case, the proportion is entirely inadequate.

I will attempt to show that the technical resources do exist by assessing the present practice we use in competency assessment, and try to give an idea of what it would take to bring everyday practice in line with the state of the art. In order to get a clearer picture of what would be involved in a systematic attack on the problem of competency assessment, we need to form some kind of a picture or map of the scope of the task. This we will do by first formulating a set of criteria that an assessment procedure must meet in order to be viable, and then examining the various kinds of assessment problems we must solve, in the light of these criteria.

Three Phases in the Assessment Process

In brief, we will find that any assessment device, procedure, or technique for assessing a competency must have three elements, involving three phases:

1. A standard *task* to be performed by each person to be assessed, the performance of which will elicit a demonstration of the competency;
2. A procedure for obtaining an objective documentary *record* of the performance of the person being assessed; and,
3. An objective procedure for quantifying or *scoring* the record.

The standard task. The nature of the task (or tasks) that any given test or other measurement device requires a student to perform is of course a critical element; what the device measures depends ultimately on it.

The primary function of the standard task is to elicit a demonstration of the competency from any student who possesses it. This may be accomplished by structuring the task in such a way that its successful performance depends on the use of the competency. Ideally, command of the competency should be both a necessary and a sufficient condition for successful completion of the task. In other words, no one who lacks the competency should be able to perform the task; and no one who has the competency should fail to perform it. This is in most cases a more difficult criterion to fulfill than it might appear to be on first glance, but it is nonetheless important.

It is also important that all students being assessed should be confronted with comparable tasks—tasks that are equal in difficulty and that require the same competency. And it is generally desirable to base an assessment on multiple tasks— to have each student perform more than one standard task, demonstrate the competency more than once—for the sake of reliability. This is because of the fact that the necessary and sufficient condition is rarely satisfied in practice. If it is possible to succeed in a task without using the competency (as, for example, by guessing the answer to a multiple-choice item), we use several tasks (or items), assuming that the competent student will succeed in more tasks than the incompetent one.

The documentary record. The importance of the objective documentary record of a performance is often overlooked; but it is secondary in importance only to the proper definition of the task.

The record is important, for one thing, for the protection of the student (and, in a different sense, of the assessor). If for whatever reason a student challenges the accuracy or fairness of an assessment of performance, it is critically important that a record of the performance be available for review. The Board of Examiners of the New York City Board of Education has over the years been sued many times by candidates who have failed the teaching license examination. Most of these suits are settled on the basis of re-examination of candidates' answer sheets. These answer sheets are the documentary records of the performances in question. With such a record at hand, it is possible to answer the critical question, which is whether or not another candidate who had performed similarly would also have failed to be licensed—whether the assessment was fair. Without such a record, it would be difficult or impossible to answer this question.

The documentary record is also important as a basis for scoring the performance. Having such a record makes it possible to exploit the technology of educational measurement, the methods of item analysis, and the other procedures for improving tests that psychometricians have developed and refined for many years. Without such methods of refinement, assessment devices would remain very crude and primitive; with them we can make competency assessment procedures reach or approach the level of validity and reliability that is necessary for the uses made of them.

The two essential characteristics that a record must have are (a) that it be accurate and (b) that it be objectively scorable. In order to be scorable, a record must be based on the same behavioral units or categories as are used in defining the competency, since it is on the presence or absence of these behaviors or indicators of competence in the performance that the score must be based. In most cases, this requires a degree of specificity in the definition of a competency that is rarely achieved at present. Without such specificity, accurate assessment of a competency is not possible.

If a record is scorable in this sense, then accuracy (the second essential) becomes a matter of objectivity in recording, indicated by consistency between different records of the same performance. If the performance recorded and the one that occurred are the same, then the record is accurate.

When students record their own performance by making marks on an answer sheet, as is the case with a paper-and-pencil test, the record *is* the performance and its accuracy does not come into question. This appears to account for the fact that conventional test theory, which is derived almost entirely from work with paper-and-pencil tests, has so little to say about the importance of the performance record. When the performance is of such a nature that the record must be made by an external observer rather than by the student being assessed, the question of accuracy in recording becomes important.

Neither a paper written in response to an essay examination nor a videotape of a teacher's behavior in the classroom is a documentary record in this sense, because neither of them is expressed in the units or categories on which scoring must be based. In either instance, objective scoring is impossible unless someone first codes the answer or the videotape in terms of the appropriate behavior categories.

Scoring the record. The only requirement for this step in the assessment process is that it be objective, and (given a quantifiable record) this is relatively easy to achieve. A proper performance record can be scored by a clerk or a computer—and, indeed, should be.

Practicability

In designing procedures for assessing teacher competencies it is important to be conscious of the three essential elements just described and to design the assessment so as to conform as closely as possible to all three. But it is equally important that the procedure designed be practicable.

Practicability is a characteristic which is technically unrelated to the validity of a procedure or technique, but which has much to do with whether it is feasible to use the procedure for the purpose for which it is designed. The most valid technique in the world has to be used or it is worthless.

A technique that is to be used to route the individual student through a teacher-preparation program, recycling when necessary to assure mastery of competencies sequentially related to other competencies must meet high standards of practicability. It must be inexpensive to administer and, if possible, self-administered, so that students can be assessed promptly at the moment when they need to be assessed. An assessment procedure that requires the use of other personnel is going to cost more and need to be scheduled in advance. If a procedure requires that a supervisor assess the student's performance in interaction with a group of pupils, as in microteaching, for example, the assessment will have to be scheduled at a time convenient to the supervisor and the pupils, which may not be when the student needs it. It is also important that it be possible to assess the same student more than once on the same competency in order to measure change. This is particularly difficult to do with microteaching because equivalent samples of pupils are hard to find.

The most valid technique in a set of alternative ways of assessing a competency is often the least practicable, so trade-offs must be made. A more valid procedure that is impracticable can yield less net valid data than a less valid procedure that can be used more often, or at more critical points.

It is important to bear in mind another principle—it is often possible to assess more than one competency on the basis of the performance of a single task. When the nature of the task is such as to reduce its practicability, this can be a useful expedient. Just as a client's performance on an instrument like the *Minnesota Multiphasic Personality Inventory* can be scored to measure not one but a profile of personality variables, so a record of a single performance of a student in interaction with a group of pupils can be scored on not just one but several performance competencies (if the task is properly defined).

Five Types of Competencies

From a methodological standpoint, it is useful to distinguish three major kinds of professional competencies that need to be assessed: professional knowledge, professional skills or abilities, and professional attitude or value positions. Competencies defined as skills or abilities can be further subdivided into three types: (a) perceptual or information-gathering skills; (b) performance or implementation skills; and (c) decision-making skills. We have subdivided the domain of teacher competencies into these five divisions because the problems involved in assessing competencies of the same type tend to be similar, while those involved in assessing competencies of different types tend to differ. The way we would assess teachers' knowledge of general science or of learning psychology (for example) is very different from the way we might assess the teachers' skill in questioning pupils or in managing transitions.

Assessing knowledge competencies. The present state of the art of performance assessment is such that we probably know more about the measurement of knowledge than we do about the measurement of any of the other types of competency that contribute to overall teacher competence.

The teacher-competency tests that state legislatures mandate are usually perceived by the legislators as tests of general knowledge and knowledge of curriculum content, and the tests are intended mainly to exclude from certification candidates who may be described as ignorant or illiterate. Whether or not we can agree with the implied assumption that general knowledge and literacy are properly regarded as competencies or whether they should be viewed as pre-existing teacher characteristics that ought to be assessed before the student is admitted to teacher education, we can hardly deny their importance.

Our interest here is in measuring the professional knowledge competencies a teacher acquires in training. The principal difficulty encountered in the development of knowledge tests has to do with our requirement that possession of the competency or competencies—in this case the knowledge or knowledges—specified should be necessary and sufficient conditions for passing the test.

It is generally recognized that all cognitive tests show substantial positive intercorrelations with one another—that there seems to be a single general factor which makes some people score high and others low on any cognitive test (whether of knowledge or ability). Knowledge, by its very nature, must be specific to content (I can know who wrote the *Divine Comedy* without having any idea of the atomic number of barium). Since this general factor is in all cognitive tests it would seem better described as a general ability than as any kind of knowledge. A pragmatic definition of it would be the ability to get high scores on cognitive tests, regardless of content.

The validity of a knowledge test depends, of course, on what content it measures—that is, on the kinds of test questions a student must answer correctly in order to score high. The ability to answer certain kinds of questions correctly must be relevant, but the ability to answer other kinds of questions correctly must be irrelevant; otherwise the test will measure general ability rather than knowledge per se.

Ability tests also differ from knowledge tests in that what they measure is defined ultimately in terms of some other kind of behavior—so that their validities are established not on the basis of item content but on correlations of scores with some kind of nontest behavior. The general test-taking ability we have been discussing is an exception in that it does not refer to any nontest behavior; it direclty affects performance on tests of all types—tests of other abilities as well as tests of knowledge. Group intelligence tests can be regarded as tests mainly of this general ability.

How great is the effect of this ability on scores on a typical test? Let us take an example. A well-constructed aptitude test, when validated against an independent criterion, may show a validity coefficient as high as .60. This would mean that about a third of the variation in scores (a proportion equal to the square of .60 or .36) reflects variations in the aptitude the test is supposed to measure. It also means that about two-thirds (64%) of these differences reflect other factors. These factors are usually referred to as errors of estimation and treated as random or chance errors.

The reliability coefficient of such a test will usually be about .90 (or higher). This means that 10 percent (1.00-.90 = .10) of the variations in scores reflect chance errors (guessing, etc.). This leaves 54 percent of the variation (.64-.10), more than half of it, unexplained. We know that this 54 percent is due neither to chance errors nor to the aptitude the test is used to measure. It reflects variations in true scores of students that are entirely unrelated to the aptitude the test purports to measure. It measures the ability to do well on the test regardless of the aptitude or knowledge that the test measures. The test scores of two students with identical aptitude but different general abilities may be expected to differ more than the average scores of two students with identical general ability but different amounts of aptitude. As a matter of fact, the test is a much better measure of general ability than it is of the aptitude it is designed to measure. The same thing would be true of any test with the same validity and reliability as this one; very few tests are any better. This has nothing to do with the nature of the aptitude— it applies to any cognitive test with these statistical characteristics.

What concerns us here is the fact that any test designed to measure knowledge with a validity of .60 and a reliability of .90 must also measure this general ability more validly than it measures the competencies of concern. One implication of this is that any state that uses total scores on the National Teacher Examinations Common Examinations (or any similar test) as a basis for certifying teachers is in effect certifying teachers mainly on the basis of their general test-taking ability: and could presumably do just about as good a job of teacher selection if they used a group intelligence test (like the SAT) instead. I find this very disturbing.

If we are satisfied to choose teachers on the basis of general ability there is no need to wait until they have spent time and money completing a teacher-preparation program before we find out whether they are bright enough to become teachers. Intelligence as measured on group tests is stable enough so that it can be measured before the student is admitted to the teacher-education program in the first place. The chance that anyone who reaches the junior level in college lacks the amount of intelligence needed to become a competent teacher is not great; but there is even less likelihood that such a student will acquire it during two years of teacher education. It seems immoral to let students waste two years of their lives in a futile effort to acquire knowledge which is irrelevant to their chances of being certified because their general ability is too low.

If we want to certify teachers on the basis of knowledge, we must find some way not presently being used to isolate the information about knowledge that test scores contain from this general factor. There are two strategies we might try. One is based on the fact that students' knowledge may be expected to change with training, while their general ability should stay the same. This suggests that we might try to separate knowledge from ability by looking at changes in scores on tests (and items) from before to after training, rather than at their status at one point in time.

Item analysis procedures presently used are designed to maximize individual differences between students' standings on a test at one point in time. Items that do not discriminate between high and low scoring individuals are usually discarded. Since the students tested usually differ much more in general ability than in knowledge, conventional item analysis procedures are likely to lower the sensitivity of the test to knowledge differences and increase its sensitivity to differences in general ability. Therefore they are more likely to decrease than increase the validity of the test, even though they may increase its reliability. Item analysis should be based on longitudinal data and it should retain items on which students show maximum gains during instruction, and reject items on which they do not. This should make the test more sensitive to knowledge and less sensitive to ability differences in students. It is to be expected that this reduction in the amount of systematic irrelevant variance will be reflected in lower reliability and higher validity. Unfortunately, it is easier to calculate the reliability of a test than its validity, so that the decrease in reliability is more visible than the increase in validity.

A second possible strategy for reducing the effect on scores on knowledge examinations is based on the premise that students of equal general ability will usually differ in their knowledge of different content areas, particularly when one of the areas of knowledge is esoteric, as professional knowledge should be to anyone not trained in the profession. In practical terms, this means that even though the total score on a battery of knowledge tests (like the NTE) may be regarded as a measure of general ability rather than of knowledge, information about candidates' professional knowledge may be found in differences between scores on different subtests. General test-taking ability tends to be cancelled out when one subscore is subtracted from another. In the case of the NTE Common Examinations, the difference between candidates' scores on the professional knowledge sections and their scores on the general knowledge sections, which will be virtually unrelated to their general ability, is of particular interest. A student with a given total score whose subscore on the professional knowledge subtests is higher than the score on the general-knowledge subtests must possess more professional knowledge than a student with the same total score whose subtest scores are equal. The difference between the two scores contains the valid information about professional knowledge, while their total contains the information about general ability.

Like gain scores, such contrasts tend to be substantially less reliable than the subtest scores that are contrasted. And as with gain scores, the reduction in reliability may be expected to be accompanied by an increase in validity. There is probably no more firmly established empirical fact about teacher evaluation than the fact that a teacher's total score on the NTE Common Examinations has no relationship to how competent or effective the teacher is (Quirk, Witten, & Weinberg, 1973). The contrast score we have proposed, since it is independent of the total score, measures something else, something that may be related to teacher effectiveness.

If there is any reason to believe that professional knowledge competencies might be important for a teacher to have, it is important to find some way of separating these knowledges from the general ability to earn high scores on any cognitive test that is the main component of scores on all such tests. The fact that the ability seems to be stable while the knowledge can be (and should be) changed leads me to suggest that knowledge-test items ought to be selected on the basis of changes during instruction. The fact that general ability strongly affects scores on subtest in all areas of knowledge leads me to suggest that contrasts between scores on subtests in different areas of knowledge might be used to assess knowledge, rather than scores on the subtests themselves.

An alternative to the paper-and-pencil test. The experience of taking a multiple-choice test is very different from the experience of interacting with a class. It may be possible to design a test which elicits the same knowledge that interactive teaching demands; but there the resemblance ends. As we have seen, students can do very well on a test of knowledge competencies by using an ability which is of little or no help when they are engaged in interactive teaching. For this reason, we have sought for some other way of measuring teacher knowledge, and have had some success with the one I propose to describe now.

Students who take this test are provided with answer sheets very similar to those that accompany multiple-choice tests, with spaces to mark alternative responses to the 125 items. The items to which they are to respond, however, are not presented in a booklet but in the form of 35mm slides and a cassette tape. If the test is being administered to a group of students, the slides are projected on a screen from a carousel projector which is synchronized with a cassette player. If it is being administered to a single student, a slide-tape viewer is used which also synchronizes the slides to the cassette.

Each slide presents a brief verbal description of a problem situation that a teacher might encounter, which is simultaneously heard from the tape. After the description has been read through, it remains visible while a series of possible courses of action are presented, one by one, on tape only.

The students must decide whether each suggested action is appropriate—is one they might follow in that situation—or inappropriate—that is, one they would not follow. Other options are either to mark "?" or not to respond at all.

The series of alternatives is presented one at a time in rather rapid succession, at intervals of from three to five seconds. None are repeated; each one must be judged by itself. All, some, or none of the alternatives may be either appropriate or inappropriate ways of responding to the problem. A few seconds after the presentation of the last alternative, a new slide appears with a new problem.

A sample problem reads as follows: The principal unexpectedly appears at your door just as you have begun a class discussion, says to go on with whatever you are doing, and sits in the back of the room. What might you do next?

The first alternative is: Try to do as (s)he says and continue as though (s)he were not there.

The best way for students to respond to each alternative, we suggest in the instructions, is on the basis of how they would actually behave in that situation. There really is not enough time to follow any other strategy before the next alternative appears: Invite him or her to leave.

And before the student has enough time to give this second possibility much thought, the third appears; and so on.

After the last alternative to this sample problem, a slide appears that reassures the students that if there was not enough time to think, then the test is working as it should, because that is the way teaching is. Teaching involves mainly decisions based on insufficient information that must be made too quickly to permit adequate thought—just like those in the test.

The first of thirty problems is then presented. The series of problems follows a sequence that begins when the teacher takes over a class for the first time and continues with a series of problems that come up during an arithmetic lesson, a social studies lesson, etc. After about 45 minutes, the students will have been confronted with 125 alternatives to evaluate.

The first instrument of this type that we constructed was designed to assess what teachers had learned from three different inservice training packages. Rather than construct a separate test for each, we used the same one for all three. To confront a teacher with problems related to one training unit at a time would be unrealistic indeed; what we tried to do was to present a set of problems that seemed typical of a teacher's day. Among them were problems related to each of the three training units—as well as to others the teachers may or may not have studied. Among the alternative responses to a problem we tried to include at least one which was either correct or incorrect according to one of the training packages. It was from the teacher's response to these alternatives that we derived the teacher's scores.

Many of the choices the teacher made were not scored at all. Some of them were unscorable—that is, we ourselves had no basis for deciding whether the suggested action would be appropriate or not.

That is how classroom life is: not all of the problems that come up have known solutions; not all of the choices a teacher makes can be definitely scored as correct or incorrect. The training packages these teachers had studied were highly prescriptive; they made definite recommendations about how a teacher should respond in certain situations. Such situations were included in the test, and the prescribed responses were scored as appropriate in those cases, so that a high score on the key for a package would indicate that a teacher had assimilated the knowledge that package was designed to impart; and a low score would indicate that (s)he had not assimilated it.

Although their main objective was to communicate knowledge related to research or theory, the packages also advocated certain value positions, took stands on what teachers ought to do. We found that we could measure these objectives in the same way that we measured knowledge: by presenting problems and alternatives that involved values rather than knowledge. In other words, our test samples the decisions students would make when confronted with tasks whose performance required competencies very similar to the knowledge and value positions involved in interactive decision-making. The test was not designed to measure either perceptual competencies or implementation skills, nor was it designed to assess directly the ability to synthesize all of these that we call decision-making skill. The decisions it required the student to make looked like interactive decisions, but the choices offered were so narrow, and so directly related to knowledges and values, that we believed that little or no decision-making skill was required for successful performance.

This type of exercise is highly practicable; it is not much more costly or difficult to construct and administer than a paper-and-pencil test and it yields an objective record which can be scored like any other answer sheet. Yet it has much greater face validity than any multiple-choice test. Practicing teachers who take the test react positively—they perceive it as both fair and relevent. We like to think that it helps preservice students see the connection between knowledge and practice better than a multiple-choice test would. I have no data to support the assertion that this is a valid and effective way to measure knowledge and values relevant to interactive teaching, but I am inclined to think that it is. It must be more valid than either the attitude inventory or the multiple-choice test which it replaces.

A note on assessing professional values. In a democratic society, individuals' right to their own values and attitudes is a fundamental human right, and one that they do not relinquish by seeking admission to a profession, even though the adoption of a set of professional values is seen as part of the process of becoming a competent practitioner. This requirement is defensible only to the extent that certain value positions are necessary to the achievement of solutions to professional problems that are acceptable to the profession. A candidate who cannot or will not take these positions is an incompetent problem solver in the same sense as one who cannot master the knowledge and skills necessary to the achievement of acceptable solutions to professional problems.

I suggest that assessment of values in the context of problem situations similar to, and intermingled with, situations used to assess knowledge is preferable to the use of questionnaires because the relationship of values to teaching practice is more apparent.

Assessing Skills and Abilities

The relationship between professional skill and effectiveness seems intuitively to be much more direct than the relationship between professional knowledge and effectiveness; knowing what ought to be done is certainly very different from being able to do it. Fewer teachers fail because they are ignorant than because they cannot apply what they know to the problems they encounter in their teaching.

The definition of skill implied here is the one we shall use: the ability to use knowledge in the solution of problems. Professional skill, then, is the ability to use professional knowledge in the solution of professional problems.

The domain of professional skills that teachers would find useful is as vast as the domain of professional problems that they may expect to encounter in professional practice. It is so large that the only way in which we can profitably discuss strategies for assessing professional skill is in terms of types or categories that correspond to the optimal strategies for assessing them.

Jackson (1965) has made a most useful distinction between what he calls *interactive* and *preactive* teaching skills. Interactive skills are the ones that teachers use while interacting with pupils. Preactive skills are those teachers use when they plan, evaluate, or are otherwise engaged in teaching activities while no pupils are physically present. Skill in the actual conduct of class discussion is, of course, an interactive skill; skill in defining objectives appropriate to the status of a class and the goals of the school is a preactive skill. As Jackson points out, the two kinds of skill involve very different abilities: Preactive teaching is much more deliberate, thoughtful, and less subject to time pressure than interactive teaching, which calls for prompt, almost intuitive responses with no time for deliberation. Procedures for assessing the two kinds of competence will define quite different kinds of tasks or problems to be performed.

An analysis of the professional problem-solving process suggests that different kinds of skills are involved at different stages in the process. Before professionals can apply knowledge to the solution of a problem, they must be able to perceive the elements in the situation that are relevant to the definition of the problem. Professional problem solvers must also be able to decide what needs to be done in order to solve the problem at hand. And, finally they must be able to implement the solution.

Thus we will discuss skill assessment in terms of *perceptual skills, decision-making skills,* and *implementation skills.* In examining the problems peculiar to each type of skill we will confront most of the problems involved in assessing teacher skills and abilities.

Assessing preactive teaching skills. Since preactive teaching does not involve live pupils, but is done by the manipulation of things like test papers and curriculum bulletins, it is relatively simple to construct tasks or problems that simulate those encountered in preactive teaching. Some form of the *in-basket test* is indicated (Frederiksen, 1960).

For readers not familiar with this particular assessment device, a brief description may be in order. A student taking the test would receive a packet of materials simulating the content of a teacher's *in-basket*—or more appropriately, perhaps, the contents of the brief case the teacher takes home to work on during the evening. The contents of the teacher's brief case may include papers or compositions to grade, letters or memoranda that need replies, recommendations from the school psychologist to be acted on, and so on. The teacher may be required to construct a lesson plan, to make up a test, or to do a similar activity.

A single problem may involve tasks that call for the demonstration of perceptual, performance, and/or decision-making skills. The ability to interpret standardized test scores, for example, is a perceptual skill that can be assessed in this way. The ability to write test items would be a performance skill, also assessable in this way. The procedure is flexible enough so that each type of skill may be isolated or it may be tested in combination with others.

The in-basket technique is probably best adapted to use as part of the terminal assessment made of students when they become candidates for graduation and certification. For assessments made during training, for instance, assessments of mastery of a skill that is prerequisite to entering another course or module, this approach is too cumbersome—not only to construct but to administer.

Because these skills involve symbol manipulation rather than interaction with pupils, they may be relatively accessible to assessment with specially constructed paper-and-pencil tests. The problem of controlling for general ability discussed in connection with knowledge assessment needs to be dealt with. The format used for another purpose by Sorenson looks promising (Sorenson, Husek, & Yu, 1960).

The assessment of interactive skills. The need for practicable solutions to problems in the assessment of interactive skills is perhaps greater

than that in any other area of competence. Lack of interactive skill accounts for most failures of teachers, as well as a large share of the damage that incompetent teaching does to the educational enterprise. A lack of objective procedure for diagnosing deficiencies of this kind may be the main reason why we cannot eradicate them early in the teacher's preservice training. Too many students pass all of their courses with flying colors only to discover in their first student-teaching experience that they lack critically important interactive teaching skills they were supposed to have acquired in earlier courses; and too many graduate without acquiring them.

The ability to measure a skill accurately and often is a prerequisite to developing that skill in students. The range of individual differences in the responses of students to training is so great that it is not safe to assume that students have mastered the competency until they have been reliable assessed and found to have reached a level defined as mastery. In addition to being objective, reliable, and valid, the assessment procedure must also reach a level of practicability well above what present techniques achieve.

Just about the only procedures we seem to have for assessing teacher skills are based on tasks defined in ways that require the use of pupils (or peers playing the roles of pupils) in some variation on microteaching (Allen & Ryan, 1963). All such techniques are expensive, cumbersome, and therefore not very practicable. The logistics involved prevent most of us from using microteaching very often. As a result, training in these critical competencies must proceed largely in the dark, without the frequent, detailed, diagnostic feedback that is so essential to effective training. The main reason why so many students reach the final stage in their training so ill-prepared is because not enough assessments of their interactive skills have been made to detect deficiences in the earlier stages.

The strategy I am going to propose for improving this situation depends in part on the separation of the three types of skills—perceptual, decision-making, and implementation skills—for assessment (as well as for training) purposes. I suggest that the first two (at least) can be assessed by means that are less cumbersome and costly than those presently used.

Assessing perceptual skills. Perceptual skills are skills essential to the recognition and diagnosis of problems. Diagnosis involves detecting a discrepancy between the way things are and the way they should be. It involves competencies of two types: professional values of the teacher which indicate the way things ought to be, and perceptual skills which indicate the way things are.

The role of perceptual skills in interactive teaching has not been emphasized to the extent that their role in preactive teaching has, although the concept of the teacher who has eyes in the back of her or his head testifies to the popular awareness of its usefulness. Kounin has referred to this as "with-itness" (1970).

Using videotapes to assess perceptual skills. Ever since closed-circuit television and the helical scanning videotape recorder became generally available, there has been interest in the use of videotaped episodes of classroom interaction in teacher evaluation; indeed, the interest in film tests antedates these technological developments (Beaird, 1967).

It seems to me that both the strengths and the weaknesses of this medium arise from the role that perception plays in any use we might make of it. Its primary use is to measure how skillful students are in "reading" classroom behavior—how much of what goes on in the classroom they are aware of. The method is simple: students are shown an episode and then questioned about what they have seen. Let me present an example from our own experimentation with this type of exercise.

The students taking this test are provided with answer sheets like the ones used with a multiple choice test with numbered spaces, in each of which are spaces for marking one set of alternatives: in this instance, just two, marked *true* and *false, agree* and *disagree,* or perhaps merely *yes and no.*

The tasks are presented on a television screen rather than in a test booklet. After titles and instructions, the students might see the following episode:

> The camera focuses first on a teacher at a blackboard discussing a diagram of a fish. It then scans a class of teenagers, most of whom are passively attending, although two girls near the rear seem to be whispering or giggling whenever they appear on the screen.

After a few minutes the picture fades and a series of numbered statements appear briefly, one by one, and the students mark "agree," "disagree" or "?" in the corresponding squares on their answer sheets.

88. The teacher asked at least one question that called for divergent production.
89. As soon as the teacher noticed the two girls whispering (s)he should have directed a question to one of them. (Whispering girls reappear briefly on the screen.)
90. The girl at the end of the front row was more interested in the lesson than most of the students were.
91. The teacher's explanation of the way fish eggs are fertilized was a procedural one.
92. The drawing on the board showed too much irrelevant detail (the drawing reappears on the screen).
93. The main concept that the teacher was trying to develop was a bit too difficult for most of the pupils.

It should be mentioned that (like the slide-tape exercise described earlier) this test was designed to measure a number of different competencies simultaneously, so that statements made about the same episode relate to different competencies. Thus, only statements 90 and 93 were intended to measure perceptual skill in this instance. In both cases, the student is expected to have perceived and remembered what happened. Statement 90 could have been accompanied (like statements 89 or 92) by a reappearance of the appropriate part of the videotape. This would have been appropriate if we had wanted to test whether the students were able to recognize the relevant cues when asked to do so; as the item stands, it seems to measure whether they use the ability without being reminded to do so.

Statements 88, 91, and 92 were designed to measure knowledge of instructional strategies. Correct responses would require the students to know these concepts not merely in the sense of being able to define them, but in the sense that they could recognize instances of their use. Statement 89 was designed to assess a professional value position (as the word "should" in the statement suggests) referring as it does not to the way something is, but they way it ought to be. If the students perceive the whispering as deviating too far from what they consider acceptable classroom deportment, they will agree with the suggestion that the teacher intervene. Note that the behavior in question reappears on the screen (in case some candidates may have failed to see it the first time).

I would like this exercise better if the statements offered about it appeared to cover more of the range of things competent teachers observe, keep tabs on, as they teach. Not all of the statements would have to be scorable, though most of them ought to be (for efficiency's sake). It seems to me that when preservice teachers have an experience like this (or any other type of evaluation, for that matter) they should get a strong impression of the way a competent practitioner works—in this case, of what (s)he monitors while teaching. In the case of the slide-tape exercise, they should become aware of the kinds of options that flash through a teacher's mind as these problems arise. In a sense what I am suggesting is that as the students becomes "test wise" to these kinds of tests, they also become wiser about the practice of their profession.

Assessing decision-making skills. Skill in decision-making means the ability of teachers, once a problem has been diagnosed, to call upon their professional knowledge and prescribe an experience for the learner that (a) is within the range of implementation skills and resources at their disposal, and (b) can be defended as following approved or "best" practice within those limitations.

A prescription may be said to follow approved practice if it is consistent with (a) research, (b) tenable theory, or (c) generally accepted practice. Strictly speaking, (b) is defensible only when (a) does not exist, and (c) is defensible only when neither (a) nor (b) exists. An important part of professional knowledge consists of knowing the state of the art of approved practice. Approved practice, as I understand it, does not usually prescribe the solution to a professional problem; rather it prescribes the process to be used in reaching it.

The principal difficulty we encounter when we try to assess skill in interactive decision making has to do with this very question of approved practice. If we try to observe the students interacting with a class (or even a microteaching group) there are so many uncontrolled variables in the situation that is very difficult to arrive at a dependable assessment of what the students should have done—what best practice in that specific situation is. What we usually do is accept the judgment of the supervisor as correct. This is undesirable because it puts a premium on the students' learning to do what they think the supervisor would do rather than what they believe is correct; and because our inability to define a standard task equivalent for all students, or to define the nature of success in performing the task as a basis of scoring the performance, make this assessment strategy almost completely unacceptable.

A computer simulation. We are currently experimenting with a computer-based simulation of classroom interaction as a basis for assessing this skill. In such a simulation, we have complete control over the situation so that the nature of correct behavior or approved practice is known beforehand, and there is no problem in scoring a student's behavior.

In addition to solving this central dilemma, the classroom simulation has other important advantages, not least of which is that every student teaches exactly the same "class"—is confronted with exactly the same task. The overwhelming problem in previous efforts to assess competencies that can be demonstrated only in interaction with pupils has been the fact that no two classes (or microteaching groups) are the same—nor is any one class the same the second time it is taught. As I have pointed out, this makes it extremely difficult to get a consensus on what the student should have done so that a defensible score can be assigned to his record. This problem does not affect the simulation; and even if it did, we can at least be sure that all students' records would be scored with the same key. The simulation makes it also possible to get comparable measures of the effects each student has on the "pupils"—how much they "learn"—and for a student to teach the same class twice, so that change can be measured rather precisely.

Let me describe the current working model, a rather crude first attempt but one that illustrates what can be done. The student acting as "teacher" is first given an instruction sheet containing a set of arithmetic problems with answers. The instructions explain that this is the homework assignment of the class, and that the teacher's task is to answer any questions the pupils may have about it; or if they have no questions, to ask some questions to make sure the pupils know how to do the problems.

The teacher then enters a booth which contains a television monitor on which are displayed the names of the five pupils in the class. The teacher may now interact orally with the pupils. For example, if (s)he says "Does anyone have any questions about the homework?'' vertical lines (simulating raised hands) will appear beside one or more of the pupils' names, indicating which of them have questions.

The teacher may then call on any one of the pupils and that pupil will ask a question. The ''hands'' will go down, the pupil's name will be marked (to indicate who is speaking), and a voice will be heard asking a question. The teacher may then answer the question, and continue to interact with the pupils for as long as the exercise is scheduled to last. The teacher can say anything (s)he cares to say. What the pupils say is determined (a) by what the teacher says, (b) by the program in the computer, and (c) by which pupil is involved.

Each pupil behaves as an individual; some act brighter than others, some act as though they know more than others, some act shyer than others. What a pupil says, whether (s)he raises her or his hand, whether (s)he answers a question correctly, all depend on these characteristics (plus an element of chance to simulate what we do not know about pupil behavior).

As the interaction continues, pupils learn—they grow in knowledge. How much they learn depends entirely on what the teacher does. The more closely the student's behavior follows ''approved practice,'' that is, the more it conforms to the model entered into the computer, the more the pupils learn and the higher the teacher's score.

At the end of the exercise, the computer prints out a record of the performance of the teacher as well as of its effects on the pupils which can be scored to indicate how accurate the student's desicions were—that is, how closely they agreed with ''approved practice'' as defined in that problem. Different teaching problems or tasks can be set by reading different sets of pupil characteristics and/or different definitions of approved practice into the computer.

Assessing implementation skills. Implementation or performance skills bear a different relationship to professional decisions than either perceptual skills, knowledge, or value positions. The last three are direct inputs to decisions and are therefore antecedent; the first enter into decisions only in the sense of defining the alternatives available to the teacher. In order to assess a student's ability to implement a decision, we must define the task by identifying the decision supposed already to have been made, and asking the student to carry it out.

Demonstration of an implementation skill is elicited by asking the teacher to demonstrate it, and thereby rendering the teacher's possession of any of the other types of competency irrelevant to successful performance. In order to find out whether a student can operate an 8mm projector, the best thing to do is to provide a projector and a film and ask the student to operate it.

The major difficulties encountered in attempts to implement this simple approach relate to creating an appropriate setting. If we are unable to provide both a projector and a film, assessing a student's ability to thread a projector becomes difficult; if we are able to provide them it is simple.

This is generally true of any implementation skill; whether or not we can assess a particular skill validly, reliably, objectively, and practically depends on what it takes to create an appropriate setting, that is, on what conditions are necessary to make it possible for the student to demonstrate it. Practicability requires us to use the simplest (and cheapest) setting possible in each instance. As usual, those involved in interactive teaching tend to be the most difficult to set up. A good many interactive skills can, however, be assessed outside of the classroom perhaps with the student's peers playing the role of students. Capie and Butts have provided a useful analysis of this problem (1977).

Note that this is the first kind of assessment we have discussed in which records of performance must be made by observers. In most cases it is possible, by the use of low-inference instruments, to have other students act as recorders as one of the learning experiences they all undergo, and it is, therefore, not necessary to pay them. The major cost involved in this type of assessment will, therefore, be that involved in developing the instrumentation—observation schedules—for recording the performances. The skills the students will need to develop in order to be able to record performance will be ones the students would need to master as part of their own professional development. Learning to judge how closely a performance resembles competent performance would seem to be a vital first step on the way to learning to perform competently.

Assessing the ability to solve interactive teaching problems. So far our strategy has been to divide and conquer; we have divided the central teacher competency, the ability to solve professional teaching problems, into several phases and assessed the competencies involved in each phase separately. By taking full advantage of the diagnostic information such an approach yields we should be able to insure that every student possesses every competency (s)he needs before being admitted to student teaching. But this is no guarantee that the student will perform successfully either as a student teacher or as a professional practitioner after graduation.

We need, therefore, to make a final assessment of the student's ability to use all of these competencies in the classroom before we recommend that the student be certified as fully competent. This assessment will have to be based on the student's performance as a student teacher, since this is the only time when a preservice teacher takes charge of a full class of pupils. No simulation will do, because there is no way in which the unique relationship between teacher and class can be assessed except in the classroom itself.

What task can we set for the students to elicit demonstration of this crucial competency—the ability to use their competencies to solve problems on the job? As we have seen there is one task that every teacher must perform continuously: the task of maintaining a classroom environment favorable to learning. This is one task or problem, then, that we can expect to find teachers working on whenever they are teaching, so that it should be possible to assess teacher's ability to solve this problem whenever we can observe a sample of their teaching behavior.

Our evaluation of the student teacher's competence in solving this problem must be based on observation of process—of what the teacher does or does not do to maintain the environment— rather than on product, on how successful the teacher is in maintaining the environment. Variations in manageability of classes, which operate to lower the reliability of the assessments, may be expected to affect the results a student teacher achieves much more than they affect the means that the teacher uses to achieve them; measures of process—of what the teacher does to maintain the environment—should be more reliable, than measures of the quality of the environment that the teacher maintains.

Even more important is that, although the goal of our efforts is to make teachers effective in maintaining constructive classroom climate, we can only approach this goal by achieving objectives that are defined in terms of teacher behaviors. These teacher behaviors must reflect competencies which we help teachers acquire on the assumption that they will make the teacher effective. If student teachers fail to maintain a suitable environment, unless we are observing the process used, we cannot be sure whether they fail because they are not behaving as they have been trained to behave, or whether they are behaving that way, but are failing because our assumption that this is the way to be effective is erroneous. If the students do what we have trained them to do and fail, it is the program that is at fault, not the students. This is important to know.

In addition to the fact that the problem of environmental maintenance is one that every teacher works on all the time, there is another reason for choosing it as the one on which this phase of competency assessment should be based: There is a growing amount of empirical knowledge about how a teacher should behave in order to create and maintain a classroom learning environment favorable to learning. From the ecological research of Kounin (1970) and some experimental research based on it (Anderson, Evertson, & Brophy, 1979), as well as from process-product studies (Medley, 1977; Brophy, 1979; Good, 1979), especially those done by Soar and Soar (1979), we are close enought to being able to define "best practice" in this area to be able to measure competence with considerable confidence.

Anyone who has followed this discussion to this point does not need to be reminded of the importance of using a low-inference technique to record what the student teacher does during this assessment. So far as I know, there is no existing instrument with a key for scoring this competency whose validity has been established; but there are several observation schedules around whose objectivity and practicability has been established that could be used to obtain scorable records (Simon & Boyer, 1967). The next step is to choose one of them and develop a scoring key for it.

There is a second teaching task which, like the environmental maintenance problem, demands the continuous attention of the teacher: the problem of maintaining pupil involvement in learning tasks. This would be another excellent focus for assessment of competency in problem-solving during student teaching, if we had an adequate empirical base for defining competent teacher behavior in this area. Research in how competent teachers solve this problem has not yet produced enough dependable findings (Fisher et al., 1980; Medley, R. S. Soar, & R. M. Soar, 1975), but when it does, problem-solving competency assessments should be based on both kinds of problems.

Concluding remarks

Our approach to competency assessment has involved a heavy dependence on simulations, mainly for the sake of practicality. The simulations I have described have represented increasingly close approximations to the actual teaching act, culminating in the use of a sample of the performance of students with classes temporarily placed under their care as part of their student-teaching experience. The focus in every technique proposed has been on dealing with teaching problems; in most cases, with interactive teaching problems.

This focus on problems was adopted mainly because of my belief that it increases the validity of the assessments, but also because I am convinced that this constant preoccupation should make the relevance of what the students are learning obvious to the students, so that after graduation they do not go around saying that nothing they learned in college had anything to do with the problems they face on the job.

I would like once again to emphasize that the specific techniques described above should be looked upon as tentative first steps, not as the ultimate solution to the problem of competency assessment. I believe that these examples do point the way to go; but am not sure how far along the road they take us. As soon as we stop thinking in terms of multiple-choice tests and rating scales, a whole new vista opens up. If these examples give readers a glimpse of this new terrain, they will have served their purpose.

SUMMARY AND CONCLUSIONS

The contribution a teacher makes to the effectiveness of a school program depends on many factors, among which there are only two that are under the teacher's control and for which the teacher is accountable: the teacher's competency and the teacher's motivation or drive.

It is the responsibility of the teaching profession to ensure the competence of its members; in particular, to see that no teacher who lacks the minimum competence needed for safe practice is admitted to the practice of the profession. This chapter addresses the question of how the profession can best meet this responsibility, and of what needs to be done to discharge it effectively.

A distinction is made between competence and performance, and between each of these and effectiveness. *Teacher effectiveness* is defined in terms of the impact the teacher has on the pupils the teacher teaches. *Teacher performance* is defined in terms of the behavior of the teacher on the job. *Teacher competence* is defined in terms of the repertoire of professional knowledges, professional skills, and professional value positions the teacher brings to the job.

Both how well a teacher performs and how effective the teacher is depend on situational or contextual factors as well as on teacher competence and motivation, and are therefore more the concern of the school system and the community that employs the teacher, more under their control, than under the control of the profession. The profession, therefore, can be held accountable only for that part of teacher performance and teacher effectiveness attributable to the level of competence—or incompetence—of the teacher.

Attempts to infer teacher competence from either of these other two factors seem ill advised, because situational and contextual influences, operating as errors of measurement, make it difficult to form reliable judgements of teacher competence from either of them. The widespread tendency to confuse the three terms, to equate effectiveness, performance, and competence, is both unproductive and unjust.

The only agency that has the opportunity and the resources needed to make an accurate assessment of the competence of the individual teacher before admitting that teacher to professional practice is the institution that trains the teacher. This can be done as a part of the formative and summative evaluation that is integral to any sound program. This gatekeeping function is already performed by these institutions; but the fraction of the resources and emphasis the institutions commit to this function is far too small in comparision with that they devote to the training function. The present crisis of confidence in teacher education and widespread demand for competency testing indicate public awareness that, as a result of this neglect, the teacher education institutions are not meeting this responsibility but are admitting too many incompetent teachers to the practice of teaching.

As more attention is paid to the gatekeeping function it will be necessary to develop new assessment devices and procedures, more valid, more reliable, more objective and more practicable than the combination of paper-

and-pencil tests and performance ratings on which present-day assessments are based.

An analysis of the domain of competencies—that is, of the professional skills, knowledges, and value positions a teacher needs in order to solve the problems encountered in professional practice—was made in terms of the assessment problems involved. It was recommended that different competencies be assessed separately so that a qualitative as well as quantitative description of each teacher's repertoire of competencies may be obtained. Such information will be useful not only for diagnostic purposes, but also as a basis for research designed to increase our knowledge of "best practice" of the profession.

A number of illustrations of specific techniques for assessing competencies, as well as discussions of the general problems involved, are presented. Most of the procedures involve efforts to simulate problems teachers encounter that call for the use of the competencies being assessed, and are perhaps better adapted to formative evaluation than summative evaluation.

No claim is made that the treatment of the topic presented is either exhaustive or definitive. At best it may have touched on many if not most of a set of often neglected issues which the profession must face squarely and soon, and perhaps have suggested directions in which solutions to some of them may lie.

For more than a century we have been trying to improve the way we train teachers, with mixed results; as near as I can tell we have not done anything to improve the way we evaluate them for some 65 years. Can we hope to turn out better teachers until we learn to distinguish them from poorer ones? Perhaps a greater emphasis on the gatekeeping function will be the key to improving the training function as well.

REFERENCES

Allen, D. W., & Ryan, R. (1969). *Microteaching*. Reading, MA: Addison-Wesley.

Anderson, L., Evertson, C., & Brophy, J. (1979). An Experimental Study of Effective Teaching in First Grade Reading Groups. *Elementary School Journal, 79*, 193–223.

Barr, A. S. (1930). What Qualities are Prerequisite to Success in Teaching? *The Nation's Schools, 6*, 60–64.

Beaird, J. H. (1967, February). *Film Tests as Predictors of Teaching Behavior*. Paper presented at American Educational Research Association, Monmouth, OR: Teaching Research Division, Oregon State System of Higher Education (mimeo).

Boyce, A. C. (1915). *Methods for Measuring Teacher's Efficiency*. 14th Yearbook of the National Society for the Study of Education, Part II. Bloomington, IL: Public School Publishing.

Brophy, J. E. (1973). Stability of Teacher Effectiveness. *American Educational Research Journal, 10*, 245–252.

Brophy, J. E. (1979). Teacher Behavior and its Effects. *Journal of Educational Psychology, 71,* 733–750.

Capie, W. R., & Butts, D. P. (1977). *Evaluating Teachers Using Teacher Performance.* ERIC Document No. ED 139 630.

Clark, D. L., & Marker, G. (1975). The Institutionalization of Teacher Education. In *Teacher Education: The 24th Yearbook of the National Society for the Study of Education* Part II. Chicago, IL: University of Chicago Press.

Elam, S. (1971). *Performance-based Teacher Education: What is the State of the Art?* Washington, DC: American Association of Colleges for Teacher Education.

Fisher, C. W., et al. (1980). Teaching Behaviors, Academic Learning Time, and Student Achievement: An Overview. In C. Denham and A. Lieberman (Eds.), *Time to Learn.* Washington, DC: US Department of Education.

Frederiksen, N. (1960). In-basket Tests and Factors in Administrative Performance. In *1960 Invitational Conference on Testing Problems.* Princeton, NJ: Educational Testing Service.

Good, T. L. (1979). Teacher Effectiveness in the Elementary School. *Journal of Teacher Education, 30,* 52–63.

Howsam, R. B., Corrigan, D. G., Denemark, G. W., & Nash, R. J. (1976). *Educating a Profession.* Report of the Bicentennial Commission on Education for the Profession of Teaching of the American Association of Colleges for Teacher Education. Washington, DC: American Association of Colleges for Teacher Education.

Jackson, P. W. (1965, November). The Way Teaching Is. *NEA Journal,* 10–13, 62.

Johnson, C. E., Elliot, C. D., & Capie, W. (1980). *An Introduction the the Teacher Performance Assessment Instruments: Their Uses and Limitations.* Athens, GA: College of Education, University of Georgia, Teacher Assessment Project.

Joyce, B. R., & Harootunian, B. (1967). *The Structure of Teaching.* Chicago, IL: Science Research Associates.

Kounin, J. S. (1970). *Discipline and Group Management in the Classrooms.* NY: Holt, Rinehart and Winston.

Medley, D. M. (1977). *Teacher Competence and Teacher Effectiveness: A Review of Process-Product Research.* Washington, DC: American Association of Colleges for Teacher Education.

Medley, D. M., & Mitzel, H. E. (1959). Some Behavioral Correlates of Teacher Effectiveness. *Journal of Educational Psychology, 50,* 239–246.

Medley, D. M., Soar, R. S., & Soar, R. M. (1975). *Assessment and Research in Teacher Education: Focus on PBTE.* Washington, DC: American Association of Colleges for Teacher Education.

Millman, J. (1972, Winter). Teaching Effectiveness: New Indicators for an Old Problem. *Educational Horizons,* 68–73.

Mitzel, H. E., & Gross, C. F. (1958). The Development of Pupil Growth Criteria in Studies of Teacher Effectiveness. *Educational Research Bulletin, 37,* 178–187; 205–215.

Popham, W. J. (1971). Performance Tests of Teaching Proficiency. *American Educational Research Journal, 8,* 105–117.

Quirk, T. J., Witten, B. J., & Weinberg, S. F. (1973). Review of Studies of the Concurrent and Predictive Validity of the National Teacher Examinations. *Review of Educational Research, 43,* 89–113.

Ryans, D. G. (1960). *Characteristics of Teachers.* Washington, DC: American Council on Education.

Simon, A., & Boyer, G. E. (Eds.) (1967). *Mirrors for Behavior: An Anthology of Classroom Observation Instruments.* Philadelphia, PA: Research for Better Schools.

Soar, R. S., & Soar, R. M. (1979). Emotional Climate and Management. In P. L. Peterson and H. J. Walberg (Eds.), *Research on Teaching: Concepts, Findings, and Implications.* Berkeley, CA: McCutchan Publishing.

Sorenson, A. G., Husek, T. R., & Yu, C. (1963). Divergent Concepts of Teacher Role: An Approach to the Measurement of Teacher Effectiveness. *Journal of Educational Psychology, 54,* 287–294.

Veldman, D. J., & Brophy, J. E. (1974). Measuring Teacher Effects on Pupil Achievement. *Journal of Educational Psychology, 66,* 319–324.

5
Changing Teaching Performance*

David H. Gliessman
Indiana University at Bloomington

Demonstrating that teaching performance *can* be changed is not the main concern of this chapter; that it can be done has been documented in numerous studies of microteaching (Turney, Clift, Dunkin, & Traill, 1973) and other methods of training (Gliessman & Pugh, 1981). The first task in this chapter is to identify the variables, common to different training methods, that appear to account for change in performance. The second task is to formulate alternative hypotheses about the processes that might provide a basis for integrating these variables. The third and final task is to develop the implications of these ideas for teacher training.

We must first, however, deal with a matter of terminology. The term *teaching performance* is used in this chapter to refer to the conduct of instruction: posing questions, providing explanations, giving directions, showing approval, engaging in the myriad instructional acts that a teacher performs in the classroom. The term is not meant to encompass the effects or products of instruction, such as student achievement or personal growth. Neither is it meant to encompass such teacher characteristics as attitudes and expectations. Rather, teaching performance is concerned, to use Dunkin and Biddle's (1974) terms, with *process variables* rather than *presage* or *product variables*. Defining performance in this somewhat restricted sense allows one to draw upon a considerable body of empirical literature on the

---

* The author is indebted to his colleague, Gary M. Ingersoll, for originally identifying some of the basic issues in this chapter and for reacting critically to its content.

modification of teacher behavior and the acquisition of teaching skills. It is from this literature that the variables to be discussed have been drawn.[1]

THE PLACE OF CLASSROOM PRACTICE

We can best begin by attending to the place of practice, with brief consideration of its uses and values in teacher training. A perspective on this issue is imperative because practice, especially when defined broadly to include general classroom teaching experience, has traditionally been viewed as the quintessence of training. It is here where previously learned concepts do or do not come together and where skills fit or fail to fit. Whatever the values, shortcomings, or irrelevancies of the teacher education program, it is held to be through practice that one really learns to teach. The essentiality of practice is reflected in one recommendation for the improvement of teaching:

> Practice, practice, practice...frequent, varied, and criticized practice. Observation, immediate feedback, and practice again to perfect the original performance. Practice in a variety of situations. (Bush, 1977)

While this quotation clearly implies means of controlling rather than simply providing practice, its spirit is familiar. A confidence in the efficacy of practice underlies (or at least is necessary to) the trend toward earlier, more extended, and more intensive field experience. The perceptions of education students, too, tend to validate its essentiality. Field experience and particularly student-teaching experience generally are perceived by education students to be the most valuable (often the *only* valuable) component of their professional training.

The evidence to support this commitment, however, is quite tenuous. While classroom teaching experience appears to lead to changes in perceptions and attitudes (unfortunately often in a negative direction; see Peck & Tucker, 1973), there is little evidence of change in performance concurrent with classroom experience (Elliott, 1978; Zeichner, 1980). Based upon her

---

[1] Viewing performance in terms of behavior and skills results in a further problem of terminology. Neither phrase, changing teacher behavior or acquiring teaching skills, is entirely satisfactory as a way of defining the objectives of training. The term *behavior* is too general, encompassing the full range of teacher behavior, noninstructional as well as instructional. Teacher behavior is better used to refer to the focus of observational studies of teaching. The term *skill*, once one decides that it can be used to refer to overt behavior (strictly speaking, it refers to competence or proficiency in performance), has inevitable connotations of physical or manual dexterity. Investigators of teacher training, however, use both terms, sometimes interchangeably. In some cases, the idea of modifying behavior best describes the changes in performance that are attempted. In other cases, the idea of establishing and refining previously undemonstrated skills better describes a change in performance. In the present chapter, both terms will be used without an effort to distinguish them.

extensive review of the literature on field experience, Elliott concluded that the commitment to such experience was much more a matter of faith than a matter of evidence, a conclusion concurred in even by its staunchest proponents (e.g. Bennie, 1982).

But we have been discussing practice in a very broad sense. In a complex setting over an extended period of time, variables other than repeated performance are likely to influence any teaching skills that are measured. A clearer picture of the effect of practice might emerge from studies in which extraneous variables are better controlled. In fact, the evidence from such studies is more definitive. On the one hand, it suggests that positive changes in certain attitudinal and dispositional behaviors (e.g., toward greater warmth and interest in students) occur with repeated laboratory and classroom teaching experience (Jensen & Young, 1972). On the other hand, the evidence fails to show that practice in itself results in targeted changes in performance. In a selective review of studies based on conceptual training (i.e., studies in which teaching skills are treated as concepts to be acquired), Gliessman and Pugh (1981) reported that practice resulted at best "...in levels of skill acquisition no higher than those resulting from conceptual instruction alone." Furthermore, practice was the *only* means of training that, when used alone, failed to result in changes in performance.

What can be concluded from this evidence? Whatever the perceptual and attitudinal changes that accompany practice (they appear to be sometimes positive and sometimes negative), it appears highly questionable to assume that practice in itself is the critical variable in stimulating changes in teaching performance. In a sense, practice appears to be more nearly a condition than a means of training. It provides setting, occasion, and context for trial performance; however, it is necessary to look elsewhere for the means of influencing or changing that performance. Fortunately, we have more than a little empirical and theoretical knowledge about change in performance upon which to draw. To describe a few of the means of change, the instructional and intervention variables that have been shown to influence teaching performance, is the primary task of this chapter.

MEANS OF CHANGE

Training variables have been referred to above as instructional and intervention variables. The distinction between these two is in immediate purpose and focus. Very generally speaking, instructional variables are designed to teach something about teaching behavior. More specifically, the immediate objective in using instructional variables is the acquisition of concepts about, and changes in perception of, specified teaching behaviors and skills. These behaviors and skills typically are portrayed through filmed or videotaped protocols. The conceptual and observational outcomes of instruction based on these and similar materials are paramount; for that reason, instructional variables will be referred to as conceptual and observational variables.

Intervention variables, on the other hand, are intended to directly modify behavior. Rather than the filmed or videotaped behavior of another person, the point of departure as well as the focus of intervention is the behavior of the teacher himself or herself. Typically, though not always, the teacher's behavior is recorded and replayed on videotape or audiotape. With these general distinctions in mind, we are ready to look more carefully at each class of variables.

Conceptual and Observational Variables

It is perhaps an indication of how firm a hold the doctrine of practice has had in teacher education that investigators have only recently turned their attention to the role of knowledge and understanding in changing teaching performance. The recent development of systematic study in this area is somewhat surprising since teacher educators traditionally have assumed that conveying knowledge through lecture, discussion, and demonstration would in some way affect teaching performance. While one would be hard pressed to support such a general assumption, it does seem evident that a clear conception of the behaviors or skills one is to exhibit facilitates the use of those behaviors and skills. To put it another way, teaching performance can be influenced by clearly defined and delineated concepts.

The evidence for this proposition, while not abundant, is positive and reasonably consistent. In the studies reviewed by Gliessman and Pugh (1981), instruction treating teaching skills as concepts to be acquired, in the absence of practice, significantly increased the use of those skills. A further finding, already discussed in our previous discussion of the place of practice, confirms the importance of conceptual instruction: in two of the three studies that included a practice condition without conceptual instruction, gains in use of specified skills were not demonstrated. Thus, it appears that instruction directed at concept acquisition is an effective, perhaps necessary, means of influencing performance.

To demonstrate the conceptual changes that are assumed to mediate change in performance is a more elusive task; there is, however, some indirect and direct evidence of such changes. Indirect evidence can be found once again in the studies reviewed by Gliessman and Pugh. In more than half of the comparisons in the five studies reviewed, significant gains or differences in skill acquisition were accompanied by corresponding gains or differences in concept-acquisition scores, always favoring the groups receiving conceptual instruction.[2] The fact that a better grasp of skills as concepts

---

[2] Concept acquisition in training studies is typically assessed through accuracy in identifying, categorizing, or recognizing a skill in a filmed or printed classroom protocol.

tended to accompany more frequent use of the skills themselves is at least consistent with the hypothesis that concepts mediated behavior change. Evidence directly supporting that hypothesis is reported in one of the studies reviewed (Gliessman, Pugh, & Bielat, 1979). In this study, not only were both conceptual and skill differences reported favoring teachers who received conceptual instruction (as compared to teachers in a noninstructional group) but, more important, *level* of concept acquisition in the instructed group was positively and significantly related to skill scores. Thus, teachers who showed greater mastery of the skills as concepts tended also to use the same skills with greater frequency.[3]

In training studies, conceptual variables and observational variables tend to be interrelated through a common use of filmed or videotaped examples of teaching behavior as a component of instruction. Examples appear to play a significant role in concept acquisition, possibly in conveying subtle characteristics of a teaching skill that are not easily coded in a definition (Gliessman & Pugh, 1978). The same examples may affect performance more directly by providing models of specified teaching skills. It is not always clear in fact if investigators intend the use of models to contribute primarily to conceptual learning or to observational learning; in any event, it is likely that both conceptual and observational effects result from the use of examples or models.

A few investigators, however, have used models explicitly as a basis for the observational learning of teaching skills (Koran, Koran, & McDonald, 1972). The rationale for such a training strategy generally is derived from social imitation theory, a theory stressing the imitative basis of human behavior (Bandura, 1972). Briefly, this theory posits, and its supporting evidence indicates, that people acquire complex social and emotional behavior through imitation; such imitation may be accompanied by greater or lesser awareness and may follow from filmed as well as live models. The effect of filmed or videotaped teaching models on teaching performance has been demonstrated by several investigators, but most directly by Lange (1971) who increased preservice teachers' use of an in-

---

[3] Another conceptual variable that adds a potentially important dimension to conceptual instruction is that of the level of cognitive complexity of the individual teacher or variations in conceputal level among a group of teachers. Hunt (1971) hypothesizes that the form of instruction (particularly degree of structure) ought to be adapted or matched to cognitive level for optimal effectiveness. He hypothesizes specifically that teachers of high-cognitive level profit from a low or moderate degree of structure, while those of low-cognitive level profit from a high degree of structure. Although these hypotheses are still speculative, one study at least indicated that teachers of higher cognitive level chose to attend a greater percentage of low-structure training sessions than did teachers of lower cognitive level and also were more likely to apply the principles learned (Cohen, 1979). If further supported, the implications of Hunt's reasoning would entail assessing the cognitive level of teachers in training to determine how highly to structure instructional variables.

direct or student-centered teaching style by showing them a brief film modeling that style. The fact that the subjects in this study received neither practice nor analytic training strongly supports the hypothesized effect on performance of viewing the filmed model.

How might one account for the effect of conceptual and observational variables on teaching performance? Those who have investigated the effects of conceptual variables have tended to argue that the critical task in acquiring a teaching behavior or skill is learning to discriminate its characteristics (Gliessman, Pugh, & Bielat, 1979; Wagner, 1973). In short, acquiring the concept of a skill enables one to understand what one is to do in using that skill and perhaps how one can do it well. To acquire a behavior or skill itself, in the sense of being able to perform it, is a lesser problem because most teaching skills are neither unique to teaching nor unfamiliar in every-day affairs. Rather, teaching behaviors appear to be fairly common social behaviors—verbal, social, emotional—that are likely to have been adequately "practiced" through day-to-day social contacts. The crucial task of training is to conceptualize these behaviors, particularly to discriminate among them, as teaching skills.

It is not thereby implied that the concepts referring to teaching skills are always easy to acquire or to master. For one thing, individual behaviors or skills are components of larger instructional acts, procedures, and styles whose characteristics may be both subtle and complex. A case in point is the construct of *indirect influence* which Lange (1971) addressed in his training study. Indirect influence comprises a set of teaching behaviors the principal components of which are asking questions and conveying support or approval. Neither of the latter are particularly difficult concepts but they are organized into a relatively complex teaching style that is not easy to grasp conceptually.[4]

Some teaching behaviors may be difficult to treat as teachable concepts because they contain many nonverbal, expressive, even emotive elements. These behaviors may be especially well taught through the use of models. Here again, the fact that highly familiar component behaviors are involved is an important condition of learning. Bandura (1972) hypothesized that the component behaviors of complex social and emotional behaviors often have been acquired previously by the learner. To be able to exhibit those complex behaviors essentially requires that the component behaviors be integrated into a larger act. This explains why some complex behaviors can be exhibited on the basis of observation and without rehearsal or trial.

---

[4] This complexity may reflect in part that indirect influence is not really an internally consistent construct (see Dunkin & Biddle, 1974).

Intervention Variables

By far the most common intervention variable in studies of teacher training is feedback, that is, information given the teacher about the characteristics or effects of his or her performance. Although feedback can be continuously provided during the course of instruction (for example, by means of a television display visible to the teacher that registers cumulative skill frequencies; see, for example, Semmel & Sitko, 1976), it is typically and most easily provided on a delayed basis following teaching. The means of doing so is videotaped or audiotaped replay of the teacher's performance, descriptive or evaluative information about that performance, or some combination of the two.

It is important to distinguish feedback in this sense from feedback as a basic aspect of learning, especially perceptual-motor learning. In the latter case, feedback encompasses the visual, auditory, kinesthetic, and other cues by which learners correct their directional responses, target tracking, and other perceptual-motor skills. Among some theorists, feedback processes are assumed to account for much of the self-correcting or adapting character of human behavior. So interpreted, such processes would certainly apply in the same pervasive sense to a teacher's adjustments and adaptations to events in the classroom. As an intervention technique, however, feedback refers to a more general process with many verbal elements. The key to that process is some means of conveying information to a teacher about his or her performance.

Perhaps because the importance of feedback in basic learning processes has been so well established, few investigators have felt it necessary to directly examine its use in changing teaching performance (for example, by contrasting the effect of practice when feedback is and is not provided). Indirect evidence suggests, however, that it is a significant variable. Replaying performance on different media, for example, has shown differential effects on performance (Turney, et al., 1973). While it is difficult to distinguish the most and least effective media (general trends favor videotape, but the evidence is not consistent across studies), the fact that the use of different media has shown discernible differences in skill acquisition indicates that feedback itself is a significant variable. Similar conclusions may be drawn from systematic attempts to vary other aspects of the form and content of feedback.

In different studies, widely varying media have been used as a basis for feedback: videotape (Kleucker, 1974), audiotape (Davis & Smoot, 1970), verbal report (Good & Brophy, 1974), computer-generated summary (Bondi, 1970), computer-generated television display (Semmel & Sitko, 1976). The specific teaching behaviors that have been modified vary from such highly complex behaviors as varying the level of questions asked according to pupil responses (Moore, Schaut, & Fritzges, 1978) to much less complex behaviors such as the use of approval or acceptance (Kleucker, 1974).

A major alternate class of intervention variables draws upon behavioral learning models for principles that apply to changing teaching behavior. The paramount and perhaps most familiar of these principles is that of reinforcement: behaviors or responses that result in confirming, satisfying outcomes tend to recur while those that do not tend not to recur. Applied experimentally and with some success to the control of pupil-social behavior, these precepts also have been applied to the modification of teaching behavior. Such applications have met with some success on the conventional criterion of change in performance in the training setting itself (though with far less success when the more stringent criterion of generalization of changes in behavior to other settings is used; see Robinson & Swanton, 1980).

The basic sequence of behavioral training entails (a) the analysis of a teacher's behavior to identify the response elements that need to be established, modified, or eliminated; (b) the use of positive reinforcers to increase the rate of desirable responses and the withholding of reinforcers for those response elements that should be extinguished. Through the latter, as well as such processes as modeling, cuing, and "shaping," teaching behavior can be modified (McDonald, 1973).

Strictly interpreted and applied, behavior analysis and behavioral training may have particular value in changing teaching behaviors that for some reason are difficult to establish, to modify, or to extinguish. An example is behavior that is not entirely under the teacher's conceptual control, such as habitually attending only to a few pupils in a large class. The general principle of reinforcement, that satisfying consequences increase the likelihood that a response will be repeated, is of course widely applicable in teacher training. Videotape replay, for example, appears to provide an excellent setting for modifying teaching behavior through a supervisor's selective use of approval and praise.

Intervention variables are clearly complex variables. Even the apparently straightforward act of viewing one's own performance on videotape incites some highly complex, little understood processes (Fuller & Manning, 1973). Gaining an understanding of these processes would entail unraveling a tangled skein of anxieties, satisfactions, ego defenses, and confirmations. It is evident, however, that intervention through the use of feedback or reinforcement contains both informational and affective elements. Feedback is informational in nature: what skills were used or not used; how students reacted to a particular teacher behavior; what instructional style was displayed. Feedback that is confirming also has reinforcing properties, of course, but its function in training is primarily informational. The use of praise or approval, on the other hand, introduces a stronger affective element. Such social reinforcers may convey more or less information depending upon the refinement with which they are used but they typically do elicit affective responses. Thus, training interventions in general vary in complex ways on both informational and emotional dimensions.

An important characteristic of any intervention is generally accepted to be the degree of *focus* or *specification* it achieves (Fuller & Manning, 1973; McDonald, 1973). For purposes of developing specific skills, the more precise the focus (that is, the more attention is drawn to specific behaviors or critical aspects of behavior), the more effective intervention is likely to be. That a high degree of focus is something to be achieved rather than assumed is evident in a study reported by Diamond (1978). She found that the content of supervisor-trainee conferences analyzing videotape replays typically was vague, lacking in focus, and restricted in the range of behaviors considered.[5]

Integrating Hypotheses

It is reasonable to consider the effects of integrating these major variables into a unified training methodology. Would not combining observational learning with the use of feedback, for example, be of greater effectiveness than the use of either variable alone? This has in fact been done in the minicourse and other systematic microteaching methods. Ideally, such training entails a sequence of skill definition, skill modeling or exemplification, practice, and videotaped or audiotaped feedback through several cycles of training. Present evidence, however, fails to show any consistent advantage for such complex training methods compared to training based upon single variables (Gliessman, 1981). Failure to demonstrate such an advantage probably can be attributed to a number of factors, among them less than optimal continuity in training elements, selection of essentially simple target skills, and inadequate evaluation criteria.

The design of an optimally effective training sequence, however, requires that careful thought be given to the rationale underlying it. What

---

[5] An interesting variation in the provision of feedback was attempted by Tuckman, McCall, and Hyman (1969) who drew upon Festinger's (1964) theory of cognitive dissonance; this theory posits that discomfort resulting from disharmony between one's beliefs or perceptions can motivate change in beliefs and perceptions, behaviors, or both. The investigators faced teachers with evidence of discrepancy between self ratings and observer ratings of relative directness or indirectness of teaching style. Aware of a discrepancy, the teachers exhibited change in both perceptions and behavior toward greater consistency between perceived and observed teaching style. The procedure and results of this study, especially if they are replicated, suggest a useful approach to working with highly experienced teachers who may be less receptive than teachers in training to directed change.

provides the "warp," so to speak, of the training fabric? There are at least two different views on this question. In the case of practice-based methods such as microteaching, it is practiced behaviors or skills that are assumed to be the connecting thread of the training process. This leads to an emphasis on repeated practice as a critical element in training (Sadker & Cooper, 1972). Given this assumption, it is reasonable to view training elements such as definition, modeling, and feedback principally as means of facilitating practice of the appropriate behavior or skills.

There are others, however, who discern the connecting thread in training to be, not behaviors or skills, but the cognition or understanding of the trainee. What the trainee brings to practice and takes from practice conceptually is the most critical aspect of training. MacLeod and McIntyre (1977) have elaborated this view in positing that complex conceptual schemata tend to control teaching behavior, while changes in that behavior result from changes in schemata. Thus, practice through microteaching or classroom teaching is essentially a means of producing changes in one's cognitive structures. Similarly, Hargie and Maidment (1978) argue that it is the cognitive discrimination of behaviors and events in microteaching (and, for that matter, in classroom practice) that is the important precursor of practice, product of practice, and mediator of change.

There may well be other processes that connect the variables in training. Whatever view one takes on this issue, however, it is clear that it should be seriously addressed before the design of a training sequence is begun. Failure to do so may help to account for the less than optimal effectiveness of present training sequences.

PERSPECTIVES AND IMPLICATIONS

What has been accomplished by delineating these variables? Are the planning and effort required to apply them to training justified? One way of answering these questions is to consider a not so obvious but probably common alternative: trial and error. Trying varied approaches to solve a problem in teaching is a reasonable way to behave; it should not be rejected out of hand. Some teachers probably acquire a large number of skills, most teachers a few skills, through just such a process. But its limitations are evident, the principal one perhaps being the repercussions for teachers and students alike of ill-conceived, ill-advised teacher responses. Trial and error is likely, too, to be a decidedly inadequate way of meeting the rush and confusion of events in teaching. While some teachers have succeeded and survived through trial and error, many have not. The attrition rate among teachers during their first two or three years may in part reflect the fact that novice teachers can be overwhelmed by demands for which they have failed to acquire adequate responses.

The Conduct of Teacher Training

Granting that a less random, more dependable means of acquiring skills is needed, what implications for training can be drawn from the variables that have been considered? To begin, it should be evident that to a great extent these variables are already a part of the experience of professional preparation and practice. Processes like modeling and reinforcement, after all, are common phenomena in human behavior. The difficulty for teacher education is that their occurence is so often unplanned or random. Conditions may exist that influence performance but in undesirable directions. In contrast, conditions that are known to influence performance may not exist at appropriate times or in appropriate places. Consider two contrasting examples: modeling and feedback.

The teacher/student teacher relationship is one that is rich in modeling potential. While the significance of it can be overstated (see, for example, Copeland, 1980), the placement of novice with professional seems fallow ground for imitative behavior to grow. In the specific case, the problem is predicting what behaviors and attitudes will be modeled and what values they will reflect. In some cases these will be fortunate; in other cases, not so fortunate. Copeland (1980) and Zeichner (1980) have recently pointed out that teachers find widely different ways of adapting to the social and bureaucratic climate of the school. Modeling itself tends to be an uncontemplated process, further complicating these variations. In teaching, as in much of life, modeling occurs without much conscious direction on the part of either model or modeler. The result is a high degree of unpredictability about the behavior and attitudes that will be modeled by an individual trainee.

Formally arranged feedback, on the other hand, apparently is a novelty in teacher training or in teaching practice. Except for some attempts at student evaluation, teachers apparently receive little informational feedback that is objective and thorough. Supervisors drop in at odd moments, observation by colleagues has never become a tradition, and videotaped recording in classrooms often has been actively resisted. The result is that teachers receive little feedback that could improve teaching skills. This shortcoming does not distinguish teaching from other professions, of course, but it is a shortcoming nonetheless.

A major problem in teacher training is how to assure a greater degree of control over the variables that influence teaching performance. Unless ways are found to accomplish this, the novice teacher is left facing the dilemma so well put by Stones (1979):

> Student teachers are invited to make the most prodigious leaps from lectures on theory to action in the classroom. Frequently they are expected to start by a brief skirmish with the realities of the classroom before encountering any theory at all. Often theory and practice are institution-

ally segregated, a practice that probably reflects a division in the minds of the providers as well as signaling...that theory is theory and practice is practice....

One of the main consequences of the divorce between theory and practice is that neophyte teachers have little option but to turn to experienced practitioners for models.

With due respect to the experienced practitioner *and* to the novice teacher, this condition places an unreasonable burden on the former to display all the desired skills and on the latter to perceive those skills correctly. How, then, can the conditions of practice be better controlled?

To some extent, such control can be gained by greater awareness on the part of teacher trainers. Teacher educators should, for example, be aware that their selection of concepts and the clarity with which they are taught are important variables in training. Similarly, cooperating teachers might be better aware of the power of the social reinforcers they themselves control as means of influencing the performance of student teachers. In a larger and more direct sense, however, some new ventures in training are probably in order. The time is right for a renewal of interest in technology that peaked and declined during the early 1970s. It is time to look again at the argument for the use of technology posed in B. O. Smith's *Teachers for the Real World* (1969). In this seminal book, Smith emphasized the control and immediacy that the use of filmed protocols and television recording can provide. The capacity to exemplify skill concepts and model teaching behaviors through filmed classroom protocols, as well as to replay teaching performance for analysis, are technological achievements that never have been fully exploited. The evidence suggests that these innovations are effective. In this chapter, evidence supporting the use of feedback based on videotaped recording has already been presented; the instructional rationale and the effectiveness of filmed protocols have been similarly supported (Gliessman & Pugh, 1978). More recently, a computer technology based on the microcomputer and vidiodisc promises an exponential increase in the control and power of these elements of training.

Like the systematic use of film and videotape, microteaching has fallen to a low estate in teacher education. Its decline can be attributed in part to the shift in focus to field experience, but also to skepticism about the transfer of skills exhibited in the laboratory to the classroom itself. The supposed separation between laboratory and classroom, however, need not be inevitable. Copeland's (1977, 1980) findings are particularly informative. He explored the factors that affect the classroom use of a teaching skill acquired through microteaching. He found (as have others) no direct transfer of skills from microteaching to the classroom setting. However, microteaching training interacted with supervisory intervention and to a greater extent with classroom ecology to positively influence performance of the same skill in the classroom. Classroom teachers who modeled the skill or had received supervisory training tended to facilitate the use of that skill by their student teachers. Perhaps more fundamental was the classroom environment itself; an environment that was supportive of a teaching skill facilitated the use of that skill by student teachers. This suggests that congruence between the classroom ecology and an acquired teaching skill facilitates the use of that skill.

Copeland addressed squarely the problem of the application of skills to the classroom. Intertwined with this problem is the larger question of what skills are defensible as objectives of training since, as we shall see, the characteristics of skills tend to influence the extent to which they are adopted by teachers. Research on teacher training has not fared well when judged in terms of the validity of skills addressed; it is instructive next to see why.

Research on Teacher Training

In his book *The Scientific Basis of the Art of Teaching* (1978), Gage comments that research on teacher training and on teacher effectiveness have been conducted apart from and without much reference to one another. In this contention, he is quite correct: few investigators of training methods rationalize their selection of teaching skills in terms of research on teaching effectiveness and very few evaluate the impact of the teaching skills they develop on such product variables as student learning. At the same time, investigators of teacher effectiveness spend little time speculating about the methods that might be used to develop the teaching skills they have identified.

This mutual isolation is particularly unfortunate for one attempting to draw implications for teacher education from research on training. While investigators in teacher effectiveness have increasingly tended to identify complex skills or *competencies* as important teaching variables, training investigators have consistently addressed essentially simple teaching skills or collections of skills as objectives of training. The majority of the investigations of training methods (and it is a substantial majority) address two sets of skills: asking questions at higher cognitive levels and using an indirect style of teaching. Rather than higher order questions and student centered teaching, studies of teacher effectiveness have tended to identify competency areas such as monitoring, maintaining work involvement, and providing substantive feedback as teaching variables associated with student achievement (Peterson & Walberg, 1979). The result is that research on training has generated considerable evidence on acquiring teaching skills of questionable or at least undemonstrated importance. While it is not entirely fair, since successful training methods probably do not tend to be skill specific, one can understand why teacher educators might tend to take the results of training research lightly.

Research on teacher training should increasingly take into account the results of research on teacher effectiveness, addressing the skills and competencies that are found to contribute to student learning. Since such skills and competencies are more likely to be complex than simple, training methods and interventions will need to be correspondingly sophisticated. Recent investigations of teacher adoption of recommended practices (Mohlman, Coladarci & Gage, 1980; Needels, 1980) suggest that practices that appear to be complex and difficult to implement are less likely to be adopted than those that are explicit and readily described. Such findings underline the need for instruction and intervention that make the complex attainable.[6]

There is encouraging evidence in two studies that complex, interactive teaching skills can be acquired. In each study, a carefully designed intervention strategy produced significant changes in teaching performance. The teaching skills addressed were essentially responsive, that is they followed from the teacher's immediate assessment of student responses to questions or other initiations. By providing somewhat different forms of feedback based on classroom observation to the teachers of these classrooms, the investigators were able to help teachers modify their responses to two different groups of elementary level pupils: (a) those who seldom volunteered answers to questions or initiated contributions and those who seldom were given the opportunity to respond a second time after an initial failure (Good & Brophy, 1974); (b) those who appeared to need attention or who had answered questions incorrectly (Moore, Schaut, & Fritzges, 1978). In the first study, teachers significantly increased their interactions with low participation pupils and extended their interactions with students who had initially responded incorrectly. In the second study, teachers increasingly directed their attention to pupils who needed attention and adjusted the level of questions posed to pupils who had previously answered incorrectly. Thus, the provision of systematic feedback proved an effective means of change in complex sets of teacher responses.

SUMMARY

Changing teaching performance—modifying teaching behavior and developing teaching skills—appears to be less a result of practice than it is a result of instruction and intervention. While practice affords a necessary condi-

---

[6] Another finding, supporting the importance of joining training research with effectiveness research, is that teachers are more likely to adopt practices that appear to them to have an adequate rationale. An important part of such a rationale is evidence on the importance of specific skills or practices for student learning.

tion of training, instructional and intervention variables must be introduced to effect change in behaviors and skills. Among the instructional variables that have been demonstrated to be effective are those directed at the acquisition of concepts and at observational learning. Among the intervention variables that have been found effective are the use of feedback and reinforcement. These variables may be integrated into more complex training methods on the basis of behavioral, conceptual, or other processes. However, it is likely that thought must be devoted to the nature of such integrating processes before more highly effective training sequences can be designed and developed. A major implication for teacher training is the desirability of reinstituting controlled conditions, such as the use of media- or computer-based, simulated training methods. Research on teacher training, on the variables identified in the present chapter as well as others, should increasingly focus on the development of complex skills, especially those related to increased student learning.

REFERENCES

Bandura, A. (1972). The role of modeling processes in personality development. In C. S. Lavatelli & F. Stendler (Eds.), *Readings in child behavior and development* (3rd ed.). New York: Harcourt Brace Jovanovich.

Bennie, W. A. (1982). Field-based teacher education—a reconsideration? *Teacher Educator, 17*(4), 19–24.

Bondi, J. C. (1970). Feedback from interaction analysis: Some implications for the improvement of teaching. *Journal of Teacher Education, 21,* 189–196.

Bush, R. N. (1977). We know how to train teachers: Why not do so! *Journal of Teacher Education, 28*(6), 5–9.

Cohen, M. W. (1979). *Teacher's belief systems and training effects.* Paper presented at the annual meeting of the American Educational Research Association, San Francisco.

Copeland, W. D. (1977). Some factors related to student teacher classroom performance following microteaching training. *American Educational Research Journal, 14,* 147–157.

Copeland, W. D. (1980). Student teachers and cooperating teachers: An ecological relationship. *Theory Into Practice, 18,* 194–199.

Davis, O. L., & Smoot, B. R. (1970). Effects on the verbal teaching behaviors of beginning secondary teacher candidates' participation in a program of laboratory teaching. *Educational Leadership: Research Supplement, 4,* 165–169.

Diamond, N. A. (1978). *An analysis of explicit evaluative discourse in supervisor-teacher micro-teaching conferences.* Paper presented at the annual meeting of the American Educational Research Association, Toronto, Canada.

Dunkin, M. J., & Biddle, B. J. (1974). *The study of teaching.* New York: Holt Rinehart, & Winston.

Elliott, P. G. (1978). Field experiences in preservice teacher education. *Bibliographies on educational topics,* (No. 9). Washington, DC: ERIC Clearinghouse on Teacher Education.

Festinger, L. (1964). Cognitive dissonance. In E. E. Sampson (Ed.), *Approaches, contexts and problems of social psychology*. Englewood Cliffs, NJ: Prentice-Hall.

Fuller, F., & Manning, B. A. (1973). Self-confrontation reviewed: A conceptualization for video playback in teacher education. *Review of Educational Research, 43*, 469–528.

Gage, N. L. (1978). *The scientific basis of the art of teaching*. New York: Teachers College Press.

Gliessman, D. H. (1981). *Learning how to teach: Processes, effects and criteria*. Washington, DC: ERIC Clearinghouse on Teacher Education.

Gliessman, D. H., & Pugh, R. C. (1978). Research on the rationale, design and effectiveness of protocol materials. *Journal of Teacher Education, 29*(6), 87–91.

Gliessman, D. H., & Pugh, R. C. (1981). Developing teaching skills through understanding. *Action in Teacher Education, 3*, 11–18.

Gliessman, D. H., Pugh, R. C., & Bielat, B. (1979). Acquiring teaching skills through concept-based training. *Journal of Educational Research, 72*, 149–154.

Good, T. L., & Brophy, J. E. (1974). Changing teacher and student behavior: An empirical investigation. *Journal of Educational Psychology, 66*, 390–405.

Hargie, O. D., & Maidment, P. (1978). Discrimination training and microteaching: Implications for teaching practice. *British Journal of Educational Technology, 9*, 87–93.

Hunt, D. E. (1971). *Matching models in education*. (Monograph Series No. 10) Toronto, Canada: Ontario Institute for Studies in Education.

Jensen, L. C., & Young, J. I. (1972). Effect of televised simulated instruction on subsequent teaching. *Journal of Educational Psychology, 63*, 368–373.

Kleucker, J. C. (1974). Effects of protocol and training materials. *Acquiring Teaching Competencies: Reports and Studies*, (No. 6). Bloomington, IN: National Center for the Development of Training Materials in Teacher Education, Indiana University.

Koran, J. J., Koran, M. L., & McDonald, F. J. (1972). The effects of different sources of positive and negative information on observational learning of a teaching skill. *Journal of Educational Psychology, 63*, 405–410.

Lange, D. N. (1971). An application of social learning theory in affecting change in a group of student teachers using video modeling techniques. *Journal of Educational Research, 65*, 151–154.

MacLeod, G., & McIntyre, D. (1977). Towards a model for microteaching. *British Journal of Teacher Education, 3*(2), 111–120.

McDonald, F. J. (1973). Behavior modification in teacher education. In C. E. Thoresen (Ed.), *Behavior modification in education* (72nd Yearbook, Part I). Chicago, IL: National Society for the Study of Education, University of Chicago.

Mohlman, G., Coladarci, T., & Gage, N. L. (1980). *Comprehension and attitude as predictors of implementation of teacher training*. Paper presented at the annual meeting of the American Educational Research Association Boston, MA.

Moore, J. W., Schaut, J. A., & Fritzges, C. J. (1978). Evaluation of the effects of feedback associated with a problem-solving approach to instruction on teacher and student behavior. *Journal of Educational Psychology, 70*, 200–208.

Needels, M. (1980). *Directed teacher change*. Paper presented at the annual meeting of the American Educational Research Association, Boston, MA.

Peck, R. F., & Tucker, J. A. (1973). Research on teacher education. In R. M. W. Travers (Ed.), *Second handbook of research on teaching*. Chicago, IL: Rand McNally.

Peterson, P. L., & Walberg, H. J. (Eds.). (1979). *Research on teaching: Concepts, findings and implications*. Berkeley, CA: McCutchan.

Robinson, V., & Swanton, C. (1980). The generalization of behavioral teacher training. *Review of Educational Research, 50,* 486–498.

Sadker, M., & Cooper, J. M. (1972). What do we know about microteaching? *Educational Leadership, 29*(6), 547–551.

Semmel, M. I., & Sitko, M. C. (1976). *The effectiveness of a computer-assisted teacher training system (CATTS) in the development of reading and listening comprehension instructional strategies of preservice special education trainees in a tutorial classroom setting*. Bloomington, IN: Center for Innovation in Teaching the Handicapped, Indiana University.

Smith, B. O. (1969). *Teachers for the real world*. Washington, DC: American Association of Colleges for Teacher Education.

Stones, E. (1979). *Psychopedagogy*. London, England: Methuen.

Tuckman, B. W., McCall, K. M., & Hyman, R. T. (1969). The modification of teacher behavior: Effects of dissonance and coded feedback. *American Educational Research Journal, 6,* 607–619.

Turney, C., Clift, J. C., Dunkin, M. J., & Traill, R. D. (1973). *Microteaching: Research theory and practice*. Sydney, Australia: University of Sydney.

Wagner, A. C. (1973). Changing teaching behavior: A comparison of microteaching and cognitive discrimination training. *Journal of Educational Psychology, 64,* 299–305.

Zeichner, K. M. (1980). Myths and realities: Field-based experiences in preservice teacher education. *Journal of Teacher Education, 31*(6), 45–55.

6

Teacher Induction: An International Perspective on Provisions and Research*

Richard P. Tisher
Monash University, Melbourne, Australia

Teacher induction, that is initiation into teaching, may be deemed to begin when teacher trainees commence their preservice education, when they start their student teaching (Fenstermacher, 1980) or alternatively, when newly trained teachers accept their first teaching appointment. A majority of teachers' employers pinpoint the beginning of induction to this time of acceptance; that point of view will be adopted in the ensuing discussion. Attention will be directed primarily to the formal provisions made to induct teachers even though it is recognised that any initiation has both formal and informal components.

It is accepted that informal guidance, help, and advice from colleagues can be of great assistance to new teachers, but it is extremely difficult to gather information about the nature and effectiveness of informal support systems. Furthermore, there is no guarantee that a majority of new teachers will receive informal support from experienced colleagues, even when, as one North American study has shown (Newbury, 1979), that support is required or sought. Some experienced teachers prefer to remain as uninvolved as possible, display a reluctance to help their new colleagues, and believe new teachers should cope on their own. For these and other reasons, formal steps are taken by many educational authorities to induct new members. Attention will be directed here to the nature and effects of these efforts that, by and large, appear to occur during the first year of teaching. If it is accepted that teacher induction refers to the formal initiation of newly trained teachers into the profession and by which they come to be, at a basic level,

---

* This chapter is a revised version of an invitational address presented at the annual meeting of the American Educational Research Association, New York, March, 1982.

professionally competent and personally at ease, then induction may not necessarily end after one year. There is a general consensus that from one to three years may be involved.

Insight into the nature and effects of induction may be obtained by studying the formal provisions underlying induction or the characteristics and qualities of new teachers during their early professional years. A number of investigators from European countries (Broeders, 1980; Frech & Reichwein, 1977; Gabriel, 1957; Müller-Fohrbrodt, Cloetta & Dann, 1978; Phillips, 1932; Taylor & Dale, 1971; Veenman, 1982; Veenman, Berkelaar & Berkelaar-Tomesen, 1983), North America (Cruickshank & Broadbent, 1968; Corcoran, 1981; Dreeben, 1970; Hunter, 1967; Isaacson, 1981; Lortie, 1975; Pataniczek & Isaacson, 1981; Zeichner & Grant, 1981; Zeichner & Tabachnick, 1981), Australia (Hogben & Petty, 1979; MacArthur, 1981; Otto, Gasson & Jordan, 1979; Power, 1981; Telfer, Fyfield & Taylor, 1979; Tisher & Taylor, 1982), and New Zealand (Battersby, 1981; Murdoch, 1978) have compiled information about new teachers' concerns or problems, job satisfaction, and control ideology. A smaller number in the United Kingdom (Bolam, 1973; Bradley & Eggleston, 1975, 1978), New Zealand (Battersby, 1981; Murdoch, 1978), Australia (Tisher, Fyfield, & Taylor, 1979) and North America (Zeichner, 1979a) have dealt with formal induction provisions. Very few, if any, have gathered empirical information about the underlying processes, although there are some attempts at explanatory theories (Lacey, 1977; Zeichner, 1979b). It may be that insights about these processes can also be gleaned from the literature associated with the socialization of persons into other cultures or groups (Biddle, 1979). This chapter will not examine the explanatory theories. The ensuing sections deal only with the nature, underlying assumptions, and perceived benefits of formal provisions for induction; some of the qualities, characteristics, and concerns of beginning teachers; and some of the author's perspectives about induction and associated research that have emerged from surveying the international literature.

THE NATURE OF TEACHER INDUCTION

Teacher induction appears to be formally fostered more in some countries than in others. For example, educational authorities in Britain and Australia were initiating and formulating policies and writing about formal induction provisions in the 1970s. In the same period, there were a few experimental induction programs in the United States but, by and large, the commitment to formal provisions was not as great or as consistent as in Britain and Australia (Zeichner, 1979a). In Australia, Britain, and New Zealand, there are formal provisions for inducting teachers which are predicated on a number of grounds: new teachers experience difficulties and need help in their first years of teaching; there are weaknesses in preservice teacher education; and the desire of employing authorities and professional associations to maintain some control over teacher education. These formal provisions, and for that matter, in experimental programs in the United States, are comparable. New teachers in these countries may benefit from some or all of the following:

- Printed materials which contain information about conditions of employment, facilities available to teachers, school policies, rules, and administrative procedures. These printed materials are frequently issued when new teachers accept their first appointment.
- Reductions in teaching load. This is achieved by either a reduction in actual allocated time for teaching in each week, or a reduction in the size of the classes taught, or (in secondary schools) a reduction in the range of classes taught (e.g., to ninth grade only), with a corresponding reduction in the amount of lesson preparation.
- School orientation visits prior to commencing teaching. The visits may be to the actual school to which the teachers are appointed or to others in the nearby region.
- Released time to attend regular one day or half-day inservice workshops or to visit other schools.
- Regular (weekly or monthly) counselling meetings within the school. The meetings are generally organised and conducted by an experienced colleague or a visiting consultant specially appointed for the purpose.
- Lengthy (4 to 8 days) conferences or workshops conducted by experienced colleagues and other resource personnel in locations away from the school.

Conferences, workshops, and counselling meetings involve discussions, seminars, group work, simulated exercises, lectures, critical incidents, and role playing. By and large, the issues that figure prominently include those that appear in a normal preservice education program: Namely, lesson planning and preparation, classroom discipline and management, questioning and review strategies, and procedures for evaluating pupil progress and motivation in the classroom. Furthermore, where counselling meetings are involved, experienced colleagues visit classrooms and observe lessons given by new teachers. To a lesser degree, new teachers are permitted to visit and observe lessons given by their experienced colleagues.

The consultants or colleagues who are appointed to conduct conferences, workshops or counselling meetings are sometimes, but not always, specially trained for their role in induction. Training provisions exist in Britian and Australia (Thurstans, 1979; Young, 1979), where it is also assumed that a professional tutor will be based in the school, released from some normal teaching duties, and in contact with resource units (e.g., regional teacher's centers) that can provide specialized assistance (Young, 1979). In one Australian state the training of induction tutors is conceived as part of inservice education for experienced teachers. The strategy is to train three experienced teachers as induction tutors whose responsibilities for the professional development of new teachers in their school lasts for a specific number of years, after which time another three experienced colleagues are trained to assume the responsibilities. Each tutor receives a substantial resource folder (Queensland InService Education Committee, 1981) containing ideas for school-based induction programs and for professional development.

Whereas education authorities rarely declare the objectives for their formal provisions for induction, it may be assumed that these objectives could include:

1. To extend the teachers' knowledge about the school and the educational systems and how both function;
2. To increase the teachers' awareness and comprehension of the complexities of teaching situations and to suggest alternative ways of coping with these complexities;
3. To acquaint the teachers with support services and resources within the school and the region;
4. To help the teachers (generally through counselling activities) to apply knowledge they already possess, or could obtain for themselves, to the daily tasks or problems which confront them. (Tisher, 1980, p. 81)

If it is accepted that these are purposes of induction, then either by intention or oversight education authorities are casting induction tutors in the role of providers, rather than collaborative problem solvers. The creative potential of beginning teachers appears to be ignored; there appears to be little overt recognition that beginning teachers may be fresh resources of ideas, for example with respect to new teaching methods or new advances in subject matter. Provisions for induction in several countries appear to be based on a deficit-dependency model about new teachers (Dean, 1977; Stammers, 1979). New teachers are regarded as deficient with respect to their knowledge of the educative process, instructional strategies, and their ability to teach. They are viewed as dependent upon more experienced colleagues— colleagues who, more readily than teacher educators, are the best sources of practical information about teaching and better able to help newcomers fit into the profession (McCabe, 1979). Clearly a deficit-dependency model places a greater emphasis on the constraining rather than the creative features in the socialization process associated with induction. If induction is to be of high quality, then more allowances need to be made for the creative potential of new teachers.

FORMAL PROVISIONS AND BEGINNING TEACHERS' CONCERNS

Research about induction provisions and their effects indicates that, even when the formal provisions exist, a proportion of new teachers do not receive them; those that do express satisfaction in having received them, but only about half of these see much value in the activities (Tisher, Fyfield, & Taylor, 1979; Zeichner, 1979a). There is no compelling evidence for the superiority of one induction provision over another (Zeichner, 1979a), although different forms of released time are much better than no provision at all (Bradley & Eggleston, 1978), and beginning teachers believe that other new teachers should not be denied a variety of induction provisions (Tisher, Fyfield, & Taylor, 1979). Table 1, which is based on data from a national survey in Australia, illustrates some of these findings. It is appropriate to note that although a minority of new teachers are afforded the opportunity to observe experienced colleagues' methods of teaching, a majority recommend that future new teachers should not be denied that provision.

With respect to the provision of released time from teaching duties in order to consult with experienced colleagues, engage in supervised programs

TABLE I   Provisions or Opportunities for Beginning Teachers

Opportunity or Provision	Percentage of Beginning Teachers Who	
	Recommended the Opportunity	Were Given the Opportunity
Accepting advice in classroom management or help in producing programs	86	74
Receiving written materials on school matters	86	74
Observing other teachers' methods of teaching	82	44
Receiving written materials on conditions of employment	80	51
Exploring local educational resources	74	48
Accepting evaluation	73	55
Participating in organized consultation with experienced school personnel	68	53
Conferring informally with beginning teachers from other schools	65	59
Attending group meetings for beginning teachers at school	65	42
Visiting other schools for observation/ consultation	62	20
Attending group meetings for beginning teachers elsewhere	56	45

Source: Tisher, Fyfield, and Taylor, 1979, p. 61.

of professional activities, visit other resource centers, or plan teaching activities, Bradley & Eggleston (1978) claim, based on the results of an experimental study in Britain, that although different types of released time are better than none at all, supervised released times appear to be superior to unsupervised release. They note that new teachers who were provided with supervised released times became more confident and less frustrated with teaching than their peers who were provided with unsupervised release.

Whether different induction provisions affect teaching skills, teaching strategies, classroom interaction patterns, or pupil achievement is a moot point. The findings from several experimental studies are equivocal with respect to teaching strategies and skills (Zeichner, 1979a) and the research literature lacks information on the effects of the provisions on pupil achievement. Beginning teachers, who generally are satisfied with their teaching appointment, tend to become more custodial than they were during their preservice training and believe they are managing their classrooms more adequately than their principals do (MacArthur, 1981; Tisher, Fyfield & Taylor, 1979). This is not to imply that they believe there is no room for improvement. On the contrary, as Table 2 shows, a significant proportion of those who believe they are controlling their classes adequately worry about the task. All teachers in fact perceive problems with teaching—those in their first years of teaching perceive more problems than their experienced colleagues. What is significant for educational administrators and induction

TABLE II   Percentages of Teachers Managing and Worrying about Teaching Tasks at the End of Their First Year of Teaching

I Teaching Task	II Concerned	III Managing Adequately	IV* Those Managing and Concerned
Teaching groups with wide ability range	63	55	26
Teaching slow learners	62	48	22
Evaluating own teaching	55	64	25
Motivating pupils	54	67	26
Discovering level at which to teach	47	73	25
Teaching specific skills	41	64	23
Controlling classes	39	78	22
Assessing students' work	37	80	20
Devising schemes of work	35	86	25
Teaching immigrants	30	36	11

* Column IV indicates the overlap between columns II and III

Source: Tisher, Fyfield, and Taylor, 1979, p. 49.

counsellors is the fact that across nations, for elementary and secondary teachers, the lists of most salient problems are remarkably similar. In recent international reviews of 57 studies, Veenman (1982) and his collaborators (Veenman, Berkelaar, & Berkelaar-Tomesen, 1983) conclude that the six most highly ranked perceived problems of beginning teachers are: classroom discipline, motivating students, handling individual differences, relations with parents, addressing problems of individual students, and assessing student' work. This list is comparable to that obtained in a representative national sample of Australian elementary and secondary teachers (Tisher, Fyfield, & Taylor, 1979). Table 2 contains the relevant findings and distinguishes between the proportions of new teachers who, though worried about an issue, believe they are coping with it adequately. This feature is rarely highlighted in studies of beginning teachers' concerns.

REFLECTIONS

As a consequence of surveys of the international literature, correspondence and visits with induction researchers in several countries, involvement in a national study, and interactions with beginning teachers over a number of years, the author has formed perspectives about induction. Some of these are presented here for consideration in the hope that they will foster more effective teacher induction in the future.

The first years of teaching are extremely important ones, affecting the professional and personal development of teachers because "learning to be a teacher is not just learning a job—it is learning a new way of being yourself" (Claxton, 1978). Formal induction provisions need to recognize this dual aspect of teacher development, while making allowances for the creative potential within new teachers. The deficit-dependency assumptions, which, as was noted earlier, underlie many of the induction provisions, can be misleading and lead to an inadequate realization of new teachers' creativity. This is not meant to imply that formal provisions for induction should be abandoned. Induction, in fact, cannot be left to chance, which is what may occur when informal procedures are advocated at the expense of formal ones. Formal provisions (listed in Table 1) have a vital role even in these years when fewer new teachers are being hired.

That new teachers express satisfaction with induction provisions, but at the same time do not always see value in some of them, has implications for organizers of induction programs, especially when those reactions are compared to findings about trainees' perspectives on preservice education. There is undoubtedly a range of teaching issues which are appropriately included in preservice courses and a range which can with advantage be left to the induction period. These are issues which only have meaning when the need for them is seen in practice. Teacher educators, educational employing authorities, and induction organizers should change their perspectives of what preservice teacher education and induction can realistically accomplish so that each will complement the other to a greater extent.

To date, even though induction tutors or counsellors are specially appointed for the purpose, little is known about the quality and effects of their work and, when they exist, their training programs. A great deal of research is required on these matters and, no doubt, more developmental work is required on tutor-training programs. Too little effort has been expended to develop tutors' skills in counselling and to select those experienced teachers with appropriate qualities to counsel and collaborate with new teachers.

The nature and the quality of induction and the work of induction tutors are affected substantially by contextual characteristics including school facilities and values. But even though many people have recognised that induction is context specific, little research has attempted to document this association. The task is undoubtedly a complex one and will require ingenious researchers who will adopt new research styles. Conventional research methods involving experimental designs and surveys will only yield mildly definitive results that do not compel policymakers to act. Yet action is required if induction is to be more effective. In order to maintain and improve induction, and at the same time increase our understanding of the effects of the formal provisions, projects which combine developmental activities and research should be initiated. This can be achieved by establishing action research projects in which a collaborating team conducts an innovative induction program based on the best practical and experimental evidence available, while, at the same time, a formative evaluation of their efforts is undertaken. While research information is being generated, something practical is also being done for teacher induction.

One other matter that needs further study is teacher job satisfaction. Knowledge about its relationships with teacher anxiety, absenteeism, and expectations would help a great deal in shaping induction provisions and conditions of work. With respect to expectations, Wanous (1976) maintains that certain aspects are more important to overall job satisfaction than others. These are expectations about intrinsic characteristics of teaching (e.g., opportunities for personal growth, intellectual stimulation, and independent action); they are more likely to decline during induction than expectations about extrinsic characteristics (e.g., teaching load, school administrative duties).

Teacher induction is an important process that cannot be left to chance, that requires further development and research in order to make it more effective. The research and development tasks are complex and challenging, but there are many exciting things to be done.

REFERENCES

Battersby, D. (1981). *The first year of teaching: A grounded theory study.* Doctoral thesis, University of Waikato, New Zealand.

Battersby, D. (1982). The professional development of beginning teachers: Some recommendations from a New Zealand study. *South Pacific Journal of Teacher Education, 10* (2), 22–31.

Biddle, B. J. (1979). *Role theory expectations, identities and behaviors,* New York: Academic Press.

Bolam, R. (1973). *Induction programmes for probationary teachers.* Bristol, England School of Education, Research Unit, University of Bristol, 1973.

Bradley, H. W., & Eggleston, J. F. (Eds.). (1975). *An inquiry into the induction year.* Nottingham, England: School of Education, University of Nottingham.

Bradley, H. W., & Eggleston, J. F. (1978). An induction year experiment. *Educational Research, 20,* 89–98.

Broeders, A. (1980). *Beginnende leerkrachten: werksituatie en arbeids satisfactie.* Doctoraalscriptie, Instituut voor Onderwijskunda, Catholic University, Nijmegen, Holland.

Claxton, G. (1978) *The Little Ed. Book.* London: England: Routledge & Kegan Paul.

Corcoran, E. (1981). Transition shock: The beginning teacher's paradox. *Journal of Teacher Education, 32*(3), 19–23.

Cruikshank, D. R., & Broadbent, F. W. (1968). The simulation and analysis of problems of beginning teachers. Report to the Office of Education, Department of Health Education and Welfare, Bureau of Research. Brockport, NY: State University of New York.

Dean, J. (1977). Making in-service effective. *British Journal of In-Service Education, 4*(1).

Dreeben, R. (1970). *The nature of teaching.* Glenview, IL: Scott, Foresman & Co.

Fenstermacher, G. D. (1980). What needs to be known about what teachers need to know? In G. Hall, et al. (Ed.), *Exploring issues in teacher education: Questions for future research,* Austin, TX: University of Texas, R.&D. Center for Teacher Education.

Frech, H. W., & Reichwein, R. (1977). *Der vergessene teil der lehrerbildung: Institutionelle bedingungen und inhaltliche tendenzen im referendariat der gymnasiallehrer.* Stuttgart, Germany: Klett-Cotta.

Gabriel, J. (1957). *An analysis of the emotional problems of the teacher in the classroom.* London, England: Angus and Robertson.

Hunter, J. S. (1967). *The beginning teacher one year later.* Washington, DC: U.S. Department of Health Education and Welfare.

Hogben, D., & Petty, M. F. (1979). From student to primary school teacher: Attitude, stability and change. *South Pacific Journal of Teacher Education, 7,* 92–98.

Isaacson, N. S. (1981). *A description of the nature and extent of support systems as perceived by beginning secondary teachers.* Doctoral dissertation, University of Oregon.

Lacey, C. (1977). *The socialisation of teachers.* London, England: Methuen.

Lortie, D. C. (1975). *School-teacher: A sociological study*, Chicago, IL: University of Chicago Press.

MacArthur, J. (1981). *The first five years of teaching*. ERDC Report No. 30. Canberra, Australia: Australian Government Publishing Service.

McCabe, J. J. C. (1979). Some implications of induction for initial teacher training. *British Journal of Teacher Education, 5,* 157–164.

Müller-Fohrbrodt, G., Cloetta, B., & Dann, H. D. (1978). *Der praxisschock bei junger lehren,* Stuttgart, Germany: Klett-Cotta.

Murdoch, R. P. (1978). *Professional development: The induction and education of beginning teachers*. Christchurch, New Zealand: Christchurch Teachers' College.

Newbury, J. Mc. (1978). The barrier between beginning and experienced teachers. *Journal of Educational Administration, 16*(1), 46–56.

Otto, E., Gasson, I., & Jordan, E. (1979). Perceived problems of beginning teachers. *South Pacific Journal of Teacher Education, 7*(1 & 2), 28–33.

Pataniczek, D., & Isaacson, N. S. (1981). The relationship of socialization and the concerns of beginning secondary teachers. *Journal of Teacher Education, 32*(3), 15–17.

Phillips, M. (1932). Some problems of adjustment in the early years of a teacher's life. *British Journal of Educational Psychology, 2,* 237–256.

Power, P. G. (1981). Aspects of the transition from educational student to beginning teacher. *Australian Journal of Education, 25,* 288–296.

Queensland In-Service Education (Secondary) Committee. (1981). *Teacher induction program—Secondary,* Brisbane, Australia: Queensland Education Department.

Stammers, P. (1979). Whose INSET is it? *British Journal of InService Education, 6*(1), 5–9.

Taylor, K., & Dale, J. R. (1971). *A survey of teachers in their first year of service*. British, England School of Education, University of Bristol.

Telfer, R. (1981). Some variables associated with teaching problems.*South Pacific Journal of Teacher Education, 9*(2), 13–21.

Thurstans, I. (1979). Teacher-tutor training: A summary of the development of training programmes for teacher tutors in the induction processes in the U.K. in R. P. Tisher, (Ed.), *More effective induction in Australia: New Directions,* Faculty of Education, Monash University, Melbourne, Australia.

Tisher, R. (1980). The induction of beginning teachers. In E. Hoyle and J. Megarry (Eds.), *World yearbook of education 1980: Professional development of teachers*. London, England: Kogan Page.

Tisher, R. P., Fyfield, J. A., & Taylor, S. M. (1979). *Beginning to teach*. Volume 2, ERDC Report No. 20. Canberra, Australia: Australian Government Publishing Service.

Tisher, R. P., & Taylor, S. M. (1982). New teachers' job satisfactions. *South Pacific Journal of Teacher Education, 10*(1), 9–16.

Veenman, S. (1982). Problemen van beginnende leraren: Uitkomsten van een literatuurecherche. *Pedagogische Studiën, 59,* 458–470.

Veenman, S., Berkelaar, A., & Berkelaar-Tomesen, J. (1983). Problemen van beginnende leraren in het basisonderwijs: Een exploratief beschrijvend onderzoek. *Pedagogische Studiën, 60,* 28–37.

Wanous, J. P. (1976). Organisational entry. From native expectations to realistic beliefs. *Journal of Applied Psychology, 61,* 22–29.

Young, W. H. (1979). The professional tutor: An innovation in initial training, Induction and in-service education for teachers. In R. P. Tisher, (Ed.), *More effective induction in Australia: New Directions.* Faculty of Education, Monash University, Melbourne, Australia.

Zeichner, K. M. (1979a). Teacher induction practices in the United States and Great Britain. A paper presented at the Annual Meeting of the American Educational Research Association, San Francisco, CA.

Zeichner, K. M. (1979b). The dialectics of teacher socialization. Paper presented at the Annual Meeting of the Association of Teacher Educators, Orlando, FL.

Zeichner, K., & Grant, C. (1981). Biography and social structure in the socialization of student teachers: A re-examining of the pupil control ideologies of student teachers. *Journal of Education for Teaching, 1,* 298–314.

Zeichner, K. M., & Tabachnick, B. R. (1981). Are the Effects of University Teacher Education "Washed Out" by School Experiences? *Journal of Teacher Education, 32*(3), 7–11.

7
Teachers of Teachers*

Heather Carter
University of Texas at Austin

Throughout the United States, public and private institutions of higher education are accredited to prepare candidates for the teaching profession. Each institution, regardless of its status, has many faculty members involved in the teacher-preparation program. Some of these teacher educators, may hold faculty appointments in an academic area, but most will be in the schools, colleges, or departments of education. These individuals are charged with at least four important responsibilities: transmission of the skills held by the profession; gatekeeper for the profession; codification of the basic knowledge upon which the teaching profession is based; and, service to the profession. Certainly, these responsibilities are shared by those who serve as teacher educators in public schools, state agencies, and private and professional organizations. However, the concern of this chapter is limited to university-based teacher educators who hold faculty appointments within the schools, colleges, or departments of education. The background of these persons, the mechanisms by which they joined the ranks of university-based teacher educators, and their current four-fold mission will be examined. The discussion is based on a descriptive study on teacher educators conducted at a major research university.

In this study, a univerity-based teacher educator was defined as a faculty member in a tenure track who had taught at least one required undergraduate professional education course during the preceeding twelve

* This study was supported in part by the National Institute of Education Contract OB–NIE–G–80–0216. The opinions expressed herein do not necessarily reflect the position or policy of the National Institute of Education and no official endorsement by that office should be inferred.

months. Two, one-hour focussed interviews were conducted with each of the 28 participants.[1] These interviews were designed to collect data regarding the precollegiate and collegiate training, professional background, and the current professional activities of the teacher educators in the sample. Considerable caution should be used when interpreting the data, since the sample size was small, and since all members were teacher educators at the same institution. Some confidence in the data is gained by noting that they corroborate the findings of Jackson (1968), Lortie (1975), Joyce, Howey, Yarger, Harbeck, and Kluwin (1977) and Howey, Bents, and Corrigan (1981).

BACKGROUND OF TEACHER EDUCATORS

Preprofessional Experiences

Physicians, lawyers, nurses, and social workers typically have had little experience, if any, of being in their clients' roles. For example, few physicians, at the onset of their career, have been patients for anything but routine examinations and minor problems. Teachers, however, have been clients for thousands of hours on a regular basis in precollegiate settings over a period of 12 or 13 years. Added to this, teacher educators, during their undergraduate preparation, have been clients in a university for at least another four years. Over that extensive period, many assumptions are developed by the nascent teacher educator about the role and responsibilities of teachers and teacher educators. This early direct exposure is potentially a powerful source of influence upon teacher educators as they carry out their responsibilities.

In the study, the sample of 28 teacher educators was comprised of 18 males and 10 females. There were 24 Anglo-Americans, two Mexican-Americans, one Black-American, and one Asian-American. Ten had received their doctorates prior to 1970 and 17 since 1969.[2] One did not hold a doctorate. Most described themselves as coming from low to middle socioeconomic status (SES) families; among those receiving their doctorate more recently there appeared a trend to be of middle SES origins. The majority of the teacher educators were the first or second born in families of one, two, or three children.

The elementary schools these teacher educators had attended were generally in nonurban settings where the students were from one ethnic

---

[1] A full account of this study is available in the final report of the investigation (Carter, 1981). That report includes more detailed data on the sample together with the interview schedules.

[2] Significant differences were observed among participants who had received their doctorates prior to 1970 and those who had received them since 1969. The differences include values, research thrusts, background, and expectations.

group. None had attended racially-balanced schools. For a few, high school had brought the first direct experiences with students from other ethnic groups, but for the majority, their high school peers were from the same ethnic background. Six had attended private or parochial schools for all or part of their precollegiate years. Most of the teacher educators in the sample expressed a general satisfaction with themselves during that period. Few significant decisions regarding future careers or academic programs to be pursued had been made by these individuals at that time. At a critical developmental stage in their lives, these persons had experienced a relatively homogeneous social setting, one not greatly challenged by extremes of wealth or poverty, or by variations in ethnic or cultural background, or by extremes of lifestyle. They shared the view of the school as a purveyor of knowledge, knowledge which they desired and which could be attained. A secure situation contributed to the teacher educators' decisions to enter the teaching profession and influenced their philosophies regarding the preparation of teachers.

Most of the teacher educators interviewed had attended small state-supported institutions where all but three had acquired a teaching certificate upon completion of undergraduate work. Only half, however, had majored in education. Six had majored in the social sciences, four in English, two in science, one in mathematics, and one in fine arts. These persons assessed the experiences they had had during those years very positively, stating that it was the first occasion on which they had really considered learning to be meaningful. While valuing the challenges and experiences encountered in their academic fields, the future teacher educators saw less value in their education courses. They indicated that they had learned about teaching; they had not learned how to teach. They believed they had learned how to teach primarily by teaching and, to a lesser extent, by modeling teaching behaviors they had seen others exhibit. Several persons indicated that, of their preservice professional education courses, the student teaching experience had been the only one that had permitted them to have actual contact with pupils:

> I had no other experience with children. I think I could have learned a great deal if I had had more experiences in the school...had I been given guidance...had I been asked to try other teaching strategies.

It was generally during the years at college that these subjects had decided to pursue a teaching career. Many had not entered college anticipating that they would be teachers and had not selected education as their major field of study. Generally, they did not recall a specific decision to become a teacher, but rather they had drifted into the field and had found it to be satisfying. This is consistent with the eased entry characteristic of teaching as described by Lortie (1975, pp. 17-19). By the end of their collegiate experiences, although possessing some anxiety, they had looked forward with optimism to a teaching career. They had anticipated making practical contributions to society.

Professional Experiences

The teaching profession places high value on the role of the practitioner as reflected in requirements for appointment as a faculty member in a teacher-education institution (National Council for Accreditation of Teacher Education [NCATE], 1979). Of the 28 educators interviewed, only one had no school-teaching experience. That person's assignment as a faculty member did not involve direct work in the public schools. The majority of the subjects had had between two and six years of school-teaching experience prior to becoming teacher educators. The majority had taught in urban schools, but only one subject had taught in a specifically inner-city school. Persons who received their doctorate prior to 1970 had more varied experiences than the more recent degree recipients.

The rewards experienced by the teacher educators while public-school teachers were consistent with those described for teachers by Lortie (1975). All but six stated that student interactions were the most valued and rewarding aspects of teaching:

> Getting to know kids, having interactions with them, and all those things that give one pleasure when interacting with other people.

Closely related to this reward was the impact that the participants felt they had had as teachers:

> I felt that I was accomplishing something that was important, and it gave me a good feeling about myself. I knew that I was making a contribution.

Both of these rewards were intrinsic. No reference was made to any form of extrinsic reward.

Schoolteaching, however, had not been without its frustrations—frustrations which for some ultimately contributed to their leaving schoolteaching and becoming teacher educators. The two most frequently mentioned sources of frustration were the perceived bureaucratic excesses and the isolation of the classroom teacher. The former is at the roots of Wittlin's (1965) questions regarding the professional status of teachers.

> The professional status of the schoolteacher is altogether questioned on the grounds of his limited autonomy, of his restrictions in decision-making concerning what and how he teaches, and of his position as a strictly supervised employee. (p. 93)

Isolation was the focus of the book, *The Lonely Teacher* (Knoblock & Goldstein, 1971), concerning the interpersonal relations of schoolteacher and pupil.

The intrinsic rewards in teaching, according to the teacher educators sampled, had been great during the schoolteaching years. They had believed they were making a genuine contribution, they had enjoyed the interaction with pupils and, for many, teaching had been easy, although time and energy consuming. Frustrations, however, had been great and had caused most of them to be less than satisfied with this level within the teaching profession. They had therefore decided to leave the public-school classroom.

ENTRY TO TEACHER EDUCATION

Lortie (1975), when discussing recruitment resources for teaching, speaks of attractors and facilitators to the profession. The same terms can be applied when considering entry into the role of teacher educator. Attractors are the advantages offered to the person in the role of teacher educator; facilitators are the conditions and factors that help people move into this occupation.[3]

Attractors

The attractors for teacher education included both the rewards that were experienced in classroom teaching together with alleviation of the frustrations that had been encountered. The interaction with students was a source of great reward in classroom teaching and one that could be retained as a teacher educator:

> I really loved teaching and I wanted to stay in touch with it. I knew that if I went into science education I could still keep in contact with schools and I could still keep in contact with students.

While indicating that, as classroom teachers, they had felt they were able to make a contribution, there was a recognition that this could be wider when teaching at the collegiate level:

> The justification I would use for being a college teacher instead of an elementary teacher is that I discovered a few ideas, or have been taught a few ideas which lots of teachers don't know and ought to know and could do a whole lot better if they knew...If I can pass them on to

[3] The assistance of Mark Isham and Roscoe Stribling is acknowledged in the development of this section. A more complete description of these entry mechanisms is provided in a paper presented at the American Education Research Association Conference, Los Angeles, CA, 1981 (Isham, Carter, & Stribling, 1981).

someone else so that kids get a better education, then I am not just influencing a few kids, but in some small way hopefully influencing lots of
teachers in what they do for kids.

By becoming a teacher educator, the participants were able to retain the personal rewards of classroom teaching while deriving benefits not available to
classroom teachers.

A major source of frustration as classroom teachers had been the perceived bureaucratic constraints. These were of particular aggravation when
they had been seen as infringing upon or undermining teachers' professional
competence in issues such as course content, teaching procedures, or time
usage. As university-based teacher educators they believed they would be
more autonomous:

In terms of how I would go about my job, I would be on my own. I
would be able to do anything I wanted to do and in any way I wanted to
do it.

The second major frustration experienced as a classroom teacher had
been the lack of collegial interaction.

I had no time to interact with other professional people. On those occasions when I did find time we discussed either social matters or teaching
conditions or discipline problems. We never talked about any kind of
professional issues.

Lack of intellectual stimulation was voiced by participants as an indication of the perceived isolation of the classroom. Interaction with students
was important, but interaction with adults was considered to be more stimulating and some saw the possible consequences of lack of stimulation
among their older colleagues:

Something had gone out of them after spending from 10 to 20 years in
the classroom. They were intelligent and thoughtful people but who
were both dead and cowed by 20 years on the job.

There were facets of university life that had appealed to the persons
interviewed when they were still classroom teachers. Many were attracted to
teacher education because it afforded the opportunity to combine interests
in various disciplines with interests in teaching:

I could teach both in the chemistry department and in science education.
It appealed to me to be able to do more work in education without giving up my teaching in the science field.

The attractors in no way meant that the teacher educators intended to shun their colleagues in classroom teaching. They would, however, not be committed to the routine of the classroom, but would gain several advantages.

Facilitators

Some professions require the first in a series of career decisions to be made early in life in order to successfully negotiate entrance. Other occupations, such as classroom teaching, have wider ranges of decision times that permit entrants to postpose decisions and commitments until later in life. This is certainly the case with teacher education, and late decisions were common among the sample subjects of teacher educators interviewed. Some had decided to become teacher educators while still in classroom teaching for any one or more of the attraction factors described in the previous section. These subjects undertook a systematic doctoral program lasting about three years. For many others, however, there was not a definite decision. These were already enrolled in a master's degree program or were pursuing graduate work when they managed, more by default than by design, to transform a series of courses into a program of study:

> As far as the PhD is concerned, after I got my master's degree, I simply started taking courses for my own personal satisfaction to learn more about my field. The fellow who turned out to be my major professor said, "Why don't you formalize this into a PhD program?" And that's the way the whole thing began.

The role of a university-based teacher educator is a somewhat obvious next step in a career which is marked by absence of stages (Lortie, 1975). There are few steps through which one can pass in classroom teaching. The extrinsic rewards are somewhat automatic and rare in that there are few levels or grades of teaching with differentiated rewards within either the elementary school or secondary school. The salary range is also somewhat flat. Teacher education affords a more staged profession and satisfies many of the stated needs of the persons who fill the role.

THE FOUR-FOLD MISSION OF THE UNIVERSITY-BASED TEACHER EDUCATOR

There is some general agreement about the role of precollegiate teachers. Few would deny that their responsibility is to convey the essential knowledge of the adult world to its youth. There is, too, a general belief about the role of teacher educators. These persons, presumably master teachers themselves, should pass on their skills of teaching to the next generation of teachers. This, however, is a somewhat simplistic description of their role. It is perhaps more desirable to consider them as having a fourfold mission within the profession: transmitting skills, acting as gatekeepers, codifying basic knowledge, and providing service.

Transmission of Skills Held by The Profession

"They do not know what it is like in classrooms." "They cannot teach students how to teach." Comments such as these are heard from classroom teachers who do not perceive university-based teacher educators as members of the teaching profession. Although some teacher educators question their own efficacy, they all see themselves as members of the profession. When they left the daily responsibilities of teaching in the precollegiate schools, they believed they were moving to another phase of the same profession—one in which they would have different responsibilities and one in which they could use more of their skills while experiencing fewer frustrations.

Many teacher educators seemed to be agreeing with the teachers when they stated that they themselves had learned to teach by teaching. What, then, did they believe they could teach in their courses? Did they believe that they could, in fact, help students to become teachers? The question "How did you learn to teach?" caused several persons to respond that they had never learned to teach; learning to teach was, they said, a continuous process: "The question assumes by its verb that I know how. I continue to learn how." Most of the teacher educators interviewed believed that it is possible to initiate the process of learning to become a teacher. This can be accomplished by learning some basic technical skills:

> I believe we can help teach the technical aspects of teaching. Personally I don't think that we can do much with 90 percent of what the teacher is all about. I think that 90 percent of teaching is an art.

> There's just not enough time to teach people to teach, for one thing. So we can only teach them to be aware of the variables of concern when you teach. You can teach them to be aware of things like management.

Musgrave (1979) describes the technical manner in which mass media use skills for communication:

> Teaching grows to be less of an art and more of a science as research reveals more about the process of learning and the best way to communicate information. Yet it is still true that to practice as a teacher assumes a core of specialized knowledge and skills. (p. 170)

The teacher educators in the sample, while recognizing that they had learned and still learn to teach by doing, believe apprenticeship alone is insufficient. The careful presentation of the technical core of teaching skills may make the activities involved in teaching more predictable, may alleviate much of the trauma of the induction experiences, and may decrease the attrition rate among beginning teachers (Williams, 1981).

Being a university-based teacher educator does not mean isolation from the public-school classrooms. Involvement in schools is frequently very high as part of the professional preparation of teachers. The teacher educators generally retain the belief they had held while in their preservice preparation, a belief shared by practicing teachers, that although skills may be taught in the college classrooms they have to be practiced in the public schools. Many management techniques seem very logical and very easy to apply until one is confronted with the somewhat fidgety, excited kindergarten class at Halloween, or the apathetic yet belligerent eighth graders as they come to their remedial reading class. For years, as was indicated by many participants in the study, most education courses were taught on the university campus. More recently, there has been a shift in work location, and many methods courses are now field-based. This may mean that the entire course is taught in the public-school classroom, or that part of the instruction is carried out in that location (Arnstine, 1981). Among the faculty members interviewed, there was considerable variation regarding their perceptions of the value of field experiences:

> I feel that teaching methods courses from a theoretical base with no practicum is a dead-end proposition. If we are going to have a worthwhile experience we have to do something with kids.

> I'd have less field-based education. . . My position is that university people should do what they can do best and that's not to go into public schools and tell people what to do. . . It seems that public school people are far more competent to do some things than those of us who teach at the university. There should be a separation of responsibilities.

The last extreme statement is the only one of its kind in the sample. It is worth noting that the two persons quoted structure their teaching responsibilities at the university in a manner consistent with their stated philosophical viewpoints. The first person indicated that all mornings were spent in the field and that activities related to this portion of his responsibilities occupied most of the time. The second person, however, stated that although he does work with undergraduate students, "My job as a professor is isolated from the schools. I don't work in the schools."

The variance observed among university-based teacher educators regarding the value of field experiences is a reflection of the relationship they perceive between craft knowledge, or practice, and theoretical knowledge, or concepts. Taylor (cited in Woods, 1980, p. 267) addresses this relationship:

> Practice as such will necessarily give rise to certain questions in the mind of the students...Without acquiring some concepts by means of which his experience can be ordered, the student will have nothing to report.

The relative value of theory, generally presented in structured class settings, and field experience has not yet been determined. Research directed toward this end will be of critical importance and may "improve substantially on the unaided common sense or raw experience of the teacher" (Gage, 1978, p. 93). With this progress, university-based teacher educators will still be visible in the public schools and will work with preservice teachers in these settings, but the experiences will be more structured and more productive in helping the students become teachers.

The first portion of the four-fold mission of the university-based teacher educators, the transmission of skills, is becoming more clearly defined. Apprenticeship has taken on a truer perspective, a technical core has developed, and the relative value of craft as opposed to theory is being determined.

Acting as a Gatekeeper for the Profession

Within the teaching profession, the university-based teacher educator is the primary person responsible for recommending candidates for a teaching credential. This is an important gatekeeper role. It is unusual in a profession for the same persons who teach the students in class to be responsible for recommending the licensure of those students. If they are not recommended, have teacher educators failed to achieve their teaching objectives? Are the standards and objectives of the teacher educator congruent with those of the practitioners? Possibly of most importance, do the teacher educators feel it is their responsibility to advise a student not to enter the profession if he or she is not qualified? The teacher educators in the sample were unanimous and positive in their responses when asked this last question. There was less unanimity, however, when they were asked if they were able to prevent an unqualified candidate from pursuing certification. Respondents fell into three categories: (a) Persons who felt they had "power" to prevent entry into the profession; (b) those who felt they could exert "influence," that is, nonbinding counselling or persuasion; and (c) those who felt they had no "power." Most people, and in equal proportions, fell into the first and third categories. There was, however, a marked difference in the persons who comprised these categories dependent upon the number of years they had spent as classroom teachers. Those who had taught for more than four years saw themselves as having the power to determine entry; those with four years experience or less did not perceive that power.

Power to prevent:

> I think it is my responsibility to encourage those who are interested in continuing and it is my responsibility to discourage those who are not really interested in continuing...I have always tried to talk the person into withdrawing but if he doesn't, that person usually fails...It is my individual judgement.

Essentially no power:

> Do I feel it's my responsibility? Yes, but it's hard to do....These kids are so young and I only see them for five or six months....They can change....I really get scared when I have to tell people "this may not be for you." It's easy when I see someone who's just way off base, but when I see someone who comes in committed, works hard to be a teacher, then it's hard to say "No."

Those who recognize they have the power and are willing to wield it try initially to use counselling procedures with the students. Those who ultimately decline to use the power also engage in counselling strategies. It appears that those persons who have been more directly and more extensively linked with classroom teaching are prepared to act as gatekeepers to the profession. The high level of identity these persons have with classroom teachers may permit them to feel a responsibility to control entry.

Codification of Basic Knowledge

Controversy exists regarding the definition of a profession. Traditionally, the term referred to few groups of people: physicians, lawyers, and clerics. In recent years, the term has been applied to more diverse groups including insurance agents, arborists, and welders. Goode (1969) suggests that "it would be generally agreed, I think, that the two central generating qualities are (1) a basic body of abstract knowledge, and (2) the ideal of service" (p. 277). The first category, knowledge, has seven major characteristics. Two of these are of especial interest when considering teacher educators:

> (i) Ideally, the knowledge and skills should be abstract and organized into a codified body of principles....

> (ii) The amount of knowledge and skills and the difficulty of acquiring them should be great enough that members of the society view the profession as possessing a kind of mystery that it is not given to the ordinary man to acquire, by his own efforts or even with help. (pp. 277–278)

For many years, educational research in the United States pursued a pseudoscientific approach in an attempt to acquire that codified body of principles. Unfortunately, the use of the scientific method has not produced a well-defined set of principles. This does not necessarily mean that the scientific method is an inappropriate model, although it is difficult to see how all human behavior can consistently fit into it; it may mean that educational research has not been built on the long tradition of systematic observation that precedes controlled experimentation in the natural sciences. In recent years, systematic observations using social science models have been applied to educational research (Good & Brophy, 1973; Rist, 1970). Much of this serves to highlight the complexity of classroom life (Eggleston, 1977; Jackson, 1968; Ryan, 1980), but an abstract and organized set of principles for teacher educators and the teaching profession is developing (Williams, 1981).

A manifestation of a body of knowledge should be apparent in a clearly defined philosophy of the field in which one is working. When members of the sample were asked about their philosophy of teacher education, there was a general lack of clarity. However, the responses fell into three main categories.

1. *Well-defined:*

> The philosophy I would want to exhibit would encompass all areas. I would like to model, for the students that are going out to be teachers, interest in students' affective and cognitive abilities. I think just demonstrating how I would want to interact with students would be the underlining philosophy that I would use; not only as far as interest in knowledge, but interest in the students themselves and their needs.

2. *Somewhat defined:*

> I think that teacher education should make a significant contribution to the quality of teaching that goes on in the public schools. It should not be limited to the quality of teaching; it should concern itself with the quality of the schools themselves, the environment in which education takes place, and the expectations of society on education.

3. *Vague:*

> I guess that if I could infect people, I would infect them with the power of the learner. The buried potential in every single person...I guess that's it. I guess it's a belief in learners. If we believed we would stop trying to fill vessels like we did a hundred years ago, and we would start trying to open them.

None of the persons in the sample included any theoretical or research framework for his or her philosophy. This absence may be yet another example of the pervasive influence of craft knowledge over theoretical knowledge. With reference to Goode's statement that the profession should possess "a kind of mystery that it is not given to the ordinary man to acquire" (Goode, 1969, p. 278), it is of significance to note that several writers have commented on the quality of the vocabulary used by teacher in their professional conversations—few technical terms are used (Hargreaves, 1980, pp. 132–133). This may result from the continuous need for teachers to be engaged in discussions with parents and community members. Whereas patients frequently admit a lack of understanding of physicians when they speak with them, few voice that problem after having conversations with teachers. Teachers, too, have to continuously phrase their instruction in a vocabulary suitable for students. In the interviews, teacher educators, when discussing their philosophy about teaching, appeared to lack a specialized vocabulary. They placed great emphasis upon formulating their thoughts in a language which could be readily understood and which was not shrouded in the "mystery" considered by Goode to be a characteristic of the professions. It is unfortunate that, too frequently, depth of verbal expression is measured by its level of obscurity rather than its simplicity. The verbal expression of teacher educators may well be equal in depth to that of members of other professions, but, because it is not full of specialized terminology, it is not awe-inspiring.

Teacher educators, as members of a university, have a greater responsibility than others within the teaching profession to contribute to the codification and hence extension of the professional body of knowledge by engaging in research. Twenty of the 28 persons in the sample stated that they spent a large proportion of their time in conducting research and in writing for publication. Most recognize this as part of their responsibility as university faculty members:

> Pressure to publish comes from the fact that you've signed on in a major research institution, and the role description there is that you influence, and that you will make contributions, and nobody knows a contribution unless you put it in print somewhere.

Individuals in the sample indicated that they recognised the need to conduct research, not only because they were members of the university faculty, but also because of their responsibility to the teaching profession:

> My major function I see as improving instruction, improving children's learning. My primary way of doing that is by effecting the quality of teaching. I can do that by imparting what I know to people who are to be teachers, of I can conduct research so that I can learn more about instruction. I see the research that I do as fundamental to teacher education as the courses I teach.

For the university-based teacher educators, the codification of basic knowledge requires the development of abstract knowledge, reflected in a well-articulated philosophy; the use of a clear, yet specialised, vocabulary; and the continued development of solid research.

Service to the Profession

Many definitions of a profession include its service aspect (Etzioni, 1969; Goode, 1969; Hughes, 1965). While service is generally interpreted as acting in some way to help or serve clients, other interpretations are valid. For the purposes of this chapter, service includes activities within the organization of the university or in the interest of the university, and activities related to the inservice education of classroom teachers.

Service to the University

One of the frustrations experienced by teacher educators which contributed to their leaving classroom teaching was the apparent high level of administration by fiat. They perceived that the professional opinion of teachers was seldom sought when decisions were made. Too frequently, it appeared that decisions were made for administrative ease rather than on sound educational principles. At the university, teacher educators see committee membership as a means of being involved in decision making, but many resent the resultant time commitments. One example of the negative reactions to committee and service demands came in response to the question, "What aspects of your role would you like to change? A subject replied, "Get rid of all this service stuff! Get off all committees immediately! Like tomorrow!"

Teacher educators expressing this point of view believed that these activities limited their research and teaching activities which they saw as the major responsibilities of university faculty members. Others, however, were interested in these involvements and saw them as necessary for the life of the organization:

> I'm very active politically and administratively within the university, in committee work and so on. . . . I see that as working towards, or working for, the health of the organism known as the university.

The participants who were actively involved in university service activities and who valued such involvement held appointments at the rank of associate professor. They saw this involvement as a clear stage in the decision making of the entire university. Such involvement may also be viewed by these associate professors as experiences which may help them move to another level within the profession—university administration.

As early as 1965, Barber described the necessity for professionals to become involved in legislative action: "In short, professions are included in the ranks of 'pressure groups'" (p. 29). He indicated that there is diversity in the form that this political participation can take. While organizations such as the American Medical Association have been powerful through their lobbying practices, other methods are also viable. Univeristy-based teacher educators are fully aware of the need to be involved in political activity in order to improve their status. Community service is seen as a form of political pressure:

> I think that if we ever expect to make it with the legislature, we've got to increase our service to the community. But here again we've got to remember that as a major research institution we can't provide service at the expense of research.

Service within and for the university is thus seen both in the narrow context of participation on university committees and also at the wider level of community involvement.

Inservice Activities for Classroom Teachers

Continuing education is considered important for all members of any profession. For teachers, this can be accomplished through attendance at professional meetings, reading professional journals, attendance at inservice meetings, or visits to other schools. University-based teacher educators, while not solely responsible, contribute to the first three of these procedures. They view their role in inservice meetings as a service contribution.

In the sample of teacher educators interviewed, only a few stated that they spent a large amount of time conducting inservice activities. It was indicated that the university attributed less value to involvement in inservice activities than did the teacher educators. One-hour or one-day sessions were undertaken by participants but were generally considered to be of little value:

> I spend a lot of time getting ready for inservice programs. I get about $100 a day for doing a dog-and-pony show on the road. I don't think that's teacher education. I don't think it has much value. Maybe it will have an influence eventually.

Long-term commitment to inservice education was viewed much more enthusiastically:

> I don't know how to serve the community really, other than through teachers and teaching, which becomes inservice training. I can't think of anything that would be more important probably than inservice training

if it were done properly. Done as it typically is, it is absolutely useless. So I am not interested in the typical process. I couldn't be more interested in anything if it were done appropriately.

"Appropriately" meant sustained activity with one set of teachers or with one school district over a period of time. There was considerable similarity between the opinions of the teacher educators in this sample and those of the individuals interviewed and reported on in *School-focussed Inservice: Descriptions and Discussions* (Howey, Bents, & Corrigan, 1981, pp. 65–76). References by participants were also made to successful inservice when it was jointly planned by the provider and the recipient. The procedures used in the collegial model at Michigan State University would certainly meet the desired goals of the teacher educators who were interviewed (Barnes & Putnam, 1981).

University-based teacher educators in the sample were generally not involved with inservice education in a formalized manner. This may be due largely to the lack of value placed upon it in the traditional university reward system. Nevertheless, that service is an essential part of these persons' responsibility within the teaching profession.

REFLECTIONS

This chapter has described the background of university-based teacher educators, the forces that caused them to move from precollegiate to collegiate level teaching, and the four-fold mission they undertake in their career role. Some reflections can be made taking into consideration the interplay of these three factors.

Teacher educators believe that they possess or have knowledge of skills which can be transmitted and which can help the undergraduate student to assume beginning teacher responsibilities. These skills have been developed from personal craft knowledge and from the theoretical framework behind teaching and schooling. They differ from those practiced by some teachers in public schools, thus creating a dissonance between these teachers and teacher educators. It was this very dissonance that caused many teacher educators to initially leave the public school classrooms. The resistance to change that they experienced within the sytem at the earlier stage of their careers continues to preclude their achievement of the ideals for which they strive. Tension very frequently exists in the interactions that occur between teacher and teacher educator—tension which is exacerbated by the role that the teacher educator plays in the certification process.

This tension can be seen to diminish when a teacher educator gains the confidence of colleagues in the public schools. Traditionally, two ways for teacher educators to gain this confidence have been to spend numerous hours in the schools or to engage in teaching activities within the public school classroom. There appears, however, to be two possible alternates— teacher educators can persuade teachers to test in their own classrooms the new techniques that teacher educators want to introduce; or, the teacher educator can engage in collaborative enterprises with the teachers in the public-school classroom. The growing demand upon teachers to update or extend their teaching credentials supports the first approach. The second alternative frequently occurs as a result of the teacher educator's desire to conduct research. Because of human subjects, legislation, and the reticence of school districts to permit outsiders to tamper with the curriculum or instruction of the schools, the teacher educator finds that the most expedient way to accomplish research is to work in collaboration with teachers. By extending their own knowledge, by testing out new ideas, and by being engaged in collaborative activities, the teacher can gain greater confidence in the teacher educator. At the same time, the teacher educator is able to see that some of the skills they have painstakingly developed do not always produce the results anticipated in a real-life situation.

The current climate has potential for teacher educators and teachers to overcome tension and work together toward desired goals. The teacher educators would have some likelihood of transmitting skills developed; the teacher would have some opportunity to become a more sophisticated professional.

The apparent lack of a codified body of knowledge has contributed over the years to another source of tension: that between university-based teacher educators and the system of the university. There appears to be an opportunity in the immediate future to diminish this tension. For many years, the only outlet provided to teacher educators to publish their work was in teacher magazines. This was not totally unsatisfactory to the teacher educator who saw it as a means of communicating with the broader teaching profession. However, it certainly did not satisfy the demands of the university for scholarly publication—the work did not meet either the traditional experimental or descriptive standards for research. With the development of a theoretical base for teaching, more substantial professional journals have accepted the publications of teacher educators. This theoretical base was initially developed at some of the federally funded centers for teacher education such as the Institute for Research on Teaching at Michigan State University, The Research and Development Center for Teacher Education at The University of Texas at Austin, and The Far West Regional Laboratory in San Francisco. With the development of a broad theoretical framework, opportunity is provided for individual teacher educators to develop their own research. Evidence of this occurring is obvious at annual meetings of research organizations and in major scholarly publications. Teacher educators are developing a codified body of knowledge through channels which have both scholarly and professional status. Continued development of this codified body of knowledge is essential.

Service activities present a real dilemma for university-based teacher educators. These persons frequently find the service activities in which they are required to be involved on the university campus to be similar to those they considered as trivial while in the public schools. Such activities, however, are essential within an organization, and the teacher educator must find mechanisms to cope with this apparent frustration. Off-campus, teacher educators gain satisfaction from involvement in those service activities which are of a less parochial nature and generally involve national professional organizations. Through these activities, they are able to make considerable impact upon the profession as a whole. A major service problem that frustrates some teacher educators is the relationship with the local school districts. These districts generally value service with more limited scope. While it would seem reasonable that the teacher educator could combine such local service activities with their own professional interests, there are few examples of such integration occurring. Few teacher educators have resolved the tension that derives from the need to engage in services both within the university and the local school district.

Certainly this is a prime time to consider the role of the teacher educators. The ferment that has permeated the entire teaching profession has not left teacher educators unchanged. They have developed a set of skills which is now being accepted by the teaching profession as a whole. This set of skills is part of an emerging codified body of knowledge. With continued opportunities to engage in research and to develop the body of knowledge within the university setting, teacher educators will grow in their ability to carry out their four-fold mission.

REFERENCES

Arnstine, D. (1981). The temporary impact of teacher education: Some suggestions for remedies. *California Journal of Teacher Education, 8*(2) 41–66.

Barber, B. (1965). Some problems in the sociology of the professions. In K. S. Lynn (Ed.), *The professions in America.* Boston, MA: Houghton Mifflin Co.

Barnes, H., & Putnam, J. (1981). Professional development through inservice that works. In K. R. Howey, R. Bents & D. Corrigan (Eds.), *School-focussed inservice: Descriptions and discussions.* Reston, VA: Association of Teacher Educators.

Carter, H. L. (1981). *Teacher educators: A descriptive study.* Report No. 9006. Austin, TX: Research and Development Center for Teacher Education, The University of Texas at Austin.

Eggleston, J. (1977). *The ecology of the school.* London: Methuen.

Etzioni, A. (Ed.). (1969). *The semi-professions and their organization.* New York: The Free Press.

Gage, N. L. (1978). *The scientific basis of the art of teaching.* New York: Teachers College Press.

Good, T. L., & Brophy, J. E. (1973). *Looking in classrooms.* New York: Harper & Row.

Goode, W. J. (1969). The theoretical limits of professionalization. In A. Etzioni (Ed.), *The semi-professions and their organization.* New York: The Free Press.

Hargreaves, D. H. (1980). The occupational culture of teachers. In P. Woods (Ed.), *Teacher strategies.* London: Croom Helm.

Howey, K. R., Bents, R., & Corrigan, D. (Eds.). (1981). *School-focussed inservice: Descriptions and discussions.* Reston, VA: Association of Teacher Educators.

Hughes, E. C. (1965). Professions. In K. S. Lynn (Ed.), *The professions in America.* Boston, MA: Houghton Mifflin Co.

Isham, M. M., Carter, H. L., & Stribling, R. (1981). *A study of the entry mechanisms of university-based teacher educators.* Paper presented at the meeting of the American Educational Research Association, Los Angeles, CA.

Jackson, P. W. (1968). *Life in classrooms.* New York: Holt, Rinehart and Winston.

Joyce, B., Howey, K., Yarger, S., Harbeck, K., & Kluwin, T. (1977). Reflections on preservice preparation: Impressions from the national survey. *Journal of Teacher Education, 28*(5).

Knoblock, P., & Goldstein, A. P. (1971). *The lonely teacher.* Boston, MA: Allyn & Bacon.

Lortie, D. C. (1975). *Schoolteacher: A sociological study.* Chicago, IL: The University of Chicago Press.

Musgrave, P. W. (1979). *The sociology of education* (3rd ed.). London: Methuen.

National Council for Accreditation of Teacher Education (NCATE). (1979). *Standards for accreditation of teacher education.* Washington, DC: NCATE.

Rist, R. (1970). Student social class and teacher expectation: The self-fulfilling prophecy in ghetto education. *Harvard Education Review, 40,* 411–451.

Ryan, K. (1980). *Biting the apple.* New York: Longman.

Williams, R. C. (1981). Changing teacher behaviors: From symbolism to reality. In M. Defino & H. L. Carter (Eds.), *Changing teacher practice: Proceedings of a national conference* (R.D. Report No. 9017). Austin, TX: Research and Development Center for Teacher Education, The University of Texas at Austin.

Wittlin, A. S. (1965). The teacher. In K. S. Lynn (Ed.), *The professions in America.* Boston, MA: Houghton Mifflin Company.

Woods, P. (Ed.). (1980). *Teacher strategies.* London: Croom Helm.

8

The Role of Selective Admissions Policies in the Teacher-Education Process

Marleen C. Pugach
University of Illinois at Urbana-Champaign

Professional preparation in all fields includes the responsibility both for instructing entrants and for utilizing information about their progress to make decisions regarding readiness for entering practice. In teacher education, the latter responsibility has been called the "gatekeeping function," (Medley, 1982), "control of entry," (Marshman, 1981), or "quality control," (Arnold, Denemark, Nelli, Robinson, & Sagan, 1977); all of these terms imply the importance of the selection of teacher candidates who are likely to succeed in the eventual practice of teaching. There are a number of points in the sequence of teacher preparation where this selection, or screening function, can be exercised. It can occur at the time of admission to the college or university, prior to entering the professional program, prior to student teaching, or prior to the institutional decision to grant certification. Selection can also occur at the inservice level: at the time of employment, during yearly probationary contract renewals, or prior to tenure decisions.

Various proposals have been advanced and adopted regarding selection in response to demands to improve the quality of the teaching force, most commonly in the form of teacher competence testing just prior to the granting of certification (Sandefur, 1981) and on-the-job teacher performance assessment in the first year of practice (Kleine & Wisniewski, 1981). It can be argued, however, that implementing selection at the time of program admission is the most expedient choice, before schools, colleges, and departments of education (SCDEs) expend human and financial resources for preparing candidates who may lack the fundamental dispositions to teach (Haberman & Stinnett, 1973; Turner, 1975). Further, teacher-education candidates, once admitted, are rarely denied continuation in their programs, are graduated and certified (Bush & Enemark, 1975), and go on to be appointed to teaching positions where they are denied tenure at a rate of only approximately 3 percent (Silzer, 1981). For all intents and purposes, then, gaining admission to teacher education has traditionally been commensurate with gaining admission to the profession. And whether this state of affairs will change in the future with the recent introduction of exit-level testing remains to be seen.

This chapter describes the role of policies of selective admissions for teacher education in controlling the eventual quality of practicing teachers. Selective admissions is presented not as a procedure for obtaining isolated predictions regarding potential success as a teacher, but rather as the first in a series of procedures for monitoring candidates as they progress through their programs of preparation. Improving the quality of teachers is conceptualized primarily as a function of the effects of the process of selective admissions on both applicants and teacher-education faculty.

ANALYSIS OF ADMISSIONS CRITERIA

Exactly what practices have commonly characterized the process of admissions to teacher education? Eleven studies were located which describe admissions criteria used at universities nationwide from 1957-78; the results of these surveys are summarized in Table 1. It is useful to consider this analysis from the viewpoint that beginning in 1969, the teacher shortage that spawned the rapid growth of SCDEs and the increased demand for student recruitment subsided (Ornstein, 1976). It seems reasonable to expect that standards for selection would have become increasingly stringent after that time as a means of responding to the subsequent oversupply of candidates.

Traditional Patterns of Selection, 1957–1978

The table clearly indicates that the criteria for the selection and admission of candidates to programs of teacher education have shown little substantive change over two decades. Although interest in documenting admissions practices increased in the post-1969 period of teacher surplus, with 73 percent of the available surveys having been conducted from 1972 to 1978, the data do not differ from those of earlier surveys. Students usually apply for entry in their sophomore or junior years (Leonardson, 1977; Nunney, Fiala, & Lewis, 1963; Stout, 1957; University of Kentucky, 1972). Cumulative grade-point average (GPA) has remained, as it was early on, the only common criterion used across institutions. Although reported ranges of GPA were broad, a minimum score of 2.0 on a 4-point scale typically has been acceptable for entrance (although in most cases, secondary education majors have been expected to maintain higher grade point averages than elementary majors).

TABLE I Summary of Reported Admissions Criteria, 1957–1978

| | | | | | Admissions Criteria | | | | |
Author/Date	n	Group Membership	GPA[a]	SAT/ACT	Personality Testing	Interviews	Speech Proficiency	Communication Proficiency
Stout, 1957	785	4 year	58.5% (2.0)	40%	45%	33%	22%	40%
Magee, 1961	180	Publicly supported, NCATE approved	90% (2.0–3.0)	...	...	...	...	...
Nunney, Fiala, & Lewis, 1963	91	4 year, Western US only	80% (1.5–2.6)	31%	23%	...	...	...
Carpenter, 1972	180	AACTE Members	95% (2.0–3.25)	...	13%	40%	...	...
Haberman, 1972	386	ATE members	89%	...	22%	42%	61%	62%
University of Kentucky, 1972	44	Major selected universities	82% (2.0–2.5)	...	...	...	...	...
Yevak & Carlin, 1972	179	Colleges and universities	100% (2.0–2.5)	...	...	...	63%	59%
Sinclair & Picogna, 1974	43	Identified by state personnel	44% (2.0–2.5)	...	23%	42%	21%	21%
Gress, 1977	51	4 year, Ohio only	82%	...	...	...	...	...
Leonardson, 1977	26	"Recognized leaders"	96% (2.0–2.8)	...	...	...	50%	40%
Shank, 1978	200	4 year	97% (2.0–2.5)	23%	44%	54%	74%	78%

Note: Empty cells may signify lack of quantifiable data and not necessarily absence of that criterion. Percentages represent proportions of institutions in each sample reporting the use of that criterion.

[a] Reported ranges of minimum scores are noted in parentheses below percentages; 2.0 was the most commonly cited score.

147

Assessments of personality using both standardized instruments (e.g., Sixteen Personality Factor Questionnaire, Minnesota Multiphasic Personality Inventory, Minnesota Teacher Attitude Inventory) and informal, personal interviews were also cited frequently. The post-1969 studies tended to show a combination of the two (Carpenter, 1972; Haberman, 1972; Shank, 1978; Sinclair & Picogna; 1974), which can be interpreted as increased attention to personality factors. Both before and after 1969, surveys indicated that interviews were rarely the responsibility of program faculty members (Carpenter, 1972; Shank, 1978; Stout, 1957). Traditional checks of speech and language proficiency were more characteristic of the latter group of studies (Haberman, 1972; Leonardson, 1977; Sinclair & Picogna, 1974; Shank, 1978; Yevak & Carlin, 1972), but these criteria were most often satisfied by students' receiving passing grades in required courses in rhetoric or speech communication.

A variety of other criteria have been used sporadically: departmental recommendations, health clearances, direct experience with children, letters of recommendation, etc. However, GPA has clearly been the single most favored criterion, and Gress (1977) indicated that attention to admissions criteria was directed "least frequently to unstructured evaluations and written recommendations" (p. 15).

While SCDEs readily report the existence of selection criteria, the analysis of responses from these eleven surveys illustrates that such criteria are limited in scope and that selection as practiced in most institutions has been largely nonfunctional for purposes of discriminating between applicants for teacher education. Three particular issues bear mentioning in this context. First, from the initial 1957 survey it has been consistently recognized that the most commonly used criteria were inadequate, yet active movement toward implementing alternative selection policies did not occur. For example, Stout (1957) questioned whether the evidence collected at the time of admissions was actually used in making selection decisions. Whether existing criteria functioned as screening devices was also questioned (Haberman, 1972; Shank, 1978; University of Kentucky, 1972), and these studies indicated that the typical state of affairs was based more on expediency and low cost than on utility. Despite this recognition that low standards associated with admissions criteria were failing to make functional discriminations between candidates, few efforts at instituting alternative practices were reported. Sixty-four percent of the respondents in Leonardson's (1977) survey stated that they planned to exercise stricter policies in the future but offered no specific plans being developed for that purpose. When Haberman asked institutions whether new standards or new criteria for admissions would be introduced, 69 percent responded negatively, 8 percent were considering raising the GPA minimum, and only 6 percent were planning to require more direct preadmissions experiences with children. In addition, few validation studies to aid in the identification of functional selection criteria were noted. Although five institutions in Leonardson's study claimed to have been actively pursuing research in this area, only two completed studies were cited, both of which were doctoral dissertations. Twenty-three percent of Shank's (1978) sample was reported to have completed empirical research to determine the predictive validity of criteria in use, but no particular study was offered as a reference. The existence of a teacher surplus, a logical opportunity to reconsider the standards applied to applicants, appears not to have served as an incentive for change, and the relative absence of selection research confirms minimal interest; a sense of inertia seems to have characterized the entire issue.

Second, the relationship of selection criteria to program goals was questioned (Stout, 1957; Shank, 1978). The selection and admissions process is divorced from the program itself; when interviews are required, faculty members rarely participate. And although it can be safely assumed that many of the institutions surveyed were approved by the National Council for Accreditation of Teacher Education (NCATE), the standard which explicitly requires the derivation and implementation of "objective and subjective criteria derived from the philosophy and objectives of the teacher education program" (NCATE, 1982, p. 23) has not provided inspiration or motivation for change. In facing the issue of selection, SCDEs must determine to what extent program definition and commitment now exist from which to derive selection policies, and explore the concomitant issue of the existence of a sense of purpose in their teacher-education programs.

Finally, problems with rejection and reacceptance of rejected candidates were addressed in many of the studies. When candidates are rejected, the majority have found their way back into the program which rejected them or have subsequently been accepted into other programs. Comments on rejection rates indicate that what exists is essentially an "open-admissions" policy; low standards and low rejection rates led Carpenter to comment that "the research continues to prove that teacher education continues to be the route of least resistance..." (1972, p. 31), and that rejection of candidates occurs only in cases of extreme deviance. Forty percent of the programs in Stout's (1957) sample excluded *no* applicants while 45 percent excluded between only 1 and 10 percent. In a general description of admissions policies of institutions accredited by the North Central Council for the Accreditation of Teacher Education, Brubaker and Patton (1975) report that fewer than 10 percent of all candidates were denied admission. Carpenter (1972) found that 91 percent of the institutions they surveyed had actually denied admission based on stated standards, but that 89 percent allowed unsuccessful candidates to reapply. And Haberman (1972) reported that in 1970, 749 students were accepted to the School of Education at his university and 24 were rejected; most of the 24 were later readmitted. In the following year, 929 candidates were admitted and 67 were rejected; subsequently, 20 percent of the rejected group was admitted. Clearly, rejection is the exception.

In summary, only nominal selection practices have been utilized in admitting candidates to teacher education, mirroring the belief that some criteria are better than none, even if those in use are limited in their effectiveness (Howsam, Corrigan, Denemark, & Nash, 1976). Meaningful criteria have not been applied, and the status of the teaching profession has suffered as a result (Arnold et al., 1977). The practice of selective admissons, as well as research on selection, have not held great interest for teacher education and have traditionally received little serious consideration as a means of controlling the quality of entrants to the teaching profession.

Factors Contributing to Traditional Selection Practices

It would be difficult to cite a single factor as the major cause of commonly used selection practices. Rather, the traditional reluctance of programs of teacher education to implement rigid policies of selection stems from a convergence of research, economic, and professional constraints which operate on and within SCDEs. Four specific factors have contributed to the current status of admissions policies: (a) historical precedent; (b) supply and demand; (c) low status of teacher-education programs; and (d) problems in teacher effectiveness research.

Historical Precedent. The use of limited selection criteria dates as far back as the colonial period, when policies operated in a manner similar to those being questioned today. During that period, the three prevalent criteria for teaching were: (a) the ability to retain disciplinary control over the school; (b) good moral character; and (c) academic achievement—in that order (Kinney, 1964). However, it was common for academic examinations to be waived due to the shortage of applicants. So although the examination was not always required and bore no empirical relationship to teaching success, it "served an immediately useful purpose in discouraging the wholly incompetent from applying and in identifying the utterly illiterate" (p. 42), discriminating in much the same broad way as a minimum GPA standard of 2.0.

Requirements for admissions to the early normal schools, according to Borrowman (1965), usually included no more than a knowledge of elementary school subjects. As normal schools developed into state teachers colleges, admissions standards were developed to include high school graduation, health clearance, and good moral character (Brubaker & Patton, 1975). With the teacher surplus of the 1930s, standards for selection were again raised to deal with the oversupply; the multitude of requirements as we know them today were implemented and were in common use by 1950. These included: high school GPA; formal and informal personality assessments; letters of recommendation; achievement tests; and health and character clearances. However, even with these criteria in place, Brubaker and Patton stress that "only the most obviously deficient prospects were being eliminated" (p. 6); no substantive changes had occurred. Historically, then, although teacher education has instituted criteria for admissions, it has been reluctant to enforce rigid, discriminating standards for selection.

Supply and Demand Considerations. The long period of teacher shortage, ending around 1969, probably contributed most heavily to the absence of discriminating selection policies. At that time, schools and colleges of education were expanding and sought to enroll as many candidates as possible to satisfy the needs of the growing population (Nutting, 1978). The overriding concern was the production of teachers in sufficient quantity, and few educators looked past the demands of the day to address the need for selection and quality control. In 1959–1960, for example, the National Education Association (NEA) underwrote a $50,000 project to study selective admissions (Mitzel & Rabinowitz, 1961). However, the existence of a teacher shortage effectively prevented the implementation of its recommendations. In their formative years, teacher-education programs concentrated on the recruitment of large numbers of applicants; the issue of quality control and the implications of enrolling smaller numbers of students were simply contradictory to the demand for filling teaching positions. In the post-shortage era, a time of generally declining enrollments, the number of SCDEs that flourished earlier continued to seek out students—not to keep the classrooms of the public schools staffed with highly qualified teachers, but rather to justify their existence. Thus, interest in selection is perfunctory at best, since its practice raises the very real threat of reducing the numbers of faculty positions. "Schools of education," according to Weaver, "reacted to declining enrollments like the plague. They intensified efforts to recruit and retain students, and at the same time relaxed standards in order to capture more of those who did apply" (1981, p. 17). Or as Sykes (1983) concluded, SCDEs "survive and prosper by enrolling students, not by serving as the conscience of the profession" (p. 104). The conflict of job protection and increased selectivity of applicants is probably one of the biggest obstacles to the adoption of effective policies of selective admissions.

Low Status of Teacher Education. In addition to the need to respond to market demands, teacher education has traditionally held a relatively low status position within institutions of higher education (Guba & Clark, 1978; Meyen, 1979). As professionals, the majority of teacher educators appears to have accepted passively this position, along with the low status of its entrants. Turner (1975), in fact, suggested investigating the possibility that admitting less able candidates leads to lower faculty standards for student achievement. Teacher educators have been reluctant to exercise judgements regarding student success (Morris, 1956) and on control of the profession in general (Sykes, 1983), and even if rigorous selection standards were in place, it would still be incumbent on faculty to deny continuation or certification to those it felt should not teach (Mitzel & Rabinowitz, 1961; Pratt, 1977). When faced with the task of terminating a student's enrollment, however, "education faculties seem to have a paralytic failure of nerve" (Morris, p.247).

The traditional passivity of teacher-education faculty with regard to making professional judgements at all points in the training of its candidates is perhaps best characterized by Marshman, who stated that "the current approach is one of caution, perhaps underscored by an attitude that looks to other sources of authority for parameters of decision" (1981, p.8).

Teacher Effectiveness Research. While it is not within the scope of this chapter to review the literature on teacher effectiveness research, it is critical to consider its relationship to existing policies of selection. Medley (1979) identified four phases of teacher effectiveness research: (a) studies attempting to identify effective personality traits or characteristics; (b) studies of effective methods of teaching; (c) studies of effective classroom climates created and maintained by specific teacher behaviors; and (d) studies related to mastering and appropriately using a repertoire of effective competencies (i.e., effective teacher decisionmaking). Early methodological studies, according to Medley, separated techniques being tested from teacher characteristics by using only student outcomes as dependent measures, thus contributing little to the identification of specific admissions criteria. Studies of discrete variables to predict teaching success, many of which are now used for admissions, have produced low correlations with student achievement, for example: GPA; personality variables; prior experience with children; and knowledge of content and/or methodology. Teacher effectiveness research now in progress, corresponding to Medley's third and fourth phases, attempts to take into account the complexity of teaching and the interaction of teacher, student, and context variables. Should such complex variables show stable results over time, they may still offer little to guide teacher educators concerned with identifying admissions criteria, as these variables may not readily be transformed into such criteria and may perhaps be measured best in practice.

Medley concludes that in general, the results of this research are inconsistent and have thus provided little direction for teacher education. Similarly, in reviewing representative studies, Schalock (1979) has argued that teacher effectiveness research has not yet been able to provide conclusive guidelines to aid in adopting criteria for the selection of teacher-education candidates at the time of admissions. The reluctance of teacher educators to restrict admissions on the grounds that students lack the appropriate characteristics has relied in large part on the argument that an absence of consensus exists regarding what constitutes good teachers and good teaching. Teacher educators, it appears, have preferred to wait for research to answer questions regarding which criteria to use for admissions and have postponed acting on the issue until conclusive evidence has been accumulated, thereby reducing the threat of challenge by unsuccessful applicants. This observation is in keeping with Marshman's (1981) description of teacher educators as cautious with regard to their gatekeeping responsibilities. The result, however, appears to be a classic case of "passing the buck," rather than accepting the emergent state of teacher effectiveness research and exercising reasonable alternatives—for example, implementing various models of selection and conducting follow-up studies. The situation is perhaps best summed up by Arnold et al.:

> The complexity of the problems confronted, variation in individuals and in community expectations, and a range of other factors suggest that if we are to rely upon quality control measures which are validated by research findings, we will be forced to maintain the largely unselective system which presently characterizes American teacher education. (1977, p. 8)

Current Trends in Selection

In the very recent past, media attention to education has led the public to demand an increase in the quality of the teaching force and to indict the teacher-education system for failing to exert its gatekeeping responsibilities. The response to these charges has come, as Marshman (1981) anticipated, not from within the ranks of teacher education, but rather in the form of political decisions from external sources of authority, namely, state legislatures. In addition to general exhortations to raise admissions standards, the most common specific recommendation for achieving selectivity in the admissions process has been to require testing, both for basic skills and for competency in teaching domains. At least 15 states have already acted to improve their teacher-education programs, requiring for admissions combinations of passing scores on preadmissions tests, increased GPA, or increased SAT/ACT scores (States' Reform Efforts, 1983). And in addition to these 15, many states are awaiting action on similar recommendations as a result of a multiplicity of education commissions and task forces.

In addition to relying on existing criteria with moderately increased standards, these actions are based largely on the assumption that requiring simple paper-and-pencil testing of teacher candidates is the panacea for which the educational system has been searching (Pugach & Raths, 1983). Yet recent data which correlate scores on the commonly used National Teacher Examinations (NTE) with subsequent teacher ratings, still do not indicate that teaching success can be predicted on this basis (Soar, Medley, & Coker, 1983). These new standards for controlling entry of teachers into the profession are at best minimal (Sykes, 1983), and reflect a political response to a complex set of needs and pressures within individual programs of teacher education as well as for the profession as a whole. It seems safe to assume that in isolation, implementing such testing programs will not substantially alter the nature of the problem of control of quality, although the attention this issue is enjoying may prove beneficial. If this is true, then can it be anticipated that instituting policies of selective admissions in particular will make any contribution to the effort to improve the quality of the teaching force? It is precisely this issue that must be resolved.

THE LIMITATIONS OF SELECTIVE ADMISSIONS

The preceding analysis supports the need for a major reconceptualization of the role of candidate selection for teacher education. Prior to proposing a conceptual shift, however, an assessment of the limitations of selective admissions policies is necessary to clarify the functions it can positively and consistently be expected to serve.

While it is attractive to think of selection as the opportunity to make a single, linear prediction from applicant characteristics to subsequent effectiveness as a teacher, it may be more realistic to recognize that such predictions cannot be made economically (deLandsheere, 1980); the process of candidate selection is complex, and it must be conducted over time. The preceding section on teacher effectiveness cited the low correlations obtained between discrete personality and knowledge variables and teacher effectiveness. Leonardson (1977) suggested using multiple regression techniques for purposes of selection, but this approach would still depend on the isolation of some variables and it would be difficult to include in the prediction those contextual variables which current teacher effectiveness research is finding influential. Further, it in a sense undervalues the effect of the teacher-education process to expect to be able to predict accurately who will be an effective teacher from a constellation of variables existing prior to preparation; the teacher-education experience should be a moderating variable. The function of selection should be to optimize teacher preparation, not substitute for it (Turner, 1975).

Schalock (1979) proposed using as predictors variables which more closely approximate (or, have "fidelity" to) real teaching situations, for example, a two-to-five day teaching experience with full responsibility prior to student teaching. While his suggestion is convincing, and while such predictors are critical in monitoring student progress during preparation, they are inappropriate as initial admissions criteria. Selection at the time of program admissions by definition depends on variables that are distal to the teaching act.

The concept of linear prediction is further confounded by the phenomenon that the student is developing as both an individual and a professional over time. The candidate who is admitted as a sophomore will think and react differently when he or she is a senior. Feiman-Nemser (1980) has argued for a major reorganization of research in teacher education along these lines. The mediating nature of both program impact and individual change thus reduces the power of the initial selection process.

Not only is it unlikely that linear predictions can occur, but also the degree to which selection can influence the nature of the applicant pool from which teacher-education candidates is drawn is questionable. Traditionally teacher education has attracted students of only average ability, students who appear consistently to score lower than other college majors on such measures of achievement as the American College Test (ACT) or Scholastic Aptitude Test (SAT) (Weaver, 1972). Students tend to drift into teacher-education programs (Lomax, 1971; Marks, 1975), rather than to seek admission actively, and typically teacher education has served a social mobility function for students from lower socio-economic classes (Lortie, 1975). In a compelling monograph on a developmental theory of vocational choice, Gottfredson (1981) argues that it is between the ages of 9 and 13 that children narrow their choices to an acceptable range of occupations. They do so according to external issues such as the compatibility of job prestige with their social class and their perception of the general level of effort needed to obtain a job within the acceptable range of alternatives as compared to the perception of their abilities. Specific vocational choices reflecting personal interests, one's unique values and competencies, and specific barriers to training are developed last, from the age of about 14 and over.[1] When compromises must be made regarding vocational choice, the last decision made, that is, teaching or pharmacy, will be sacrificed before the general range of acceptable jobs will be changed. Options that are rejected due to sex-role or social-class type are thus rarely reconsidered, but within the accepted group the specific job choice is not rigid. This phenomenon occurs, she argues, because job level and sex-type are "more central aspects of self-concept and are more obvious ones to one's social identity" (p. 549).

If one accepts Gottfredson's theory, it is unlikely that instituting selective admissions policies will substantially alter the nature of the teacher-education applicant pool, which is circumscribed early on. Only a major societal shift regarding the perceived status of teaching, a shift which is unlikely to occur without changes in the financial rewards and the level of education needed to complete preparation, might affect the cycle. While the social mobility function of teaching would rightfully be preserved given Gottfredson's theory, the commonly heard rhetoric of attracting only the "best and brightest" into the profession may be an unrealistic goal.

In summary, the potential of selective admissions policies is limited by the following: (a) economic predictions using a linear model are not readily available; (b) candidates develop and change during the course of their preparation due to both personal development and program impact; (c) suc-

---

[1] The earliest vocational decision, according to Gottfredson, is made regarding the masculinity/femininity of the job (ages 6–8); this is the last factor that will be compromised.

cess as a teacher may be best assessed using variables which have fidelity to the complex context of a classroom, measures which are incompatible with the notion of early selection; and (d) selection is not likely to have a significant impact on the general social class and perceived ability characteristics of the talent pool.

A RECONCEPTUALIZATION OF THE SELECTION PROCESS

Given these limitations, what can more stringent policies of admission hope to accomplish? In this section, selective admissions is reconceptualized according to its potential functions. A rationale for adopting selection criteria is presented along with guidelines for their identification in the face of research results which are either inconclusive or which lack relevance for the issue of selective admissions. Finally, a specific set of criteria is proposed within a framework which takes into account both the functions of selection and the rationale for using specific criteria.

The Functions of Selective Admissions

At least two major and two minor functions exist which support the adoption of selective admissions policies; these functions draw their strength more from the process of selection than from the predictive power of particular criteria. The importance of clarifying the processes of teacher education has been raised by Galluzo (1982); he suggests that strict adherence to product or outcome indicators rather than to processes ignores a major source of evaluation data to guide program improvement.

    Self-selection. Instituting a cluster of reasonable criteria for admissions which requires active participation on the part of applicants would provide the opportunity to evaluate seriously the personal importance of gaining admission to the program. Self-selection could have the advantage of deterring students who now casually drift into teacher education and would thus discriminate in a general way between more and less committed candidates.

    The potential value of self-selection has been raised repeatedly in the literature criticizing traditional selection policies (Arnold et al., 1977; Barnard & Thornburg, 1980; Brubaker & Patton, 1975; Davis & Yamamoto, 1968; Gress, 1977; Haberman & Stinnett, 1973); in this context, self-selection is typically suggested as a dimension of admissions only in relation to requiring introductory courses and/or early field experiences prior to program acceptance. While such preprofessional courses are desirable and necessary for providing information against which to judge personal compatibility for teaching, requiring prerequisite courses and fieldwork alone may not offer enough resistance for the casual applicant. A cluster of criteria developed at the program level, not simply those already available at the institutional level (e.g., SAT scores, grades in rhetoric courses, etc.) might provide additional opportunities for applicants to rethink their career goals.

In the few alternative selection models recently implemented and available for review, the phenomenon of self-selection appears to occur consistently. Five examples are offered.

1. Heit, Johnson, Meeks, and Paxton (1978) described a selection process at The Ohio State University for admission to the health education program. Six criteria were used in the following combination of relative weight for the admissions decisions: GPA (25%), personal interview (20%), biographical inventory (10%), intent statement (15%), grade in basic health education course (15%), and letters of recommendation (15%). No absolute cut-off for GPA was established, but an acceptable range was set. If a student showed weaknesses in certain areas, the interviewers consulted to reach a decision, taking all criteria into account. Formal admission was granted only after completion of the basic course. The authors concluded that "a serendipitous effect...appears to be that screening provides an opportunity for self-selection and decision-making which reduces the number of casual applicants" (p.150).

2. At Oregon State University, Schalock (1979) reports that since instituting the requirement of a successful two-to-five day full responsibility teaching experience prior to being accepted for student teaching at the elementary level, the number of program drop-outs increased from about 5 to 20 percent.

3. In the physical education teacher-education program at Indiana University, Baumgartner and Carlson (1974) describe a system of course-by-course evaluation of each student during the freshman and sophomore years. For each course taught by departmental faculty, students were evaluated on: general ability, potential as teacher, attendance and responsibility, professional attitude and interest, and ability in the particular course. Evaluations were completed on index cards and reviewed once a semester by a standing faculty screening committee which contacted students at the end of each semester as to their standing and probable status of their file in regard to formal admissions. If a student showed weak patterns, counseling was provided; it was also possible for a student to elect to graduate but not receive certification. While no hard data are presented, the authors argue that this policy encourages students to give consideration to the seriousness of their educational pursuits prior to formal program admission because they had a clear idea of the demands it would make of them.

4. The University of Oregon has restructured its selection process to

include the following criteria: basic skills testing in reading, mathematics and writing; personal interview administered jointly by the chair of elementary education and the head of advising; a required GPA of 2.5; and successful completion of the first professional semester. Since this process was initiated, the GPA of entering candidates has averaged 3.2 (Haisley, 1982).

5. At Northern Kentucky University, a battery of entry-level tests is required which includes: tests of basic skills in reading and writing; test of speech proficiency covering listening, speaking and articulation/pronunciation; psychological battery including Cattell's 16PF, Gordon Personal Profile and the Strong-Campbell Interest Inventory (Carter, Boyd, Rogers, & Schiff; 1980). Successful completion of a sophomore practicum is also required. Since adopting these policies in 1977, enrollment in the sophomore practicum has decreased by 25 percent and student-teaching enrollment by 17 percent.

Clearly, self-selection may be an untapped force in attracting applicants who seriously wish to pursue teaching as a career. The concept of self-selection is also consonant with Gottfredson's (1981) vocational theory, in that students considering a career in teaching would evaluate their personal compatibility and commitment to teaching specifically and would choose another occupation within the acceptable range of alternatives if the entrance criteria required commitments beyond those they were willing to make. While teacher education might still attract candidates from the same general social class and ability levels, the effort required to pursue admissions might discriminate between applicants within this range who possess higher and lower "tolerable-effort boundaries" (p.565). The sense of personal achievement at having succeeded in gaining admission might also contribute to a feeling of collegiality among candidates, since mutual completion of common, difficult experiences encourages the increased valuing of professional preparation (Lortie, 1975).

Faculty commitment. Self-selection cannot, however, function alone to guarantee the quality of program graduates. The second function of policies of selective admissions is to focus faculty energy on the integrity of the program in which they teach and on their commitments to exercising the gatekeeping role associated with it. And although Schalock (1979) assumed that "teacher educators care more than anyone else about their ability to predict who is likely to succeed as a teacher" (p. 406), apparently few now take responsibility for and participate in the process of candidate selection and retention.

Before selective admissions policies are instituted, consensus on and acceptance of program goals must be achieved. Creating a sense of purpose in teacher education is a complex task for individual programs to achieve within the constraints of the institutions in which they operate; it is likely to be dependent on the strength of program leadership. Critical to its development is creating the expectation for student success among faculty members and the prizing of program goals. Selective admissions policies may then function as rallying points for increased faculty expectations, especially with regard to the dimension of student self-selection.

Clarifying the limitations of selective admissions can introduce and reinforce the imperative for active, ongoing monitoring of student progress during the entire program. In defining program goals, a series of formal judgment points following selection must be designed and implemented with ongoing assessment and retention decisions as central considerations. With the strength of program definition as a support and an existing framework for ongoing assessment as a guide, faculty may be more willing to assert professional judgment regarding student progress. Further, as students progress in their programs, faculty should be able to draw on the accumulation of empirical data to support those judgments.

Additional functions of selection. In addition to encouraging self-selection and focusing faculty energy on the program, implementing selective admissions policies can serve two other functions. First, by requiring entry-level tests of basic skills, teacher educators can be assured that their graduates will not be subject to current criticisms of the teaching force as being poorly prepared; opportunities for remediation should be provided for candidates who show promise in other respects. Finally, if at least some SCDEs are willing to undertake the responsibility for introducing selective admissions policies independently, they may be able, if it is not already too late, to circumvent the need for external forces, namely, legislation to mandate perfunctory policies of selection.

The Necessity for Specific Criteria

Since it has been difficult to identify validated characteristics which can be utilized conclusively for purposes of admissions, the question may be raised whether the use of any criterion is defensible within the framework of self-selection and faculty commitment. Self-selection is predicated on the existence of specific entry-level hurdles which constitute selection criteria. Also, without some specific criteria in place, research on selection would continue to be relatively nonexistent. Schalock (1979) emphasized that existing programs of teacher education are the logical sites in which to conduct selection research since they are natural contexts for the collection of data related to the eventual prediction of teaching success. If each program considered itself to be a demonstration project for research on selection, the potential data bank would be impressive. Finally, Menges (1975), in a review of the literature on readiness for professional practice, cites the importance of using multiple criteria to increase the accuracy of selection decisions.

Accepting the limitation that selection criteria cannot serve the purpose of linear prediction but that they are necessary for erecting the structure of a functional process, what guidelines can be used for their adoption? Five rules of thumb seem appropriate.

Relationship to research. Selection criteria should be reasonably related to research on teacher effectiveness. For example, requiring a GPA of 3.8 might be unreasonable given the knowledge that GPA does not correlate significantly with program success. Both Gress (1977) and James and Dumas (1976), however, stress that the lack of correlation exists only after an average level of ability is reached. Thus, setting no cutoff points and accepting all applicants would also be unwise.

Proximity of meaning. Criteria adopted should be meaningful to faculty members. A grade of C in a rhetoric course may have little operational definition regarding communicative abilities, whereas the results of a writing sample required for entry and scored within the program give specific information to faculty members and can remain an active part of a student's file. In recommending higher teacher-education admissions standards, the Louisiana Board of Regents proposed using a combination of ACT scores and GPA as the pivotal criterion (Marshman, 1981). The combinations proposed were as follows: 16 ACT/2.2 GPA; 15 ACT/2.3 GPA; 14 ACT/3.2 GPA. While this is described as an attempt to institute multiple criteria, as major variables these scores provide little useful information to program faculty. The underlying assumption of the rule of proximity of meaning is that faculty members participate actively in the process.

Number and type of criteria. A reasonable number of criteria should exist reflecting a balance between objective and subjective data sources (Scannell, 1981). Enough criteria should be used to encourage serious self-selection and to provide a general picture of the applicant, but not so many as to constitute an undue expenditure of applicant time and institutional resources. For example, the test battery used at Northern Kentucky University requires extensive participation of faculty in the literature and speech departments as well as other college personnel to evaluate the psychological battery; no personal interview was required, however. This appears to be an unbalanced process, especially given the data that only 34 percent of students pass all the tests on their first attempt (Carter et al., 1980).

The role of professional judgment should be maximized as a means of moderating the impact of objective data (Arnold et al., 1977). In the past, expressions of professional judgment have been criticized precisely because of their subjectivity; the state of research on objective data should encourage the introduction of subjective measures as well. Professional judgment can be operationalized in the form of faculty responsibility for interviewing candidates and reviewing accumulated admissions data.

Relationship to program. Criteria adopted for selection should resonate with program goals (Arnold et al., 1977); Haberman, 1972). This rule necessitates specific program definition by faculty members and experimentation with selection variables directly related to program purpose. Such criteria might include additional prerequisite courses and/or field experiences, interviews, or other sources.

Recognition of student as developing adult. Haberman (1972) described this developmental aspect as the need to "assess the potential of candidates to function as continuous learners" (p. 19). Criteria in this area are now rarely used, but attention is beginning to be paid to the assessment of personal development. Sprinthall's (1980) work on the relationship of ego maturity to personal success may provide a guide for adopting such measures. Kamaka (1982) attempted to apply a management training model based on self development to teacher-candidate selection, and Bingham and Hardy (1981) utilized counseling techniques for exploring personal development in combination with other, more conventional selection criteria. The four preceding rules represent static characteristics of candidates and are used to provide data regarding primarily past achievement and personal qualities. Using measures of personal development may shed light on how candidates will respond to and interact with the dimensions of their preparation programs.

Proposed Selection Criteria

The following criteria are recommended for making selection decisions based on the preceding guidelines. It must be reiterated that these criteria will not function alone or in combination to predict efficiently the potential success of candidates. Rather, their purpose is to provide entry-level hurdles to encourage self-selection, to serve as initial points in the process of continuous judgment of student progress, and to assist faculty members in making general discriminations between applicants based on multifaceted data. It is assumed that the strength of the proposed system lies in the interaction of the criteria and the functions of the selection process and that candidates would be monitored continuously for retention at specific points throughout their preparation programs.

Basic skills testing. Successful completion of entry-level testing in the areas of reading, mathematics and written communication is recommended. Test results provide current data on skill levels which can be used to screen out applicants who, in combination with other criteria, are unacceptable to faculty. Alternatively, if applicants are acceptable in all other respects, remediation in basic skills can be provided. It is reasonable to expect those who plan to enter teaching to possess basic skills; in the past, grades in general education courses and other general measures of skill level have not been adequate to assure minimal levels of achievement. Also, taking entry-level examinations requires expenditures of time and energy on the part of applicants. If tests of basic skills are required, applicants should be allowed to sit for them at least twice; standards would have to be determined by individual institutions and the effect of the cutoff scores should be a source of data for the selection process.

Grade point average (GPA). While in the past using GPA has proved fruitless in discriminating among applicants, it was essentially the only criterion used and should never have been expected to be adequate in isolation. In the concept of selection proposed here, setting a minimum GPA would act in the same manner as a general screening device, but it would be accompanied by additional measures to build a candidate's profile. Requiring no GPA minimum would be a continued signal that an open-door policy exists. A reasonable minimum GPA, one in keeping with the research, should be set; of course, standards should be moderated by the balance of the data and provisional admission granted in cases when it is the only criterion preventing entry for those whom faculty believe are otherwise well-qualified candidates.

Personal qualities. The determination of personal qualities through the use of a required, structured interview administered by permanent faculty members can serve a variety of purposes. First, the interview gives participating faculty members direct responsibility for some aspect of selection. Next, it provides an opportunity for interviewers to make professional judgments regarding candidates' personal presentations and interactive communication skills. Most important, applicants are given an opportunity to indicate their level of commitment, their concept of teaching as a profession, and their willingness to undertake the program. Successful completion of a personal interview would be based upon the identification of desirable personal qualities by program faculty. Identification of qualities should adhere to the guidelines outlined above and should be elicited informally through the interview questions.

At least two persons should conduct all interviews; in the interests of stability, interviewers should change only infrequently. As with other criteria, successful completion of an interview should not be considered adequate as a sole judgment upon which to base decisions. Biased individual decisions might be controlled by requiring both a structured interview format and a consensus of opinions; in this way, professional judgments can be a viable aspect of selection. The Selection Research–Perceiver Academies, is conducting work with an instrument called the Teacher Preservice Perceiver Interview (TPPI), an offshoot of their original Teacher Perceiver Interview developed to differentiate job applicants for teaching. Little hard data are available on the TPPI, but the structured interview is being advanced as a sole criterion for judgment (Selection Research, n.d.). In the proposed context for selection, the interview would not function alone as a judgment point.

Developmental maturity. The importance of acknowledging candidates as developing adult learners has been addressed earlier. Criteria related to levels of development might provide one indication of the extent to which applicants will function successfully in their programs. Another concept which may be related to this criterion is the idea of "coachability" of applicants; that is, can a measure of how well applicants respond to suggestions and guidance during preparation be developed? These concepts have not been well-studied in relation to teacher education but may be an important data source for future decisions. Isolating measures which can be used meaningfully as selection criteria should be a priority.

A Recapitulation

Four basic criteria have been proposed as a basis for selection. These criteria are by no means rigid; they are guided minimally by research and maximally by their potential contribution to the selection process. The criteria are not meant to function alone to predict teaching success; such predictions are not yet within the grasp of teacher educators. Rather, they serve as a point of departure for a program of selection and retention that should exist throughout a candidate's preparation for teaching.

To implement criteria which as yet lack validation without simultaneously conducting research to determine their validity is, at worst, professionally irresponsible and, at best, to pass up the opportunity to make a contribution to the knowledge base on selection. At this time, validation studies must be conceptualized as an integral part of the selection process. Waiting for validation before implementing selection policies has not been fruitful; inverting the pattern may accelerate results. Both Schalock (1979) and Galluzo (1982) call for longitudinal follow-up studies with selection decisions as the initial data points.

The lack of validation makes two more points essential. First, it is possible that all admissions decisions should be contingent on candidates' performance under supervised conditions in the field (as is the case at the University of Oregon). Allowing all interested students to enter and counseling out unsuccessful students only after early field experiences seems too resource-intensive an approach; however, although potential success can be optimized through selection, there can be no assurances even with the use of reasonable admissions standards. An active program of selective retention can function like contingent admissions, but the awareness of a contingent-admissions policy might further the faculty commitment to screening. Finally, the proposal has stressed the interaction of data sources and the need for flexibility with respect to standards. This practice is essential in relation to retaining policies of affirmative action and continued recruitment of minority students into teacher education.

IMPLICATIONS OF SELECTIVE ADMISSIONS POLICIES

Implementing policies of selective admissions based on the concepts of self-selection and faculty commitment to continuous monitoring and selective retention has major implications for the current operation of most programs of teacher education in this country. Two likely outcomes of increasingly stringent selection policies are paramount: the expenditure of additional resources and the effect on enrollment figures.

More complex selection processes will of necessity require additional expenditures of both finances and faculty time. Funds will be needed to administer and score entry-level examinations and to support increased administrative tasks. In addition, resources to conduct and disseminate longitudinal validation studies must be secured. Administrative functions could be handled least expensively by employing graduate assistants. Expenses associated with carrying out research on selection would occur chiefly in the data-analysis stage, since the collection of data would become an ongoing part of the teacher-education process. Thus, while some additional financial resources will be required, they should not present a major obstacle to implementing selective admissions.

More pressing is the issue of lowered enrollment figures as a result of increasingly selective policies of admissions (see Carter et al., 1980; Schalock, 1979). In most institutions, funding continues to be tied primarily to the generation of credit hours, leaving most SCDEs in poor bargaining positions in the competition for the allocation of resourcs (Guba & Clark, 1978). Compromises will have to be made at the institutional level based on the assumption and subsequent demonstration that the quality of the program and its graduates will improve as a result of new admissions policies.

The number of institutions now competing for students adds to the problem. Guba and Clark (1978) identified 1,367 programs of teacher education, 93 of which, as of 1978, were of a quality so as not to obtain regional accreditation. Commitments to quality control through the process of selective admissions, even if adopted by the major producers of teachers, could be weakened considerably by smaller, less well-endowed programs accepting any student who wanted to enter—for the sake of their own existence. Inter-university competition is a situation that must be dealt with on state and regional bases, particularly to decide what types of programs will be available at which institutions given current fiscal realities; all institutions cannot realistically continue to prepare teachers for many areas of specialization.

Whether SCDEs will be willing to respond to the teacher surplus in this fashion remains a point of speculation. Weaver (1981) believes that enrollments will not be reduced voluntarily by increasing admissions standards and that SCDEs must seek new sources of students. He further argues that the solution to the problem of poor quality of students is to prepare candidates for higher paying, higher prestige, nonschool jobs. While this is certainly a practical alternative, it bypasses the problem of increasing the quality of education graduates who will work within the schools. The resolution of the issue of the surplus of teacher-education programs may be in comprehensive planning at the state level, at least with respect to publicly-funded institutions. One criterion for continued existence might be the source of motivation for change. If program faculty are internally motivated, for whatever reason, to clarify and act upon program goals, they may be more likely to renew their commitments to student success than faculty who are content to wait for externally imposed directives.

CONCLUSION

As criticisms of public education continue, attention has increasingly been focused on the quality of teachers. The need for teacher-education programs to act autonomously in instituting control of the quality of their graduates is a pressing professional responsibility. The process of selection, it has been argued, can influence the applicant pool and can function as the first in a series of faculty judgment points regarding student progress. The existence of an active program of continuous monitoring has the potential to determine the quality of graduates; as candidates progress and experience teaching responsibilities that resemble those that they will eventually hold, decisions regarding appropriateness for teaching might be more accurately made. Perhaps programs that fail to meet this challenge are best left to expire.

It has been suggested that a definitive data base regarding selection criteria could emerge from validation studies, based on a set of proposed criteria and the dimensions of the selection process, and that such studies must be conceptualized as an integral part of the policies recommended above. Proposed foci for research might include the following:

1. Is there a relationship between the phenomenon of self-selection and faculty perception of student abilities?
2. What are the effects of systematic program definition for the purposes of developing selection policies on faculty morale, student perceptions of the program, or faculty articulation?
3. Does the frequency of formal, active judgment points of student progress affect student persistence in preparation programs?
4. Does gaining entrance into a program where specific hurdles must

be cleared (e.g., passing entry-level examinations) affect student motivation and commitment?

5. What are the effects of more rigid selection policies on the perceived and real status of SCDEs in relation to the parent institution?

6. Is there a relationship between self-selection and measured levels of student ego development?

Further, substantial data could be compiled if all institutions utilizing comprehensive selection policies collaborated as demonstration projects and conducted extensive follow-up studies to determine the effects of those policies on perceived teacher success. With a systematic program of evaluation which could document improved quality of graduates, SCDEs might then be able to build a case in their parent institutions for revised allocations of resources based upon the validated success of their teacher-education graduates.

REFERENCES

Arnold, D. S., Denemark, G., Nelli, E., Robinson, A., & Sagan, E. (1977). *Quality control in teacher education: Some policy issues.* Washington, DC: The ERIC Clearinghouse on Teacher Education.

Barnard, H. V., & Thornburg, K. R. (1980). Selective admissions in teacher education: A critical reappraisal. *Teacher Education and Special Education, 3* (2), 36–42.

Baumgartner, T., & Carlson, R. P. (1974). Screening and evaluation procedures for undergraduate majors at Indiana University. *Journal of Health, Physical Education, Recreation, 45,* 83–84.

Bingham, R. D., & Hardy, G. R. (1981, February). *Prospective teacher selection and personal development: Using preservice counselors as facilitators.* Paper presented at the Annual Meeting of the American Association of Colleges for Teacher Education, Detroit, MI. (ERIC Document Reproduction Service No. ED 199 214)

Borrowman, M. L. (1965). *Teacher education in America: A documentary history.* New York: Teachers College Press.

Brubaker, H. A., & Patton, D. C. (1975). Selection and retention in teacher education: Does it exist? *Teacher Educator, 10*(3), 2–7.

Bush, R. N., & Enemark, P. (1975). Control and responsibility in teacher education. In K. Ryan (Ed.), *Teacher Education: The Seventy-Fourth Yearbook of the National Society for the Study of Education (Part II).* Chicago, IL: University of Chicago Press.

Carpenter, J. A. (1972). *Survey of the criteria for the selection of undergraduate candidates for admission to teacher training.* Bowling Green, KY: College of Education, Western Kentucky University. (ERIC Document Reproduction Service No. ED 070 758.)

Carter, K. K., Boyd, S. D., Rogers, G. W., Jr., & Schiff, P. (1980). *The Northern Kentucky University program for assessing the basic academic skills and per-*

sonality characteristics of teacher education candidates. Highland Heights, KY: Northern Kentucky University. (ERIC Document Reproduction Service No. ED 206 565.)

Davis, O. L. Jr., & Yamamoto, K. (1968). Teachers in preparation: Professional attitudes and motivations. *Journal of Teacher Education, 19,* 365–369.

deLandsheere, G. (1980). Teacher selection. *Prospects: Quarterly Review of Education. 10,* 318–324.

Feiman-Nemser, S. (1980). Growth and reflection as aims in teacher education: Directions for research. In G. Hall, S. Hord, & G. Brown (Eds.), *Exploring issues in teacher education: Questions for future research.* Austin, TX: Research and Development Center for Teacher Education.

Galluzo, G. R. (1982, April). *Program evaluation in teacher education: From admissions to follow-up.* Paper presented at the Symposium on Program Evaluation in Teacher Education, The Research and Development Center for Teacher Education, The University of Texas.

Gottfredson, L. S. (1981). Circumscription and compromise: A developmental theory of occupational aspirations. *Journal of Counseling Psychology, 28,* 545–579. (Monograph)

Gress, J. R. (1977). *A study of the reliability, validity and usefulness of identified pre-teaching predictors.* Columbus, OH: Ohio State Department of Education. (ERIC Document Reproduction Service No. ED 151 306)

Guba, E. G., & Clark, D. L. (1978). Are schools of education languishing? *New York University Education Quarterly, 9,* 9–16.

Haberman, M. (1972). *Guidelines for the selection of students into programs of teacher education* (Research Bulletin 11). Washington, DC: Association of Teacher Educators and The ERIC Clearinghouse on Teacher Education.

Haberman, M., & Stinnett, T. M. (1973). *Teacher education and the new profession of teaching.* Berkeley, CA: McCutchan Publishing Co.

Haisley, F. (1982, May 27). Personal communication.

Heit, P., Johnson, G., Meeks, L. B., & Paxton, C. (1978). A selective admissions process as a predictor of academic success in health education. *The Journal of School Health, 48,* 146–150.

Howsam, R. B., Corrigan, D. C., Denemark, G. W., & Nash, R. J. (1976). *Educating a profession.* Washington, DC: American Association of Colleges for Teacher Education.

James, T. L., & Dumas, W. (1976). College GPA as a predictor of teacher competency: A new look at an old question. *The Journal of Experimental Education, 44,* 40–43.

Kamaka, E. (1982). Model-Netics: Implications for and approaches to the selection of candidates in a teacher education program at a small private liberal arts college. *Dissertation Abstracts International, 42,* 4182A–4623A.

Kinney, L. B. (1964). *Certification in education.* Englewood Cliffs, NJ: Prentice-Hall.

Kleine, P. F., & Wisniewski, R. (1981, October). Bill 1706: A forward step for Oklahoma. *Phi Delta Kappan,* 115–117.

Leonardson, G. (1977). Selection and admission criteria to undergraduate teacher education programs. *Colorado Journal of Educational Research, 16,* 24–28.

Lomax, D. (1971). Focus on the student teachers. In T. Burgess (Ed.), *Dear Lord*

James: A critique of teacher education. Middlesex, England: Penguin Books.

Lortie, D. C. (1975). *School teacher: A sociological study.* Chicago, IL: University of Chicago Press.

Magee, R. (1961). Admission-retention in teacher education. *Journal of Teacher Education, 12,* 81–85.

Marks, S. (1975). *A description of selected characteristics of the preservice teacher as learner.* Unpublished doctoral dissertation, Indiana Univeristy.

Marshman, L. R. (1981, October 30). *Teacher education program admissions–A case analysis.* (ERIC Document Reproduction Service No. ED 210 249)

Medley, D. M. (1979). The effectiveness of teachers. In P. L. Peterson & H. J. Walberg (Eds.), *Research on teaching: Concepts, findings and implications.* Berkeley, CA: McCutchan Publishing Co.

Medley, D. M. (1982). *Teacher competency testing and the teacher educator.* Charlottesville, VA: Association of Teacher Educators and the Bureau of Educational Research, School of Education, University of Virginia.

Menges, R. J. (1975). Assessing readiness for professional practice. *Review of Educational Research, 45,* 173–207.

Meyen, E. L. (1979). Quality teacher education. *Teacher Education and Special Education, 2,* 34–40.

Mitzel, H., & Rabinowitz, W. (1961). Some observations on the selection of students for teacher education programs. *Journal of Teacher Education, 12,* 157–164.

Morris, V. (1956). Grades for teachers? *Journal of Teacher Education, 7,* 244–249.

National Council for Accreditation of Teacher Education (NCATE). (1982). *Standards for the accreditation of teacher education.* Washington, DC: NCATE.

Nunney, D. N., Fiala, F. F., & Lewis, M. G. (1963). Teacher selection in the western states. *Journal of Teacher Education, 14,* 417–423.

Nutting, W. C. (1978). *Capacity for quality teacher education programs: Guidelines for limiting enrollments.* Paper presented at the Annual Meeting, Association of Teacher Educators. (ERIC Document Reproduction Service No. ED 155 163)

Ornstein, A. C. (1976). Educational poverty in the midst of educational abundance: Status and policy implications of teacher supply/demand. *Educational Researcher, 5,* 13–16.

Pratt, D. (1977). Predicting teacher survival. *Journal of Educational Research, 71,* 12–18.

Pugach, M. C., & Raths, J. D. (1983). Testing teachers: Analysis and recommendations. *Journal of Teacher Education, 34*(1), 37–43.

Sandefur, J. T. (1981). State reactions to competency assessment in teacher education. In S. Boardman & M. Butler (Eds.), *Competency testing in teacher education: Making it work.* Washington, DC: American Association of Colleges for Teacher Education.

Scannell, D. P. (1981). *Creating conditions for professional practice in schools and departments of education.* Lawrence, KS: School of Education, University of Kansas (ERIC Document Reproduction Service No. ED 210 247)

Schalock, D. (1979). Research in teacher selection. In D. Berliner (Ed.), *Review of research in education.* American Educational Research Association.

Selection Research (n.d.). The relationship between a preservice interview and student teaching performance. (Mimeograph)

Shank, K. S. (1978). *Nationwide survey of practices in selection and retention of teacher education candidates.* Charleston, IL: Eastern Illinois University. (ERIC Document Reproduction Service No. ED 167 539)

Silzer, M. M. (1981). *Procedures in the teacher selection process and their relation to retention and turnover rates.* Unpublished doctoral dissertation, University of Illinois.

Sinclair, W., & Picogna, J. L. (1974). How are education students selected? *The Clearinghouse, 48,* 541–543.

Soar, R. S., Medley, D. M., & Coker, H. (1983, December). Teacher evaluation: A critique of currently used methods. *Phi Delta Kappan,* 239–246.

Sprinthall, N. A. (1980). Adults as learners: Developmental perspective. In G. Hall, S. Hord, & G. Brown (Eds.), *Exploring issues in teacher education: Questions for future research.* Austin, TX: Research and Development Center for Teacher Education.

States' reform efforts increase as focus of issue shifts. (1983, December 7). *Education Week,* 5–17.

Stout, R. A. (1957). Selective admissions and retention practices in teacher education. *Journal of Teacher Education, 8,* 299–317.

Sykes, G. (1983). Public policy and the problem of teacher quality: The need for screens and magnets. In L. S. Shulman & G. Sykes (Eds.), *Handbook of teaching and policy.* New York: Longman.

Turner, R. L. (1975). An overview of research in teacher education. In K. Ryan (Ed.), *Teacher education: The seventy-fourth yearbook of the National Society for the Study of Education (Part II).* Chicago, IL: University of Chicago Press.

University of Kentucky, College of Education. (1972). *A survey of current practices in the selection and retention of students in teacher education.* Unpublished manuscript, University of Kentucky.

Weaver, W. T. (1972). Educators in supply and demand: Effects on quality. *School Review, 20,* 124; 127.

Weaver, W. T. (1981, February). *The tragedy of the commons: The effects of supply and demand on the educational talent pool.* Paper presented at the Annual Meeting of the American Association of Colleges of Teacher Education, Detroit, MI. (ERIC Document Reproduction Service No. ED 204 261.)

Yevak, M. E., & Carlin, L. O. (1972). Requirements for admission to and retention in professional education programs. *Journal of SPATE, 11,* 2–10.

9

Expert or Novice? A Story About Evaluating Teacher-Education Programs With an Eye on Professional Reform*

G. Thomas Fox, Jr.
University of Wisconsin–Madison

Like all men in Babylon I have been a proconsul; like all, a slave; I have also known omnipotence, opprobrium, jail. Look: the index finger of my right hand is missing. Look again: through this rent in my cape you can see a ruddy tattoo on my belly. It is the second symbol, Beth. This letter, on nights of full moon, gives me power over men whose mark is Ghimel; but it also subordinates me to those marked Aleph, who on moonless nights owe obedience to those marked Ghimel. In a cellar at dawn, I have severed the jugular vein of sacred bulls against a black rock. During one lunar year, I have been declared invisible: I shrieked and was not heard, I stole my bread and was not decapitated...I owe this almost atrocious variety to an institution which other republics know nothing about, or which operates among them imperfectly and in secret: the lottery.

Jorge Borges, "The Babylon Lottery"

INTRODUCTION

Like Jorges Borges, I am going to tell a story; only my story is about an evaluation of a teacher-education program. Unlike "The Babylon Lottery," my story is not fiction; it is an account of what happened in an evaluation study performed six years ago and of what has transpired since then. The

---

* This story is about the first three months of an eighteen-month evaluation study. It is about the planning and designing of the study; thus, it is only the first part of a longer story. The remaining parts of the story would include: the data gathering stage of the study; the interpretive and preliminary reporting stage; a follow-up study; the writing of the final report; and events that have occurred since the final report was written.

themes of "The Babylon Lottery" and my story, however, are similar: the choice of who should have particular occupational opportunities, who will know omnipotence, and who will know opprobrium. The answer I reach is similar to Borges' answer in "The Babylon Lottery": Nearly anyone can—and should—have open to them the almost atrocious variety of opportunities now available.

I understand that I am swimming against the tide when I suggest that some criteria other than evaluative expertise be used to choose members of an evaluation team. That is why I have chosen to tell about our experience in story form. I am not writing so much to persuade you that the implications I have drawn are correct, as I am hoping to share what happened. The evaluation iconoclast Barry MacDonald (1974) has persuaded me that it is our experience that cannot be denied, whereas the interpretations or conclusions reached from our experience are more arbitrary and can be challenged. I want to share this story because I think you, too, may find the experience provocative; you may find that your consideration of who is to perform educational program evaluation to be more restricted by convention than is warranted or justified.

Corroborative evidence for this story exists.[1] I mention this because I do not want this story to remain merely a folksy tale, an interesting professional sidelight to our serious work as educators. I am convinced that this story goes well beyond the performance of our evaluation study. To me, this story illuminates, as Jorge Borges' tale does, the distribution of professional and personal opportunities—in this case, to the opportunities available for investigating educational practices.

THE BEGINNING:
WHY I WAS CHOSEN TO CONDUCT THE EVALUATION

I could begin my story with "Once upon a time, we had no experience in program evaluation." At the time we began our study, the statement was true. I had never before performed an evaluation study and neither had any of the other five faculty members who eventually joined me. Before I introduce the study team and describe our work, perhaps I should explain how this project was given to relative novices in the field of evaluation.

In February, 1975, I was called by Jim Steffensen, then Chief of the Development Branch of the federal Teacher Corps program, and his special assistant Paul Collins. They asked me to evaluate a new venture that was

---

[1] There are two published sources for corroborative evidence. The first is contained in the 21 reports of the study, called *The 1975 CMTI Impact Study* (Fox et al., 1976). The second major source is a follow-up study performed nearly three years later titled *The Residual Impact of the 1975 CMTI* (Fox et al., 1978). Furthermore, the individuals introduced in this story can be contacted. Their addresses are available from the author.

being planned for the summer of 1975: the Corps Member Training Institute (CMTI). The CMTI was to be a one month introduction to a two-year teacher internship for approximately 250 graduate students in education. The teacher interns came from more than 60 different schools of education across the U.S. (and the Micronesian Islands), each school of education being the recipient of a two-year Teachers Corps grant. Part of the grant was earmarked to educate four graduate students to make them especially capable teachers of children from low-income and minority families. These students were called *interns* by the Teacher Corps program. The other two parts of each Teacher Corps grant were: (a) to train the entire staff of experienced teachers in a few focused schools, and (b) to develop materials and procedures that could make the regular teacher education programs of the recipient colleges more effective in training teachers for schools that serve low-income and minority populations.

Teacher Corps was a federal program, begun in 1965, intended to improve the education of students from poor and minority families in the U.S. through innovative reforms in how student teachers are taught. The program was launched by the Great Society legislation of 1965; it was supported by President Lyndon Johnson, initiated by Joseph Caliafano, his presidential aide, formed in legislation by Senators Edward Kennedy of Massachusetts and Gaylord Nelson of Wisconsin, and was of particular interest to the Attorney General, Robert Kennedy. With such political support, it was perhaps only natural that by 1975 the Teacher Corps program had survived all other federal programs (and agencies) in teacher education and staff development.

By federal standards, however, the Teacher Corps program was beginning to get "long in the tooth." Its original intent to recruit and train interns had been changed by Congress to include training of experienced teachers and reforming regular teacher-education programs. These changes were to begin in the summer of 1975.

The 1975 CMTI was intended by the Washington staff of Teacher Corps to introduce the new interns to the Teacher Corps program, to each other, and to the special demands of teaching in schools serving low-income and minority populations. It was both a new and a large scale effort of the Teacher Corps program. Although the program had sponsored national conferences, it had never run a national training program on this scale. With travel expenses for 250 interns from across the nation and for a large training staff, the cost of the 1975 CMTI would be at least one million dollars (out of a yearly Teacher Corps program budget of 37.5 million dollars). In addition to the instructional purposes of the CMTI, there was a grander purpose for sponsoring this one month training program on the eve of the tenth anniversary of the Teacher Corps program. That purpose was to gain some national professional recognition for the Teacher Corps program.

I knew this before I received the phone call from Jim Steffensen and Paul Collins. I had worked as a consultant to the Teacher Corps Washington staff before, but not as an evaluator. In 1973 and 1974, I had been a consultant to the Teacher Corps Washington staff on an Office of Education sponsored evaluation of the Teacher Corps program (Marsh and Lyons, 1974). I had edited a book of educators' and sociologists' responses to the only published study on the Teacher Corps program (by Ronald Corwin, 1973). In fact, I was just completing a review of ten past evaluation studies of the Teacher Corps program (including the Corwin and the Marsh and Lyon studies). In addition, I had consulted with Teacher Corps staff revising program guidelines based upon the newly stated purposes of their program.

I also knew something about the 1975 CMTI. A few months before receiving the phone call, I had participated in an informal meeting where the feasibility of a common training program for all interns at a single site was discussed. Dr. William L. Smith, the Director of Teacher Corps, Jim Steffensen, Paul Collins, Ron Corwin, Bruce Joyce (then of Palo Alto, formerly of Columbia University, a long-time consultant to Teacher Corps and an author on teaching and teacher education), and I participated in the discussion. Questions were raised by Bill Smith about the realistic aims, instructional goals, and recommended procedures for such an undertaking. The answers to Bill's questions were generally upbeat, with agreement that the interns could use some special attention since they were now a smaller part of the Teacher Corps program than they were in the past. Discussion emphasized the need to address the organizational naivete of the interns, thereby helping them to understand, analyze, and thus work more effectively in the schools and schools of education in which they were placed. This need was uncovered in the Corwin study of Teacher Corps. We talked for about two hours on the risky and lively possibilities of a Corps Member Training Institute.

Thus, when I received the call from Jim Steffensen and Paul Collins asking me to be the evaluator of the 1975 CMTI, it was not a complete surprise. I had recently worked with Jim and Paul and had shown a critical eye and an ability to complete a task. But I had never performed an evaluation study, which clearly made me a novice in program evaluation. My combination of naivete and expertise, of course, was not uncommon to program evaluation, or indeed, to research or curriculum-development programs in education.

When I received the call from Jim and Paul, I was privately a little miffed that I had not been given an instructional role. I readily agreed to evaluate, but my background in classroom teaching and my interest in curriculum reform suggested to me that I had been given a minor feature of this instructional event. Ron Corwin, I discovered, had been given the responsibility of the first two weeks of instruction; Bruce Joyce, the second two weeks. Sensing my reticence, Paul Collins gave me advice that neither of us knew was to be so true: that the ultimate professional gain in this enterprise would be reaped by the evaluator, not by the instructional leaders of the event. To an educator like me who identified education with instruction, this claim seemed like professional treason. But I took the challenge with some professional relish. I was going to do evaluation better than it had been done before, and to enjoy it fully.

Obtaining the Contract

The next step was to meet with Jim Steffensen, provide him an outline of what I intended to do, and negotiate a contract. The design and budget was two or three pages long, and we completed the contract with a handshake. Basically we set down the purpose of the study: to record the one-month event and to determine the nature and extent of the impact of the event on the interns. We agreed that this would require a variety of procedures. I argued for a photographer since I anticipated that it would be difficult but essential to capture the interactions between young adults from a variety of racial and cultural backgrounds living and working together for a month. We compromised to the extent that the money I had budgeted for the photographer would also be used for an assistant director in the study. We also discussed the possibility for a follow-up study that could continue to investigate the impact and influence of the training during the year after the 1975 CMTI.

Basically, the hour discussion between Jim Steffensen and myself on the design, reports, and budget of the evaluation study was, as would be expected from our previous work, conducted with mutual trust. Few anxieties were expressed about the study and its relationship to the instructional features of the 1975 CMTI, and no concerns were expressed about my relative lack of experience in conducting or directing evaluation studies.

This evaluation was to be a classic case of what MacDonald (1974) has called *autocratic evaluation*. I was very clearly left with a range of possibilities for investigating the 1975 CMTI, as well as the responsibility for choosing any theoretical perspective or even ultimate purpose for the study. It was clear that Teacher Corps respected my views of what could be done with this study. I expressed my intent not only to make the study valuable to their interests in recording what happened and in deciding whether a similar activity would be warranted, but also to contribute to current understanding about the processes of teacher education and the development of teachers. This characterization of the study as being autocratic, by the way, was never accepted by the other principal investigators whom I will introduce soon. Be that as it may, it was clear that the control of this study was solely in the hands of the evaluators.

Even though I had not yet evaluated an instructional program, I had the confidence to try. I neither questioned my lack of experience in program evaluation, nor the complexity of the task. Much of such chutzpah came from my friends in the Teacher Corps program. People like Bill Smith, Jim Steffensen, and Paul Collins were comfortable at trying out the new after gaining the best they could find in a limited amount of time. My respect for the moxie needed to try something new was also gained from my postdoctorate mentor at the University of Wisconsin, Professor M. Vere DeVault. Vere, more than any other university-based educator I knew, could try almost anything new and succeed. He himself had successfully gone from music education to mathematics education and then to computer-based instruction by having imaginative ideas, relying upon a huge reservoir of common sense (he was raised on an Indiana farm), and maintaining a great curiosity about learning. Vere taught me the importance of personal audacity in the pursuit of academic understanding and, not incidently, productivity.

All in all, then, it was quite natural for me to take this opportunity to direct the 1975 CMTI Impact Study. Although I felt a bit slighted that I wasn't one of the instructional developers, I jumped into the evaluation study with some verve and vitality. I was excited. It was a new opportunity to try some of what I had learned in my own career and from analyzing others' work. Who knows? It may also help me find a regular job, something I did not have (and have not had) since I was a teacher.

Selecting an Evaluation Team

Given this opportunity to design an independent evaluation of a limited but national event in teacher education, my first decision was to involve a number of professors at the University of Wisconsin School of Education. I have been asked a number of times since then why I would have done such a thing. The answer has always been simple. First, I had (and still have) a very great respect for the team process in a difficult inquiry—in the value of dialogue and discourse in pursuing the meaning of human actions. Second, I felt knowledge held previous to the investigation was important. Since I believed that meaning was always constructed, and seldom discovered from educational inquiry, it was important to start an inquiry from as strong a knowledge base as possible. This knowledge included experience that I knew I alone did not have. I also felt a study, to be useful to the profession, must be tested in other contexts as meaning is constructed. The relevance of the results to others in teacher education would have to be continually questioned; and the best way to do that would be to involve persons in the study who were themselves engaged in teacher-education programs.

My reasons for including a number of school education faculty members were more like hypotheses than assertions. Perhaps my age also had something to do with my selection of faculty members. I had recently completed graduate school as a comparatively old student with some experience by which to judge my professors as educators. It would surprise no one that, although I respected their intelligence, I had less respect for them as educators. I felt a wider range of experience would enhance their understanding of their own role and influence on student teachers. Thus, perhaps it was possible for me to hire former professors without feeling subservient to their status, and without trying to force upon them a largely unearned role of my own.

Brief descriptions of the five faculty members I selected follow. I describe these persons in an irreverent sentence or two in order to help the reader meet each member of the team as an individual. The thumbnail descriptions are not meant to capture their entire personalities, but to place them as persons in the time and circumstance of this study.

Bob Tabachnick was a smooth-talking, senior full professor whose subject matter speciality was social studies in elementary schools. Bob was originally from New York City like many school of education professors at the University of Wisconsin–Madison. Bob had a reputation as a knowledgeable reader on a wide range of topics from physics to Shakespeare. He was the renaissance man of the department, but his reputation was fading a bit with the new emphasis on educational research. His professional background included some years in Nigeria as an expert in teacher education and as a curriculum developer. Above all else Bob is a talker, so articulate in restating your position that you (and he) would swear that it was his idea first. Just a few months before receiving the phone call from Jim Steffensen, I had approached Bob Tabachnick, the chairman of the elementary education department, with an idea and a five-page proposal for a study on the teacher graduates of the school of education. He was interested in the possibility that some empirical information on the graduates of the school of education might have a chance in directing faculty attention to the redesign of their program. Thus, I knew he was interested in the issues of this evaluation study and felt responsible for similar actions at the University of Wisconsin–Madison.

Tom Popkewitz was a junior faculty member (an assistant professor) looking towards his first promotion. He, too, was in elementary education social studies, but he was much more interested in investigative methods and the social context of educational reform and inquiry than Bob. Tom was also a New Yorker, the son of a carpenter. Although small, Tom played in the line of his high school football team where he made all-city. Like the pulling guard he was, Tom is still tough, tenacious, and single-minded. Actually, I picked Tom for two papers he had written but had not yet published. I had admired a paper he had presented with Gary Wehlage at the 1975 American Educational Research Association (AERA) conference in Washington, D.C. The paper proposed that the metaphor of work be used to analyze what teachers do and what teacher education could help them do better. The second paper was a draft of a study on a Teacher Corps project based in Madison at the School of Education and in an Indian community about 150 miles away. I thought the study unfair in critical focus; but from it I knew that he could produce a case study, and that he knew something about the Teacher Corps program. I had had Tom as a professor and knew him to be a very serious young man who was interested in naturalistic inquiry and who could be an aggressive investigator if he became involved. Within six years, Tom has had two promotions to full professor.

Gary Wehlage was an associate professor in secondary school social studies. Gary is a small town boy from Montana, an outdoors guy who hunts, fishes, and can fix cars with ease. He is quiet, deliberate, and self-effacing (especially in comparison with the rest of this team). At the time, I did not know Gary at all, except that he had presented the AERA paper on teaching as work with Tom Popkewitz that I had liked so much. I also knew that Gary and Tom had begun to teach some graduate courses together in research methods emphasizing the case-study approach. As far as I knew, he had not published much, and was, like Tom Popkewitz and me, inexperienced in conducting educational research. His background in secondary education provided a necessary perspective for the study, since some Teacher Corps interns were going into high school teaching. Since the 1975 CMTI, Gary has directed a number of studies on the retention of high school students.

Tom Romberg was the most published and experienced among us in educational research. He was a full professor in elementary school mathematics, Stanford trained, with both the propensity and the contacts to keep up with the latest trends and issues in research methodology. Tom is a big guy from Nebraska, who always looks supremely confident, whether he is looking down to talk to you or merely walking on the balls of his feet with his elbows spread wide. (He had been a basketball player and must have been a hell of a rebounder.) I did not know Tom well at all; although he taught the primary course in research methodology for graduate students, I had taken earlier equivalent courses in educational psychology. As far as I know, Tom Romberg had never performed an evaluation study before, but he was acting as a consultant to the large Beginning Teacher Evaluation Study (BTES), directed by David Berliner. His Stanford contacts were useful to us, and his self-assured nature in a field of comparatively reticent researchers made him stand out then perhaps more than he would now. His value was not only his contacts and experience, but also his comfort with a range of data analytic procedures. Only later did I discover that Tom Romberg was beginning to be enchanted with the potential of case study in educational inquiries, and that he had had some prior experience with the Teacher Corps program in its competency based infatuations of the early 1970s.

Carl Grant was a natural choice. He knew the Teachers Corps well, since he had been directing a special Teacher Corps leadership training project for more than two years. Also, one of the themes of the 1975 CMTI was in his area of professional interest: multicultural education. Carl had class.

He was from Chicago where his father was a well-known dentist and a recognized member of Chicago black society. His older brother was a principal in the Chicago public schools. Carl was the only Black member of the University of Wisconsin–Madison school of education staff, and Teacher Corps was a minority-oriented program. Carl and I were graduate students together and I liked him. I especially appreciated his common sense and managerial abilities. Carl's perceptive understanding of Teacher Corps and of his university colleagues would prove valuable to our project. Carl had been recently hired as an assistant professor in student-teacher supervision. At that time, he had no research or evaluation experience to speak of, but he knew how and he knew what was expected. Carl has recently been promoted to full professor.

Why didn't I pick faculty members who were more experienced in program evaluation? Because there were none. There were faculty members who had read about and were advising others on field-research methods, but there were no faculty members who had field experience in performing program evaluations. Thus, I chose faculty members who I thought had some of the prerequisite abilities, had gained some vicarious research and evaluation experience through their reading, teaching, and consulting, and whose professional experiences and backgrounds suggested that they would be interested and could produce final results. I was trying to form a varied team; as it turned out, three members were very interested in case study, one was experienced in quantitative analysis and research design, and one was an educational realist who knew the Teacher Corps program inside and out. Although some of these five individuals had spent ten or more years on the same faculty, none had worked together on a field study.[1]

Another early decision was to select the photographer and assistant director as negotiated with Jim Steffensen. My choice was Jeanne Tabachnick, an experienced photographer who had often photographed people in other cultures at work. She had honed many of her photographic skills in Africa, and had exhibited her work in a number of shows. She was experienced, articulate, and confident, but down to earth with an obvious practical view of the way things are. She had, it seemed to me, a sensitivity for capturing people at work that went beyond anything I had yet read (or seen) on teaching. Her open curiosity, quiet confidence of observation, and interest in people and their style of work were to mean more to our study than her photographic skills. At the 1975 CMTI, Jeanne helped focus our observation and analysis, while her photos captured the sense of community experienced by the participants at this one month training event. Although Jeanne was a professional photographer, this was her first involvement in an educational inquiry, to say nothing of an evaluation study.

---

[1] I have been asked why I did not select women faculty members; at the time of the study there was one and she was busy.

Perhaps, to be fair, I should take a stab at myself. I am an inarticulate Irishman whose tone of voice suggests more assuredness than I usually intend. In the spring of 1975, I was 38, three years beyond my PhD and with no future at the University of Wisconsin–Madison. (They had a new policy of not hiring their own graduates.) I was hoping to stay in Madison for a few more years, trying to maintain myself through consulting. For seven years in the 1960s, I loved grade school teaching, but left it to get my PhD. Like the other two Tom's (Popkewitz and Romberg, respectively), I had been a lineman and a basketball player, but any success I had was due more to natural strength than to fierce tenacity. I continue to have no faculty status at the University of Wisconsin. Except for security and for teaching, this has been to my advantage. Since the 1975 CMTI Impact Study, I have had a variety of professional opportunities that would not have been available to a junior but relatively old faculty member. I have been assisted by Linda Weiler, who was my tough administrative alter ego during the 1975 CMTI Impact Study, and Nancy Mitchell who has been an interested reader, occasional coauthor, and secretary for the past few years.

CONSTRUCTING A STUDY DESIGN

This seven-member team—five professors, Jeanne Tabachnick, and myself —began to meet immediately, since we had less than ten weeks to prepare our design for our study. Although we had never worked together on such a research project and none of us had previously evaluated an educational program, our discussions seemed to me to be unusually productive, focused, and engaging. We used comparatively lengthy meetings at first, from four to six hours, to make sure that the issues raised were understood, discussed, and resolved to a point that part of the design could be formed. Agendas were always made for these sessions and notes were kept and shared between meetings. I don't remember ever encountering an issue that we felt unprepared to discuss and resolve. Although we met severe roadblocks based on our limited awareness and lack of experience, we were never stumped.

Sometimes we resolved our differences by pretending that they were not important. An example is what we did when we tried to work together to produce a survey instrument. As we worked on defining what we were looking for in a survey and how we would integrate the survey with the case study observation and interview data, Tom Popkewitz and Gary Wehlage were getting more and more beligerent. Late one afternoon when the survey instrument began to take shape, they made it clear that *no* survey instrument would ever be accorded *any* legitimacy or credibility in their minds, no matter how painstakingly we tried to construct it nor how carefully we were prepared to analyze and interpret the results. The issue, as they saw it, was the incompatability of survey data with field data. Meaningful and discursive accounts by participants, they argued, should not be forced to compete for attention with systematically ordered responses to a survey.

After a sleepless night, I called them early the next morning and told them that such an attitude meant they were no longer involved in the study. After an awkward silence, they assured me that I had misinterpreted the extent of their dissatisfaction. We agreed they would continue to work on the survey instruments along with the rest of us. We three privately knew then, of course, that our differences in perspective were critical. Later events have shown we were right. Tom and Gary not only didn't increase their respect for survey instruments, but became more and more convinced that their powers of observation and of analyzing interviews were the primary sources of valid information. What we had really agreed to was that they would tolerate the existence of survey instruments in the study and would not use meeting time to point out the faults of such surveys. It was a false agreement with mutual benefits. I could use their interest in the problem and their involvement in field methods. Tom and Gary could use this opportunity to engage in educational inquiry in general and in program evaluation in particular.

More often, when we realized that our tentative resolution of an issue was not very acceptable, we were lucky to find some source that spoke more eloquently than we did. Two examples occurred early in our discussions. One source resolved our position on using field interviews and observations to focus on the processes of what was happening, along with survey questionnaires to help monitor how the students were building their understanding of teaching. Some of our rationale for combining these two approaches came from my criticisms of past evaluations of the Teacher Corps program, but we had no consistent, explicitly stated position. Luckily, Tom Romberg had been shown a mimeographed paper written by two men in Scotland in 1972. Although the 25-page paper by Malcolm Parlett and David Hamilton, "Evaluation as illumination: A new approach to the study of innovatory programs," was then an underground classic in England, it was not particularly well known or accessible in the U.S. The paper (published in the U.S. in 1976) came to Tom Romberg through his Stanford network.

The importance of the Parlett and Hamilton paper to the continued dialogue, design, and mutual trust of our small team can hardly be overemphasized. My hope, shared by other team members as we began to construct our kaleidoscopic notion of evaluation study, was to arrive at an easily accessible design that was compatible with out intent. The Parlett and Hamilton concept of *illuminative evaluation* was not only consistent with our hopes, it provided us with a common language, attitude, and philosophy. Our intent to integrate quantitative analysis with qualitative field methods and to loosen up the tendency only to test hypotheses that were stated before the program began now had a well articulated defense. Within three weeks of our initial discussions, we had a perspective on evaluation we all could share. We had found the Parlett and Hamilton paper, by the way, a week or two before the blow-up between Tom and Gary and myself. That we had an articulate and positive resolution did not mean we could all feel comfortable.

A second source of good luck as we constructed a study design came, again, from a Tom Romberg contact. As we were looking for a data analytic method that was compatible with our underlying assumptions and anticipation of influence, the idea of time-series design and data analysis came to Tom Romberg. In early 1975, Gene Glass (a former student of Tom's) and a few associates were just completing a book that adapted a relatively old but sophisticated method of analyzing repeated measurements. The method and design was called *time series,* a term which they had adapted from economic to educational situations. Not only was the Glass, Wilson, and Gottman (1975) manuscript available, but they were developing a packaged computer program for the analysis of time-series data. Again, it was a stroke of luck for us that made it possible to continue to make certain assumptions about the possible nature of the impact of this event, and still use some survey instruments and quantitative data analyses. Thus, within about three to four weeks, we discovered a compact rationale and articulation of our basic study intentions, as well as an innovative approach to the analysis of educational survey data.

Determining a Study Focus

Most issues we confronted, however, we could resolve based on our experience in teacher education, regardless of our inexperience in program evaluation. It was easy for us, for example, to imagine what the month of CMTI training would be like. We knew that approximately 250 masters degree candidates with little or no teaching experience from many different cultural, ethnic, and racial backgrounds in the U.S. were to receive common training at a single site. We knew such an undertaking would be filled with conflict, emotion, apathy, fear of the unknown, homesickness, professional drive, power struggles, personal agendas, and a range of intentions and perspectives on the part of both the students and their instructors. In short, regardless of the instructional intentions and design, we expected a changing, unpredictable dynamic encounter of people who would arrive not knowing anyone and leave knowing more than they wanted to know. It would be a fascinating event just to observe, to say nothing of trying to describe, accurately capture, and critically analyze.

Furthermore, our experience suggested how we could best understand the impact of this first month of training on the student teachers. We readily agreed with Tom Popkewitz and Gary Wehlage that the overall metaphor of teacher socialization would be useful. We understood, after all, that this was just the first month of training in a two year teacher-education program for the student teachers. We understood that student teachers enter such programs with certain notions of teaching and reconstruct these notions over time. We also knew that it was experience, setting, pressures, and personal responses to school and classroom surroundings that would influence their understanding of teaching—perhaps more influentially than their formal courses. Thus the socialization metaphor made sense, because it implied that a wide range of factors can impinge upon the student teachers' understandings of good teaching. Although we were new to the evaluation game, we had a complex understanding of the processes whereby students begin to become teachers. Some of this was beginning to be placed in the educational literature, but not much and not yet convincingly.

We also readily agreed to focus on the student teacher (what Teacher Corps called the intern) and on their views. The more we understood the event from the views, actions, and reactions of the interns, the better would we be able to interpret how they were influenced. But there were other reasons, such as the desire to stick with the "underdogs," those with less power in the enterprise, and to become their spokesperson(s). We also had a chance to try a new approach since none of the many past evaluations of the Teachers Corps program had focused on the interns' training, nor their perspective on training experiences. As teacher educators, we were interested in understanding how students did use such an instructional event to build their views about teaching. In addition, our intent to try to see the event as much as possible from the perspective of the interns was stimulated by another sentiment: we were curious to see if we could pull it off.

If you can imagine that our resulting discussions were intense and serious as we came to agree on the socialization metaphor, you would be partly right. The other part of our serious and intense discussions were the periodic bursts of laughter, banter, and good humor that can arise from those who not only feel fortunate in being highly involved in a new and engaging challenge, but who feel morally superior in their approach.

Stating Working Hypotheses

As we continued our discussions, we began to form certain public statements. We called these statements our underlying assumptions and took time to record them, discuss them, and make sure we could stand by them as we developed a coherent rationale for the study design. These underlying assumptions were the focus of our early discussions and became the basis for our study design and the rationale we built to defend it within the first month. First we stated what we assumed the 1975 CMTI would be like:

1. The 1975 CMTI would be dynamic and interactive;

2. It would be a cultural and social event as well as a training event; and
3. Implications for the profession would be continually constructed by both the instructors and the students.

We also stated our assumptions about the interns who were to participate in the 1975 CMTI:

1. The interns would enter the training with beliefs about teaching that may not be consistent with Teacher Corps or the 1975 CMTI goals;
2. There may be some dramatic and discontinuous changes in their beliefs about teaching during CMTI;
3. These changes may depend upon the informal, social, and cultural interactions they encounter at the CMTI; and
4. These changes in perspective towards teaching would continue to be dramatic after the 1975 CMTI ends as the interns begin to experience schools as student teachers.

We were anticipating that the interns would be transferring much from their everyday experience to their views of themselves as teaching professionals.

In these early discussions on the evaluation of the 1975 CMTI, we also felt it necessary to define teaching as making decisions about the use of limited time and resources upon fundamentally sparse information, and professional development as an ongoing process through which an individual becomes socialized into certain professional roles.

The drawing of hypotheses was one task that was relatively easy to perform, once we had agreed to some underlying assumptions and definitions. Although an issue arose as to whether we should have any hypotheses formed before we began to collect our data, the focus and direction of the assumptions made it clear that we were already beginning with some hypotheses. We were anticipating what would happen, what would be significant in what happened, how the interns would interact, how they would place meaning on their experience, and how they would fit this month into their development as teachers. Tom Popkewitz and Gary Wehlage were particularly concerned that we allow the hypotheses to be drawn from the data, as Glaser and Strauss (1967) suggested in their book on developing grounded theory. Like Glaser and Strauss, we identified these hypotheses as working hypotheses. The working hypotheses began from our previous experiences in teacher education and the Teacher Corps, and could be transformed and refocused depending upon the information provided by the study.

Eventually these working hypotheses were extended in number and categorized according to: (a) the actions and performance of the CMTI, (b) the development of interns' perspectives towards teaching during CMTI, and (c) the relationship between the training experienced at the CMTI and the interns' development of perspectives. The hypotheses were plentiful simply because we had all worked in teacher edcuation, and were drawing from our own experience in educating student teachers.

After stating our assumptions and working hypotheses, developing our data gathering methods, observation, and interview guidelines were relatively routine challenges. It became clear as we hammered out an agreement on the assumptions and working hypotheses what information we would need and how we would go about getting that information. These data gathering methods included interviewing participants, observing them at work and at play, using periodic surveys, and employing the camera for critical analysis as well as illustration. It is strange, as I sit here writing this account, to realize that we (and others who have seen our study) suggest that this was a multifaceted approach to data gathering and interpretation. Multifaceted in our case meant the above four methods, and with an analysis of the training documents and schedules, five modes of collecting information.

Hiring Graduate Students

It was about the fourth week of our discussion that we begin to hire young graduate assistants to help complete the more technical functions of our study design. In our first few lengthy discussions, we had assumed that we would be doing the data gathering, the interviewing, and the observing as well as the writing of the descriptions, interpretations, and conclusions of the study. But when the CMTI had been set for July, we realized that those who taught summer courses had a conflict that was too late to change. The solution, of course, was natural: we hired three graduate students to be observers and interviewers at the 1975 CMTI as well as assistants in completing the data gathering instruments. This was, of course, a stroke of professorial genius. The dirty work, especially the construction of the interview and observation guides, and the surveys, would basically be done by our students.

Having graduate students to complete the data gathering schedules and forms meant that they were responsible for the ultimate reductions of our study design. The final construction of the forms, and the inevitable reduction of our intentions, were their work now, not ours. We kept the authority to change the wording and format of the guides if they did not meet our standards. We met to discuss drafts, to restate our intentions, and to judge the graduate students' work accordingly. But hiring graduate students meant we would change someone else's work, not our own. We could, and did, stand aside from these products and judge them as if we were outsiders with little of our own (considerable) ego reduced.

We entered a more comfortable and efficient stage, as we criticized and redrew our students' workings of the guides and surveys. Although we probably never had to do so, we did justify their involvement as observers and interviewers at CMTI (the five professors couldn't be there; and besides, as peers the graduate students may get more honest responses from the interns), and their work on the guides and surveys (the three graduate students were, after all, the ones who were expected to use them). What could be a fairer or a more natural response than to hire graduate students within a university? The three graduate students we picked to participate in the study as observers and interviewers turned out to be, from my perspective, the most fortunate choices made in the entire study.

Iliana Ortiz was a New York City Puerto Rican who had just received her Masters Degree in Education at the University of Wisconsin–Madison. Iliana was, at least in these circumstances, a quiet, perceptive, articulate, and conscientious observer. She seemed to me to be unusually wise beyond her years, natural and comfortable in an admittedly tough role with near peers. She wrote well, but found completing her daily reports during the 1975 CMTI more difficult than the rest of us.

Reggie Jones was a New York City black who had worked in the New York schools, was looking for summer employment, and was in Madison at the time. Reggie was reserved, taciturn, and had, it turned out, a special knack for finding small bits of actions or groupings that captured essential themes of the 1975 CMTI. Iliana was small and petite, Reggie was tall and lean. Both were young (about 23) and inexperienced in school affairs, thus making them indistinguishable from the interns whom they were to interview, observe, and help us understand.

Craig Nauman was a little older, and, in addition to being a part-time graduate student, was a full time faculty member at the local technical college. Craig was a midwesterner, white, and was more personable, gregarious, and openly excitable than Iliana, Reggie, or myself. His open and interactive nature helped us all, and certainly provided us with information that we three would not have coolly observed alone.

Iliana, Reggie, and Craig developed the observation guides and the interview questions. We professors had decided that it was important to observe both the formal training sessions and the informal nature of the 1975 CMTI living experience. Iliana, Reggie, and Craig constructed various drafts of the format and the identifying categories for recording their observations. They eventually came up with two different observation sheets, one for formal training sessions, one for more informal gatherings. Both sheets left open spaces for comments, descriptions, interpretations, and hypotheses. The training observation sheet, for example, left spaces for describing "high points," "low points," and the "emotional tone" of the training session, as well as spaces for describing the purpose of the training session and the nature of the intern involvement. On the back of the sheet were spaces for observer comments and for hypotheses about the instructional session, its participants, or the 1975 CMTI itself if the session were taken as a microcosm of the CMTI.

The informal event report forms were more simple with spaces to describe the kind of meeting it was, the composition of the group, and what happened. Identifiers such as date, time, place, and observer were, of course, included on both forms. The simple forms took considerable time to construct. They were originally elaborate, but over time and successive drafts in the late spring, they became increasingly simplified. In a sense, this came about as our trust of the three constructors as observers grew.

From my perspective, the forms turned out to be efficient and well focused. Quick scans, for example, could be taken of the high and low points over a day's or a week's training. Similarly the emotional tone, instructional purpose, and the nature of intern involvement could be contrasted over time. The hypotheses generated from each event would prove to be particularly interesting as we drew meaning from our descriptions of the 1975 CMTI. We all later understood, far better than when Iliana, Reggie, and Craig were making these forms, that their dirty work would become the basis of our dirty fun in trying to understand the event and its circumstantial influence on participants.

A fourth graduate student was soon hired because, in part, she had skills and talents that none of us had. Wendy Saul was a bright, confident, verbal graduate student in the school of education who was also a writer and published poet. I don't know much about Wendy's background, but you can probably image how her talents would stand out in a school of education. Wendy took education seriously, but she also combined a gregarious nature with a bemused attitude towards educators. Bob Tabachnick and I hoped Wendy could get us beyond our arid academic prose, especially as we tried to write our survey questionnaires. Although we knew what we wanted in the survey questions, it became Wendy's job to construct the surveys to make them more closely resemble the everyday language of those we hoped would give some thought to answering the questions. This was quite a task —in volume and complexity as well as in craft. Without going into all the details, what we started to produce were five separate surveys, each covering five possible perspectives that could be taken towards teaching.

ARRIVING AT A METAPHORIC LANGUAGE FOR ANALYSIS

After a few extended discussions among the five professors and myself about the purposes, assumptions, beliefs, and hypotheses about the 1975 CMTI, we were quickly forced to consider how we would actually talk about the development of the interns' perspectives towards teaching. Although I can't recreate our discussions and the permutations and combinations of arguments, concerns, and possibilities, I can tell you we conceived five fairly well defined perspectives towards teaching. We considered these perspectives to be comparatively distinct from one another (but not necessarily independent). They were related in part to the goals of the Teacher Corps and to the intent of the 1975 CMTI. They were also relevant to the concerns we were bringing to an analysis of how student teachers were constructing their views about teaching.

The metaphoric language we eventually chose for these five views towards teaching were accompanied by some cryptic definitions. The five perspectives and their definitions were:

1. *Teaching as technique,* that is teaching is applying specific instructional and management skills;
2. *Teaching as curriculum design,* that is teaching is designing and creating learning materials and environments over time;
3. *Teaching as personal development,* that is teaching is having students recognize and reach their highest potential;
4. *Teaching as community action,* that is teaching is contributing to the goals and aspirations of the community in which the school is placed and the children live; and
5. *Teaching as organizational behavior,* that is teaching is an institutional function with expectations and norms that are to be understood, worked in, and changed if necessary.

To consider these five metaphors as our best crack at understanding how student teachers developed perspectives towards teaching was just too restricting for Tom and Gary. They wanted to wait for more evidence upon which we could construct a more autonomous, consistent, and less ambiguous set of characteristics upon which to hang our eventual judgments of the professional impact of the 1975 CMTI on the interns. Again, I eventually overruled them by fiat rather than by persuasion. I argued that between the six of us we already had experience, far more than what the 1975 CMTI would offer and certainly plenty with which to debate, argue, construct, and reconstruct a set of categories to try out in an evaluative study. I was anticipating that we would eventually arrive at other categories. But I didn't want to lose this opportunity to force us to consider before the investigation what we might find and to articulate as clearly as we were able how we would describe certain circumstances given what we knew before the study. As it has turned out, our pursuit of what we really mean by ''the development of professional perspectives'' or by ''the socialization of student teachers into the teaching profession'' continued over the duration of this study and well beyond.

I want to pause here to point out a curious professional attribute. We all had strong beliefs and strong ambitions about investigative methodology. It was method which captured our professional imagination. We imagined our success if we developed a new investigative method for evaluating educational programs. In our meetings it was difficult to modify our ambitions and beliefs about investigative method. We certainly were not prepared to revise our ambitions about method through discourse and argument. All of us were pointing our major energies, our strongest feelings, and our professional egos towards the development of a new research method.

Ironically, however, when we were discussing what we understood through experience, we were much more inclined to listen. When we were drawing upon the professional knowledge we had gained and the intelligence we could muster about our field of teacher education, we were likely to adapt, to redefine, and to reanalyze our own perceptions. Upon reflection this fascinates me now, because we could much more easily adapt what we had learned from experience than what we had gained from reading and critical analysis of others' work. The views we had built through reading were more difficult to change through dialogue and discussion than the views we had built through experience. This leads me to paraphrase what Barry MacDonald (1974) has claimed about experience. Although our experience cannot be denied, the lessons we learn from experience may be more capable of being altered than the lessons we learn from respected professional sources.

Thus, the real battles were won or lost over research method; and they were won more on authority than on argument. The real debates, however, were on the nature of professional development, and on the possible evidence for a socialization process into teaching. In the weeks preceding the study, what evaluators euphemistically call developing the study design actually became making public our understanding of teacher development. Although no one was entirely committed to the categories we eventually arrived at for describing interns' perspectives towards teaching, they did represent our best thinking during the two months of discussion and planning of this evaluation study.

I'm not certain we could have done better if we were given more time. We took much time as it was, meeting for two six hour discussion sessions a week for the first month and shorter but more frequent sessions after that. In addition, I know that I spent much time between meetings thinking about what had been said, studying the notes that were shared, and preparing for the next meeting. The others, too, have reported that this period, especially the first month, was one of the more challenging periods in their professional lives. I am suggesting that we were challenged not only to create a research method, but to arrive, through discourse, at the best approximation of our understanding of the phenomenon to be investigated. It was a time, in short, when we were engaged in interpretation of our experience, more than at any other time in the study. Although we had very little data to interpret, we had much previous experience that required analysis as we placed our evaluation study within the context of the 1975 CMTI.

FIGHTING WITH THE INSTRUCTIONAL TEAM

The context of the 1975 CMTI began to cause us more and more grief as time went on. More accurately, we were causing grief to the instructional leaders, and correspondingly to the Teachers Corps sponsors of the event. It was at least two months before we received any materials from the instructional leaders of CMTI: Ron Corwin and Roy Edelfelt, who were to teach organizational theory; and Bruce Joyce and Marcia Weil, who were to teach models of teaching. This was understandable since they, too, had similar time constraints as we did and were faced with a considerable challenge. They were to design the instruction of relatively radical (organizational theory) or new (models of teaching) content to 250 student teachers from around the country, all of whom were just entering the first days of a two-year training program. Two instructional teams of about 15 members each had to be chosen and trained, materials had to be produced, the living conditions had to be arranged and their respective instructional programs had to be resolved.

By the way, the ironies of introducing students to organizational theory while being responsible for organizing their entire living arrangements were not lost on Ron Corwin and Roy Edelfelt. From the first materials we received, it was clear that they were aware of the ironies caused by the instructional content and the instructional context. They emphasized that the 1975 CMTI could itself be a microcosm of some of the principles of organizational theory and action.

Ron and Roy's materials came well after we had stated the purposes and assumptions of our study, and after we had developed a research method and chosen a study design in which to evaluate the 1975 CMTI. Nevertheless, the materials did help in our final identification of perspectives towards teaching that we anticipated to be central to the professional development of the interns and that would also be influenced by their 1975 CMTI experiences. The objectives, aims, and general procedures listed were enough for us to check our anticipations of what the 1975 CMTI would look like from the perspective of the student teachers. About the time that we received the description of the intentions of the organizational theory strand, we sent Ron Corwin and Roy Edelfelt our evaluation intentions and study design. We were not prepared for their intense reaction against our design.

Years later I still do not understand what their concerns were, but I can relate what they said they were. Also, years after our study has been completed, and after getting to know both Ron and Roy a little better, I can interpret some of what was not said but perhaps was felt at the time.

Our adversaries were no pushovers. Ron Corwin was a well-known sociologist who had written the most respected and only published evaluation of the Teachers Corps program. Ron Corwin's study was at least a partial basis upon which Bill Smith and Jim Steffensen decided Teacher Corps should go into inservice teacher education, reduce the number of interns per project, and have a Corps Member Training Institute. Ron is a quiet, self-effacing person who becomes an articulate and very capable sociologist when placed behind a lecturn, or in the company of his peers.

In personage and demeanor, Roy Edelfelt is far more imposing than Ron. Roy looks like a bully with a square jaw, wide shoulders and body, is well over six feet all, and always carries himself as if he were an army colonel. Ron, about six inches shorter, seems to be in a perpetual slouch. Roy had worked closely with Ron on his study of the Teachers Corps as a representative of the Washington staff of the National Education Association which was a cosponsor of the study. Roy had authored many articles on teacher education and staff development. He had been on the faculty of the Michigan State School of Education before becoming the NEA national director of inservice activities and teacher education.

Although both Ron and Roy had well-deserved national reputations, they were relatively inexperienced in producing the kind of instructional program required for the 1975 CMTI. Just as we had done some research but were inexperienced as evaluators, they had taught in colleges and universities, but not in a context like the 1975 CMTI. What surprised me, however, and what I still find interesting, is that they were experienced in field study and program evaluation, but their responses to our study design never reflected any understanding from their past experience. They responded only as instructors, not as experienced evaluators.

Basically, their expressed concern about our study design was that we were planning to evaluate the impact of the 1975 CMTI in terms that went beyond their instructional goals. Of course, they were right. Much of our planning went into understanding how the 1975 CMTI would be related to the remainder of the interns' training and performance as teachers. Likewise, we considered it important to relate the CMTI not only to the Teachers Corps sponsors but also to the teacher education profession at large. In short, just as Ron Corwin had directed his study of the Teachers Corps program to federal managers and sociology theorists outside of the Teachers Corps program, so, too, were we addressing concerns, interests, and theories of teacher education that went beyond the instructional goals of the 1975 CMTI.

Ron and Roy wanted us to place much more attention on their goal statements and their process intentions. They saw little overt attention to their instructional goals in our design and nearly no relation between our emphasis on the socialization of teachers and the development of professional perspectives and their purpose to have the interns become more knowledgeable students of the organization milieu(s) in which they work. They did not believe our study had much chance of arriving at a favorable judgment or, even, of being fair, accurate, and sensitive to their primary instructional aims. Furthermore, they saw the interviews, observations, photographs, and especially the surveys as being major interventions upon the instructional environment which they had intended to create.

Their outrage was clear, pointed, and immediately taken to the top. Not only would they not participate in the study, but they did not want this study to take place on the same grounds in which they worked. The study, they said, was for us, not for them, and could be (probably would be) counterproductive to their primary aim to develop an organizational context in which the students could become major initiators. To have such an autonomous, independent evaluation going on at the same time was a clear violation in their eyes, and they were going to have none of it.

Conflict had begun. Argument, persuasion, and compromise were now obviously necessary if the study were to be performed and completed with some sense of professional pride. It became quickly clear that Bill Smith and Jim Steffensen would not take Ron and Roy's demands at face value, nor did they consider our design to be written in stone. In effect, they told Ron, Roy, and me that, as men of reason we should accept that an evaluation study would be performed as well as an instructional program implemented. Although Bill and Jim liked the idea that we evaluators had placed the 1975 CMTI into a larger context and intended to address a wider professional audience, they also acknowledged that perhaps we had gotten carried away in our enthusiasm for investigative method. They left it up to Ron and Roy and me to resolve the fine points. This wasn't easy. We never did resolve our differences and only barely buried our animosity by the time the CMTI started.

We first tried to resolve our differences over the phone and that proved fruitless. We then met in hotel rooms, and we didn't get very far there, either. We had less than a month before the 1975 CMTI was to begin and no feeling of accommodation had developed. By this time, however, it was clear to me that our intentions to conduct the surveys at least three times a week just wouldn't be acceptable even though the time-series technique we were using required about 20 points as a minimum for analysis. I understood and respected their instructional design, but was not going to reduce my attempt to address concerns of the profession at large about the issues raised by the 1975 CMTI.

Finally, Teacher Corps stepped in more directly. With a little more than three weeks before the CMTI was to begin, Bill and Jim had me attend a two day training session in Boston that Ron and Roy were conducting for their chosen instructors. Although one reason for my attending that session was to gain a more definite idea of what would be done at the CMTI and to get to know the participants, the major purpose for my presence there was for Ron, Roy, and me to come to a final resolution. Not only was there considerable time set aside for us to meet independent from the training activities (I was not, for example, to introduce or refer to our study design at all with others at the meeting), but a true-blue experienced (and expensive) mediator had been employed. The mediator was Matt Miles, a well-known consultant, author, and researcher in educational organizational change, a man of impeccable patience and quiet determination for compromise.

We met more than once those two days, for a couple of hours and it was not your normal academic discourse. I remember the four of us sitting in a fairly large suite, Ron and Roy in straight back chairs facing me in a soft easy chair, with Matt literally between us, seated sideways along the line of sight. I could lean into the soft cushions, knowing I couldn't lose that much. (Besides having the contract, didn't I have five university professors behind me?) Ron and Roy, for good reason, were more uptight and aggressive. They had more to lose, given their position, and less authority in this case. I had brought drafts of the survey questionnaires as well as definitions of the terms we were using.

The peculiar thing I remember is that Ron and Roy would not speak directly to me but to Matt who was then to relay their message to me, a few feet from them. It may not have been a classic form of mediation, but it is the closest I have come to formal negotiation. It included some considerable bargaining by Matt between sessions.

Of course, the conflict was eventually resolved, but it was resolved mainly because we all knew that Bill Smith, the director of the Teachers Corps, would not allow this to go on indefinitely. Included in our agreement was that some language of the survey questionnaires was to be changed, and specific hypotheses about the 1975 CMTI were to be stated. The questionnaires were to be given twice a week (at the beginning and end of each week) for no more than fifteen minutes at the beginning of the large group session which started each week and after the small group sessions which would end each week. We were to have a half hour to introduce our study to the instructional staff the weekend before the 1975 CMTI began, and a briefer time to introduce the study to the interns at the first general meeting.

The observers were acceptable to the extent that they blended in with the instructional setting, and were to be removed at the time that they were considered to be interventive or counterproductive to the environment being created. The photographer was acceptable to the extent that she did not interfere with the mood of the instructional setting. Interviews were tolerated if they were conducted on open time and did not interfere with any planned activities. The observation and interview guidelines were no real problem because, as Ron and Roy kept saying, they had little focus on their instructional program and thus were largely irrelevant to their concerns. If an evaluation study were to be directed to their own instructional aims and objectives, that would be the responsibility of Ron and Roy.

Thus, the final barrier was overcome in Boston; all we evaluators had to do was to complete the final versions of our questionnaire and make sure we were ready for the 1975 CMTI. You may ask, by the way, what were the reactions of Bruce Joyce and Marcia Weil (the other instructional leaders) during this time? The answer is they heard about the problems our study team was having with Ron and Roy, but they didn't participate one way or another. No materials were sent to us by them. (They said if we were interested in finding out the content and working assumptions of their instruction, we could read their book). They said they respected our autonomy, had no great pains with the study design as they understood it, and expected a fair, objective, outside accounting of the 1975 CMTI by us.

In discussions on the phone and in the few meetings we had in person, Bruce always deferred to us as the independent evaluators, whose study design and requests of time (within limits) would be respected. "No big deal," he kept saying; but then we never received any materials or instructional design from Bruce Joyce and Marcia Weil, either. My guess is that Bruce heard about the conflicts we were having with Ron and Roy with some bemusement. But to me, Bruce was always the gentleman: polite, deferring, gracious, and supremely confident about the distinctions between our two roles. Much of that was to change before this study ended. Bruce said that anything that was decided by us could be worked into his instructional scheme. When Bruce heard that we had agreed to four survey readings for each of the two-week sessions (at the beginning and end of each week), he wasn't too happy. But he accepted the agreement along with the other agreements on observations, interviews, and the photographer.

COMPLETING THE STUDY DESIGN

About two weeks after my meeting with Ron and Roy in Boston and a week before the 1975 CMTI was to begin, we had a completed version of our study design. It was placed in a three-ring notebook, titled "The Role of CMTI in the Development of Participants' Perspectives Towards the Teaching Profession," and dated June 26, 1975. We made fifty copies of this study design, including one for each of the approximately thirty instructors of the two instructional strands of CMTI and more than ten for members of the Washington staff of Teachers Corps. Including appendices such as the survey instruments, interview and observation forms, it was about seventy pages long with colored dividers separating the various appendices. The body of the study design was 23 pages long and included the rationale, the major purposes, the underlying assumptions, and working hypotheses of the study, as well as a 10 page description of the methodology.

We described four major purposes of the study:

1. To describe the training procedures and informal contacts that make up the Corps Member Training Institute;
2. To describe the development of participants' perspectives towards certain professional concerns (i.e. the nature of the internship, the nature of teaching, and the reasons for school success and school failure);
3. To determine to what extent the development of participants' perspectives may be attributed to specific features of the CMTI;
4. To continue the description of the ongoing development of their professional perspectives after the participants leave CMTI.

The fourth purpose, by the way, indicated that a final decision had been reached by the Teacher Corps that we would continue our study for the year following the 1975 CMTI.

The methodology was described for achieving each purpose. These descriptions included brief discussions of the population, the sampling techniques, the data collection procedures, and the data analytic procedures. Appendices in this three-ring notebook included:

1. Definitions of terms such as *professional development* or *teaching as technique;*
2. Descriptions of the themes which the photographer would pursue and of how photography would try to capture those themes;
3. The questionnaires and the pool of items from which the questionnaires were drawn;
4. The data recording and analysis procedures for handling the results of the questionnaires;
5. The tests for determining the reliability of the questionnaires;
6. The interview and observation forms;
7. The schedule for the questionnaires, interviews, and observations; and
8. Identification of the staff of the evaluation team.

I was proud of the study design shown in that three-ring notebook. Much had been accomplished in a short time. Five school of education professors, myself, four graduate students, and a photographer had developed a consistent plan for capturing and analyzing the anticipated dynamics of the 1975 CMTI. We had started with no experience in performing evaluation studies and little experience in working with one another, and had completed a public document that I knew could compare with those I had seen from much more expert groups.

In some ways it was better. We had spent considerable time in arguing about a language and a perspective that could express our assumptions about the role of this event within the professional lives of the student teachers. In less than three months, we had found a new attitude towards evaluation (illuminative evaluation from the Parlett and Hamilton paper), had identified a theoretical overview of the event and its position in the professional lives of its participants (socialization theory), had constructed a language with which to express our anticipations and our findings (perspectives towards teaching), and had found and adapted an overall study design (time-series design) that could integrate naturalistic field inquiry methods with scored questionnaires and their quantitative analyses. We had worked photography into the overall scheme and had developed, pilot tested, and completed a set of questionnaires that appeared to be thought-provoking for those who answered them.

We all felt a sense of triumph. Some of our pride was earned, some was not. We had experienced the excitement of dialogue and discourse, of fundamental disagreement accompanied by articulate explanation and verbal adaptation. We had used what we do best in schools of education (talk and persuade), and we produced a public product which we could defend with some pride. Our experience had proven to be valuable in drawing up our study design. Talk, discourse, persuasion, and interaction had in this circumstance proven to be tangibly productive. We had a product that was a direct result of our discussions.

We had another reason to be excited. Since we had responded to this professional challenge, we could now anticipate new professional opportunities. Professors who had not had that much opportunity for extra funding beyond their regular salaries saw how simple it all was. Pay, professional advancement, and research opportunity were recognized to be all tied together. Our quiet professional excitement about the potential for our own professional gain, could hardly be measured. You see, we knew we couldn't miss.

We realized within a few days of planning our study that the challenge had nearly no risks for us. Whether the 1975 CMTI were a success or a failure, whether it were dull or lively, whether it induced pleasant conflict or painful harmony between the various participants, was no matter to us. Our challenge was only to capture what happened and try to explain it. The instructional teams, on the other hand, could fail. Indeed, given the nature of the task and the complexity and newness of the enterprise, some failure (as well as some success) seemed inevitable. We evaluators, however, had only to produce a description and analysis of what happened. Although we had good reasons to feel triumphant about our study design, overcoming professional risks was not one of them.

EXPERT OR NOVICE?

As you know, this is just the beginning of my story. We haven't begun our study yet, but much of the study has been done. The next month in my story, July, 1975, when the CMTI occurs, is when the data will be collected. That will be, for me, the most pressured time of the entire study, since all evidence about the CMTI must be collected then. We will begin to construct our understanding about the 1975 CMTI, and what role it may play in the professional lives of the student teachers who are there. But much of that understanding will depend on the work we did in the first three months. Thus important questions can be raised about educational program evaluation this early in my story.

First, though, what kind of job do you think we have done so far? Given the sketchy details of my story, what do you think of our approach, our study design, our data gathering instruments, our focus on interns' perspectives towards teaching? How well do you think we have performed our study up to now? I trust you can answer that for yourself; so I'll tell you what I think. I think we neophytes in the business of educational program evaluation did a credible job in planning this evaluation study. I still would stack up what we accomplished in three months with what I have seen experienced evaluators produce when given a full year! The point is not that we were perfect (heaven forbid) but that we were credible, and that is what bothers me. If we were credible, why can't anyone be credible? We had no evaluation experience and very little research experience, so what experience, if any, is necessary?

One answer I draw from this part of my story focuses on the relationship between experience in the educational phenomenon under investigation and experience in educational investigation. We were experts in the former but novices in the latter. So what are the definitions of expert and novice in this case? It is not easy to determine how experience in the phenomena was related to our inexperience in evaluation method, but I can bring up some examples that begin to clarify what happened.

Clearly the experienced expert among us in investigative method was Tom Romberg, and one of the neophytes in investigative method was Tom Popkewitz. However, while Tom Romberg was interested in exploring alternative investigative methods, Tom Popkewitz was not. On the other hand, Tom Popkewitz was an expert in teacher education; he had previously run the student teaching program in the school of education. In this area, Tom Romberg was the novice. Yet, Tom Popkewitz was searching for something better than what appeared to him to be simplistic notions of socialization put forth by people like Dan Lortie; Tom Romberg considered Lortie to hold the best view about how teachers learn about teaching. In both examples, the expert was less comfortable with the state of the art, the accuracy and perceptiveness of his area of expertise. I don't intend to arrive at a general rule here but I do want to consider what past experience can bring to an investigative inquiry. It can bring certitude of what is known but discomfort with its accuracy and credibility.

Who contributed more to this study, who was involved more in this study, who was affected more by this study, Tom Romberg or Tom Popkewitz? Although Tom Romberg, our supercilious expert in research methodology gave us the basis for our continued discussions on investigative method (the Parlett-Hamilton paper), and the formal study design and data analysis proceedure (time-series), the answers in the long run are clearly Tom Popkewitz. Tom Popkewitz contributed more, he was involved more, and he was affected more by this study.

Our choice of the socialization metaphor was clearly due to the persuasion of Tom Popkewitz. From the beginning, Tom kept us focused on how to depict and how to understand what student teachers were really getting from their experiences. He was highly involved in our early discussions and debates, questioning and searching for something better than what was available in the literature on teacher education or, more generally, the literature on professional socialization. Thus, by the tenth week, Tom Popkewitz had influenced our resolution to focus on the perspectives towards teaching developed by the student teachers, and the underlying assumptions that we had developed over that time. Furthermore, as I have said repeatedly, our topic for dialogue was the nature of student teaching (not investigative method) and here Tom was highly engaged, aggressive yet flexible enough to reach for explanations better than the ones we had or the ones we could find from previous investigations or conjectural literature.

As for being affected by our involvement in the study, there is no contest at all. Tom Popkewitz changed more in professional image during the period of this study than any of us. Tom Romberg remained the knowledgeable and well informed expert on research method. But Tom Popkewitz became the tough sociologically learned educator looking for the underlying meaning in educational affairs.

These personal trends towards contribution and involvement were clearly evidenced within the planning stage of our study, within the first three months of our eighteen month study. This leads me to the next question raised by our evaluation study: What is the relationship between the planning for an educational investigation and the investigation itself?

The role of past experience and thought about the phenomenon under investigation is central and crucial to the design of a *successful* program evaluation. But, even if the planning phase of the study had been influenced by what we supposed was true from previous experience, to what extent did that influence the performance of our entire study? That question can't be answered by this part of my story, but it is a critical question to ask. Clearly our experience was essential in constructing our study design, and clearly this design will be a factor in determining the nature and substance of the data we collect and the results we report. This question is critical, in part because of many investigators' claim that the results of their studies are determined entirely by the data collected.

The possibility that this planning stage may have had a central position in the performance, interpretation, and understanding of this study bothers me. In particular, I keep asking myself, why weren't we able to engage in dialogue on investigative method? Because of our inexperience in investigation, what we learned from authorities was treated with more authenticity than what we could generate ourselves. Our understanding of research method would not allow for transformation through dialogue. Ironically, we placed our professional emphasis on method rather than on the substance of what could be learned from this evaluation study. We had decided that it was through the development of a new method that our professional reputation would be built, rather than through the development of a richer understanding of how a student teacher becomes a teacher. What was there about our own profession that socialized us in this way? If we were to improve our professional reputations, we understood it would be through method rather than through the substance of our findings. That may mean something to the state of the art of educational inquiry as well as to what it means to be a professional educator.

Novices in evaluation can accomplish a thoroughly professional job to the extent that they are willing to engage in dialogue. Contacts in investigative techniques matter. For example, we couldn't have done as well without Parlett and Hamilton or Glass and his associates' work. But that was on investigative technique rather than on the substance of the investigation. The critical distinction between novice and expert, however, was not on research method or evaluation experience. It was on the experience in the process to be investigated, and on the opportunity and the ability of the investigators to reflect upon their own experiences.

This brings me to my last question. Were we qualified, and if so, why? As you may have noticed from my story, the question never really came up with our Teacher Corps sponsors, nor, even, with Ron and Roy. Clearly our numbers had been called, it became our turn as teacher educators to perform a program evaluation. The lottery, as secret as it was, had worked. We took our turn with some vigor and we became, for better or worse professional, paid, expert evaluators of a federally sponsored national teacher education effort. The effort stood alone—in time, circumstance, and experience. It was the expensive result of a policy decision, and it would be judged by those touched by the policy as well as by those overseeing the program policymakers. Not only were we funded to evaluate this effort in terms of the Teacher Corps program, but we were given full responsibility and near autonomy for the effort. Except for the phone call from Paul Collins, the budget meeting with Jim Steffensen, and the tough negotiations with Ron Corwin and Roy Edelfelt, we were on our own for the planning months. If you have had experience in teacher education, you could probably have done as well.

A stinger exists in this last observation. If designing educational research were a professional craft different from the education of teachers, then why were we, who had so little experience, successful? Maybe we were experienced in research without having served on a research project. Is it possible that teacher education is in some significant ways the same function as educational research? Perhaps we are making two professions—teacher education and educational research—out of one. The stinger to this possibility is personally felt. Since directing the 1975 CMTI Impact Study, I became an evaluation expert as did my team members. But I'm not so sure that honor is not counterproductive to our shared educational aspirations. Our expertise reduces the possibilities for other teacher educators to be similarly engaged in future evaluation studies. My story suggests that evaluation expertise, however, is determined by the educational experiences of the evaluator, not by previous engagements with research method. If so, the almost atrocious variety that we now experience as evaluation experts must be distributed more widely. Furthermore, if evaluation were nearly the same function as teacher education, would it not also be nearly the same function as teaching? Investigative and educational opportunities that some of us experience may have to be distributed to other teachers as well as to other teacher educators. Anyone want to suggest a lottery?

REFERENCES

Borges, Jorge Luis. (1962). The Babylon Lottery. In Jorge Luis Borges *Ficciones.* New York: The Grove Press.

Bower, C., Padio, W., & Glass, G. (1974). *TMS: Two Fortran IV Programs for Analysis of Time-Series Experiments.* Boulder, CO: Laboratory of Educational Research, University of Colorado.

Corwin, Ronald G. (1973). *Reform and Organizational Survival: The Teacher Corps as an Instrument of Educational Change.* New York: Wiley-Interscience.

Fox, G. T., Grant, C., Lufler, H. S., Melnick, S., Mitchell, N., & Thompson, F. (1978, June). *The Residual Impact of the 1975 CMTI.* Madison, WI: University of Wisconsin–Madison. Prepared under contract to Teacher Corps, Washington.

Fox, G. T., Grant, C., Popkewitz, T., Romberg, T., Tabachnick, B., & Wehlage, G. (1976, September). *1975 CMTI Impact Study: Technical Reports Numbers 1-21.* Madison, WI: University of Wisconsin–Madison. Prepared as part of Teacher Corps, Office of Education contract No. 300-75-0100 (University of Nebraska–Omaha).

Glaser, B. G., & Strauss, A. L. (1967). *The Discovery of Grounded Theory.* Chicago, IL: Aldine.

Glass, G. V., Wilson, V. L., & Gottman, J. M. (1975). *Design and Analysis of Time-Series Experiments*. Boulder, CO: Colorado Associated University Press.

Joyce, B., & Weil, M. (1972). *Models of Teaching*. Englewood Cliffs, NJ: Prentice-Hall.

MacDonald, Barry. (1974). Evaluation and the Control of Education. In B. MacDonald and R. Walker (Eds.), *Innovation, Evaluation, Research and the Problem of Control*. East Anglia, England: SAFARI Project Interim Papers, Centre for Applied Research in Education.

Marsh, David, & Lyons, Margaret. (1974, July). *A Study of Teacher Training at Sixth Cycle Teacher Corps Projects. Volume I. Methodology and Findings*. Los Angeles, CA: Pacific T&TA Corporation. U.S. Departmentof Health, Education and Welfare, Contract No. CIC-0-73-5174.

Parlett, M., & Hamilton, D. (1976). Evaluation as Illumination: A New Approach to the Study of Innovatory Programs. In G. Glass (Ed.), *Evaluation Studies Review Annual, Volume I*. Beverly Hills, CA: Sage Publications.

Popkewitz, Thomas. (1975, November). Reform as Political Discourse, A Case Study. *School Review, 84* (1), 43–69.

Popkewitz, T., & Wehlage, G. (1977). Schooling as work: An approach to research and evaluation. *The Teachers College Record, 79,* 69–86.

Tabachnick, J., & Lemes, B. (1975, September). *Together: A Photographic Essay*. Part One of Interim Report, 1975 CMTI Impact Study. Madison, WI: University of Wisconsin.

10

The Case for Extended Programs of Initial Teacher Preparation*

George Denemark
University of Kentucky

Norma Nutter
Ohio University

INTRODUCTION

Public education in the United States is currently experiencing a crisis in public confidence. Parents, legislators, a broad range of special interest groups, the news media, and the general public are questioning whether our schools are teaching children the basic skills necessary for their adult lives and whether they are maintaining proper discipline. At the same time, public schools have increasingly been expected to solve major problems of social equity (for example, education of the handicapped, racial and ethnic minorities, and linguistic minorities) and a host of other social problems, ranging from alcoholism to drug abuse to consumer skills.

In the words of Ernest Boyer, former U.S. Commissioner of Education:

> ...as the authority of other institutions has eroded, we ask teachers to stand in for parents, supplement the police, and combat racial and class discrimination. They are called upon not only to teach the basics, but monitor the playgrounds, build respect for authority, counsel the delinquent, impose discipline and be moral mentors to our youth. And when they fall short anywhere along the line, we condemn teachers for not meeting our idealized expectations.

* Based on a manuscript prepared initially for presentation to the Forum of Education Organization Leaders, Washington, DC and circulated subsequently as a publication of the ERIC Clearinghouse on Teacher Education in February, 1980

203

In consequence, confidence in teachers has declined and teacher frustration has increased. And as teachers organize themselves and go on
strike, frustration of the public grows more intense.

The teaching profession is caught in a vicious cycle, spiraling down-
ward. Rewards are few, morale is low, the best teachers are bailing out,
and the supply of good recruits is drying up. Simply stated, the profession of teaching in this nation is imperiled. (Boyer, 1982)

As the training arm of the teaching profession, teacher education must
respond to this crisis. However, a number of obstacles hinder our efforts to
respond. This chapter deals with one of the main obstacles—inadequate
resources for teacher education—and, in particular, with the inadequate
time available for effective teacher education within the existing institutional patterns.

The importance of education to societal and individual well-being
demands that teaching, which many view as a profession in terms of its
social significance, become a profession in reality. We believe that a critical
element in establishing professional status for teaching is an adequate base
of knowledge which, when properly transmitted to the practitioner, elevates
the level of practice from the personal to the professional and guarantees a
level of safe practice.

Teacher education does have a substantial and growing base of knowledge to support a professional level of initial teacher preparation. However,
the major obstacle to the preparation of teachers at a level appropriate to
beginning professionals is inadequate "life space" (time, facilities, personnel, instructional and research materials, or other significant program resources). This insufficiency has contributed to the mounting public criticism
of our schools and even to the diverting of inservice education from its principal functions to the task of correcting serious deficiencies in the initial
preparation of teachers.

As we examine the case for extended programs of initial teacher preparation, we will emphasize the base of knowledge supporting teacher education, as derived from research, professional wisdom, and logical analysis.
The discussion primarily addresses programmatic or curricular implications
for teacher education, although we recognize the significance of other factors such as selection and admission procedures, student performance standards, faculty qualifications, and the reward system of higher education.
The chapter concludes with a list of several issues related to extended
teacher-preparation programs that still need to be resolved.

NEEDS AND PRESENT PROGRAM INADEQUACIES

Teachers do not now receive a fully professional preservice education. Their
preparation is not comparable in length or rigor to that of most recognized

professions, nor even that of other semiprofessions, if we consider the time alloted to strictly professional studies. More important, their education is not grounded in the basic concept that marks a truly professional education: that the graduate must have attained a level of competence sufficient to guarantee safe practice with clients.

The concept of the minimum safety level for professional practice is more than a commendable sentiment. If teacher educators were able to adhere to it, we would begin all considerations of initial teacher preparation by asking, "What should beginning teachers know and at what level of proficiency?" and determine the content and length of programs accordingly. Instead, we now begin with a given length and select content accordingly.

Present Inadequacies

Preservice teacher education aims somewhere near a level of competence sufficient for the new teachers' survival in the classroom with the least possible harm to students. When we speak of deficiencies in the preservice education of teachers, we are not making a statement about teachers, but about the failure of teacher-education institutions to serve teachers adequately. The dramatic, violent failures that cause beginning teachers to resign in midyear are dehumanizing not only to students, but also to young teachers who want to succeed—who try, but simply cannot determine how to succeed fast enough.

An even worse outcome is the ill-prepared beginning teacher who learns to survive in the classroom through inferior methods. Most new practitioners will achieve at least the minimum safety level through trial and error learning, knowledge that colleagues have time to impart, and clues and directions for professional performance recalled from their preservice program. At present, one of the declared purposes of continuing and inservice education for teachers is remediation—a purpose that tacitly assumes beginning teachers are less than fully qualified.

Several factors act to disguise or soften many of the harmful effects of inadequate preservice preparation: (a) the traditional structure of the public school puts strong pressure on beginning teachers to conceal their inadequacies and, within limits, permits that concealment (Ladd, 1966); (b) educational failure is incremental rather than sudden; (c) the total responsibility for any child's education is vested in many people; (d) children are somewhat durable; and (e) most beginning teachers do survive and reach an acceptable level of teaching proficiency. Smith, Cohen, and Pearl (1969) believe that deficiencies in initial teacher preparation have especially severe consequences for disadvantaged students, who are often taught by beginning teachers with unrealistic expectations and little understanding of their pupils.

The concept of a safe level of beginning teaching skills is usually viewed from the perspective of primary and secondary clients, and rightly so. Children, parents, and the general public are entitled to have fully competent professionals in charge of such a vital service as classroom teaching. However, other persons also have a right to expect competence—administrators, who depend on the teacher-education system and who must take the beginning teacher's credentials largely at face value; and fellow teachers, who suffer with and as a result of an inadequately-prepared colleague. Above all, practitioners themselves are entitled to receive a fully professional preservice education, so as to begin their first solo teaching assignment with both the knowledge and the skills to perform at the minimum safety level.

We know that beginning teachers suffer a good deal of anxiety stemming primarily from the discrepancy between their ideal goals and the actual techniques they find themselves using in their practice (Jersild, 1966). We also know that many of them regard the professional component of their education, except for student teaching, as having little relevance to the reality of classrooms (Hermanowicz, 1966). And we know that the biggest surprises beginning teachers say they find are (a) their lack of preparation to accommodate the broad range of student abilities and interests, (b) the fact that students are less enthusiastic than anticipated, (c) the enormity of management and control problems, and (d) the demands teaching makes on their time and energies (Hermanowicz).

A Personal Rather Than Professional Base

Most beginners do survive their first years in the classroom and become teachers who clearly are not incompetent and who do not damage students. Their success under the less than satisfactory conditions of their preparation for and induction to teaching is greatly to their own and their colleagues' credit. But does the inadequacy of their original preparation have any further consequences for them?

From his sociological studies of teachers and teaching, Lortie (1975) concluded that a major dimension of teaching practice was its strongly personal basis. In this case, *personal* implies not simply that teaching involves humane contact between persons, but that an inordinate amount of the responsibility for what happens in the classroom resides in the teacher as an individual, rather than as a representative of a profession. Instructional decisions are personal decisions based on personal observation, and the dominant justification for using and continuing to use any specific practice is personal pragmatism: "It works for me." This personal autonomy is different from professional autonomy that says, "We have determined that this works and I have determined that this is what my client's situation calls for." Lortie found that, as a consequence of the personal basis of power and control in the classroom, teachers see themselves as having no clear, concrete authority for educational practice and so lapse further into individualism and a self-defeating derogation of education. Even when teachers can see definite growth and learning among their students, they are reluctant to take credit for it because they are not sure that the gains would not have occurred without their intervention.

Because teachers lack a professional culture transmitted by a professional education system, accountability—conceived either negatively or positively and either narrowly or broadly—is a difficult concept. Teachers cannot think of education as a group effort with norms, based on knowledge and consensus, that one can reasonably expect—and be expected—to meet (Lortie, 1975). They commonly judge their professional education as "too theoretical." However, analyzing their specific complaints in light of conventional definitions of theory reveals that teachers are not objecting to theoretical studies per se; rather, *theoretical* is synonymous in their minds with *unrealistic* or *contrary to experience*. The problem is that teachers receive lofty official goals without the means to reach them (Hermanowicz, 1966; Lortie, 1975).

Both beginning and experienced teachers consistently point to two areas of need in their professional practice—discipline and motivation (Adams, 1979; Cruickshank, Kennedy, & Myers, 1974; Gorton, 1973; Ingersoll, 1976; Kennedy, Cruickshank, & Myers, 1976). Pigge (1978) found that teachers gave their teacher-education institution more credit for developing proficiencies in areas the teachers rated as less needed than in areas they rated as highly needed.

To prospective teachers, their education is a matter affecting the quality of life. The burden on teacher-education institutions is, first, to provide a firmer and more reasonable idea of what teachers can accomplish and, second, to provide the means to accomplish it. We question whether these goals can be achieved within the present system.

Certainly, teacher educators cannot blame all the faults and failures of their programs on lack of time and resources. Extending the time available for teacher education carries with it an obligation for substantive reform. However, we do believe that inadequate time and resources for initial teacher preparation have created an educational system founded on a deficiency assumption.

Minimal Professional Requirements

Examining the history of teacher education, we find an overall pattern of evolution: As the importance of education to individuals and to society grew, and as society demanded more of teachers, the length and rigor of preservice teacher education increased. In the United States, teacher education developed until, in the first half of this century, it fit into one of the established patterns of education: the four-year undergraduate college degree. The demands made on teachers and the level of performance expected of them have continued to increase; but the average time allocated to preservice teacher education has not increased by any appreciable amount in at least the past 18 years, except for the addition of approximately four credit hours in the clinical experiences component. (Compare the results of a recent study of preservice education [*The State of Teacher Education,* 1977] with the results of an earlier study [Hodenfield & Stinnett, 1961].)

Clark and Marker (1975) noted that teacher education has inherited all the problems endemic to undergraduate education: low funding based on head count and an inexpensive lecture format; low prestige within the academic community; and low rewards to faculty members for devoting their time and energy to it. In addition, by being included among other more numerous undergraduate units instead of receiving autonomy as a professional school, teacher education has acquired special problems derived from its low status in the academic hierarchy. Within the time constraint of undergraduate education, teacher education has to compete for students' time and occupies a restricted space somewhere between that of an undergraduate minor and a major.

On the average, 20 percent of the total coursework required of a secondary teacher and 40 percent of that required of an elementary teacher consist of professional studies (Haberman & Stinnett, 1973). Conversely, for 60 to 80 percent of their education, students are not recognized in any significant way as professionals in training and have no contact with the teacher education unit (Clark & Marker, 1975).

Elementary majors average 37.5 semester hours in professional studies and 11.8 hours in clinical studies; secondary majors average 25.4 semester hours in professional studies and 10.7 hours in clinical studies (*The State of Teacher Education,* 1977). Furthermore, under the certification requirements of some states, much skimpier programs are possible. For example, 25 of the states that published their minimum certification requirements in 1974 permitted secondary teacher certification with only 12 to 18 credit hours of professional studies, including student teaching. Ten states set the minimum requirement for elementary programs at 18 or fewer semester hours of professional studies, including student teaching (Stinnett, 1974). Woellner (1978) listed 22 states as still accepting 18 or fewer credit hours for secondary programs.

Such limited study cannot begin to contain a fully professional preservice education for teachers. Recently, a committee of Kentucky public school teachers, studying that state's requirements for provisional high-school certification, expressed concern over the proficiency of entry level teachers and delineated 34 skills, areas of knowledge, and experiences they felt were not adequately addressed in initial preparation programs—including the teaching of reading, individualizing instruction, group dynamics, problem solving, and early in-school experiences. The committee, working within the constraint of four years of preparation, proposed a 36 semester hour (minimum) professional preparation component for the provisional high school certificate—quite a bit more than the 17 semester hours now specified as the minimum (Harvey, 1979).

Societal Demands: Public Law 94-142

Of all current demands on public education, Public Law 94-142, The Education for All Handicapped Children Act, poses the most visible, most urgent, and perhaps most difficult challenge. The law has already been implemented faster than needed changes in teacher-education programs can take place. As a result, teacher educators have necessarily made only superficial responses to it (Reynolds, 1978, pp. 25, 28). Yet minimal, token responses—including those that teacher-education institutions have already made—will not meet either the spirit or the letter of the law; will not be accepted as sufficient by the courts; and, most important, will not be effective in achieving the desired educational equity.

Some implications for initial teacher preparation are clear: classroom teachers will need knowledge of due-process procedures, skills in preparing and using individualized educational programs (IEPs), and consultative skills for working with parents and resource specialists. Other implications are more subtle. For example, the specific requirements of PL 94-142 focus on individual achievement and academic performance; however, educators cannot overlook the fact that the reality of the law involves a social situation —social integration, to be exact—and a distinct philosophy of education (Schlechty & Turnbull, 1978). Also, most regular classroom teachers are now taught to equate educational diagnosis with norm-referenced testing. To work with handicapped students, teachers will have to gain knowledge and skills in domain-referenced assessment and task analysis (Reynolds, 1978, p. 28).

While teacher-education institutions must take steps to assist practicing classroom teachers, they must also incorporate these added skills into programs for prospective teachers. Responsibility for the education of children with special needs will confront beginning teachers on their very first day. Yet a major obstacle in preservice teacher education for PL 94-142 is the credit hour dilemma (Weisenstein & Gall, 1978). A teacher-education program faculty may judge that the needs of prospective teachers demand an expanded program, but because of state or institutional limitations they cannot add credit hours to existing programs. Thus they are forced to juggle and reallocate hours within the existing course structure, which is especially difficult in secondary programs. The education unit cannot intrude into the content areas without encountering resistance from departments outside education.

Teacher education faces the same situation for such other challenges as multicultural education, bilingual education, and consumer education. We are obligated to make more than token responses, yet we are constrained from doing so by a traditional institutional pattern.

Views Supporting Extended Preparation

While there is no clear consensus among educators on the question, we can cite a variety of proposals that favor extending initial preparation programs for teachers. With the present emphasis on accountability in education—plus the fact that teacher education is no longer under pressure simply to fill classroom vacancies—a context exists in which extended programs seem both necessary and feasible.

The American Association of Colleges for Teacher Education (AACTE) Commission on Education for the Profession of Teaching recommended a five-year initial teacher-preparation program combining the bachelor's and master's degree, plus a sixth year of supervised internship (Howsam, Corrigan, Denemark, & Nash, 1976).

Morris Cogan (1975) has recommended three full years of post-baccalaureate study, supervised practice, and supervised internship. He terms his plan a "heresy" but presents it anyway because "no one- or two-year plan of teacher education has yet been proposed that holds any promise of turning out beginning teachers who possess even minimal *initial* competencies needed in contemporary schools" (p. 213).

William G. Monahan (1977), dean of the College of Human Resources and Education at West Virginia University, thinks that adequate teacher preparation programs will require "at least two or three years beyond the junior year in college" and that such extended programs are necessary if talk about the importance of teaching is to be taken seriously.

Lawrence Cremin (1978), president of Teachers College, Columbia University, recommended a six-year program combining the bachelor's degree and a doctorate of teaching.

B. O. Smith (Smith, 1980) proposed that prospective teachers and persons preparing for other education-related employment first obtain a bachelor's degree with an academic major and other academic work to support the study of pedagogy and then complete a two-year master's degree program in education, with continuing assistance from the education unit during the first year of employment. A third year of graduate study leading to the doctorate would be available for professional specialization.

The Commission on Public School Policy in Ohio (K. Ryan, Kleine, & Krasno, 1972) recommended a five-year initial preparation sequence with

liberal and professional studies integrated from the junior year on. Graduates would receive a bachelor of arts or sciences degree and a master's degree in teaching.

A conceptual framework for a five-year program, including internship, and followed by a two-year probationary period, has been developed by Thomas Ryan at Western Michigan University (1979). In 1976, the Virginia General Assembly enacted a five-year program including a one-year internship, but its implementation has been postponed.

T. H. Bell, Utah Commissioner of Higher Education, said:

> Everything gets makeshift treatment when we try to offer to young people a basic liberal education, a subject matter specialty in a chosen field of concentration, a working knowledge of educational psychology, the basic principles of education, curriculum and methods, and student teaching experience, all in four years of college. (1979)

At the University of Kentucky, the variety of sources that have told us of the need for extended programs include a group of graduates who participated in a follow-up study (Arnold & Wilson, 1976), a group of elementary school principals who met with the University's elementary education faculty, and a committee of public school teachers of the Kentucky Council on Teacher Education and Certification (Harvey, 1979). Harry Snyder, executive director of the Kentucky Council on Higher Education, and David Ruggles, associate director of undergraduate programs, have suggested that five-year preservice teacher preparation programs be considered as a means to "allow higher education institutions to increase their contributions to professionalism among teachers under the optimal conditions which exist on their campuses," while reducing "higher education's attempt to do all things in teacher education through the higher education credentialing system" (Snyder & Ruggles, 1979).

Our Recommendation

The present system of initial teacher education is not meeting its obligations to individual teachers, the teaching profession, and the public as well as it should:

> The problem is not that we cannot prepare teachers, but that we do not prepare them. We do not prepare teachers because we are captives of a simplistic notion that we can train them as teachers at the same time that they are earning their undergraduate bachelor's degrees....We have taken a short-sighted, on-the-cheap approach to teacher education and we are getting what we paid for. (K. Ryan et al., 1972)

Teacher education, when judged by what its clients need and what it potentially can offer them in the way of professional culture, has outgrown the four-year undergraduate model. We believe that the field is backward in not taking the next step to a more fully professional model by extending beyond four years, with the amount of increased studies to be determined on the basis of the profession's requirements rather than traditional institutional patterns.

Accordingly, we recommend a six-year program of initial teacher preparation—five years of campus-based, but field-oriented, preparation followed by a sixth year of supervised internship with provision for follow-up of beginning teachers in their first year of regular employment.

SUPPORTING EXTENDED PROGRAMS

Attainment of full professional stature for teaching is much more than a matter of personal status and economic advantage for those who teach. As Howsam has said, the most critical determinants of quality in education are the schools and the teaching profession. Clearly, schools cannot improve their effectiveness "except as teacher education is upgraded and the capacity of teachers to perform with professional proficiency is achieved" (Howsam, 1979, p. 1).

Knowledge and the Professions

Specialized knowledge and education are central to three of the distinctive characteristics of a profession:

1. The profession collectively, and the professional individually, possesses a body of knowledge and a repertoire of behaviors and skills (professional culture) needed in the practice of the profession; such knowledge, behavior, and skills normally are not possessed by the nonprofessional.
2. The profession is based on one or more undergirding disciplines from which it draws basic insights and upon which it builds its own applied knowledge and skills.
3. Preparation for and induction to the profession is provided through a protracted preparation program usually on a college or university campus (Howsam et al., 1976, pp. 6–7).

Moreover, specialized knowledge and education underlie many of the remaining characteristics of a profession. Both the freedoms and the responsibilities that accrue to members of a profession derive from the unique, valuable knowledge they possess. As Broudy (1956) noted almost 30 years ago, it is immoral to assert professional autonomy for teachers unless they possess superior knowledge.

Thus, the adequacy of education's base of knowledge is central to the case for extended programs of teacher preparation. Is the base sufficient to support an extended, fully professional initial preparation program for teachers or, at least, to support a major step in that direction? We share with Gage (1978), Good (1979a), Smith (1980), and Howsam, et al. (1976) a conviction that our understanding of teaching is substantial and developing rapidly—although what we know has not been organized and institutionalized effectively and, therefore, has not been transmitted adequately to practitioners. Furthermore, we believe the present base of knowledge justifies lengthening and reforming initial teacher-preparation programs.

Some skeptics would take issue with this view, on the grounds that we are unable to demonstrate any universal principles about teaching. The argument is invalid. Absence of universals does not support a conclusion that knowledge for teacher education is inadequate. Rather, the standards for judging educational knowledge must be based on the nature of the profession. Education derives much of its foundational content from the behavioral and social sciences, which themselves are constantly struggling to accommodate the complexity of a large number of interactive variables, some of which inevitably will be unanticipated or undetected. Knowledge about teaching is probabilistic and subject to the variability of social contexts and individuals.

Cronbach and Snow (1977), in reminding us that social-science research cannot arrange the controlled situations of the natural sciences, observed that:

> a generalization will almost never prove to be true in more than, say, 75 percent of classrooms of a type (e.g., first-grade classrooms in urban settings). Such a probabilistic truth is informative, as a source of practical policies and as a basis for insight. But we cannot be content to set policy for the individual classroom in terms of an Iron Law that has a 25 percent chance of working out badly for that class. (p. 493)

And D. Bell (1966) noted that, while the knowledge of science and mathematics is largely sequential, the pattern of knowledge in the social sciences requires an understanding of linkages or interrelationships.

We cannot reject probabilistic knowledge because it supplies no universal answers, or because its application requires the exercise of intelligent and sensitive judgment. On the contrary, teaching demands important judgments in applyiing knowledge to a particular combination of individual and social needs.

A Dimension of Professional Knowledge

In the interest of brevity, we have chosen to review research data only in the area of teacher effectiveness. Obviously, the logic of building the teacher-education curriculum around its data base would require similar analyses of research in all areas of teaching and learning—inquiries relating to subject-specific and age-level-specific concerns as well as this generic component. Similarly, broad principles from the social and behavioral sciences would need to be identified from reviews of the disciplines upholding education. Moreover, as in other professions, the knowledge base in teaching is an outgrowth of professional wisdom (the systematically collected experience of many professionals) and logical analysis as well as research. All these components must be considered in the design of teacher-preparation programs. A major task of teacher education is to elevate the level of teaching practice from the personal to the professional through the expansion and use of research, professional wisdom, and logical analysis.

Let's begin with the logical notion that good teaching is associated with teachers' pedagogical knowledge and skill, as well as their knowledge of the subject matter to be taught. Some would urge that the ultimate test of a teacher-preparation program be effective teaching performance on the part of its graduates, measured in terms of impact on the learning of those instructed. This basis for assessing the effectiveness of teaching performance and teacher education seems logical and compelling. The public and their legislative representatives are increasingly intent on holding individuals and institutions accountable for how well they perform, rather than what they promise.

Other Influences on Learning

Certainly, we must base judgments about effective teaching and teacher education on more than a litany of impressive objectives or evidence that teachers possess certain characteristics or follow recommended procedures. We cannot judge teachers successful simply because they employ approved methods, if their students are not making adequate progress in learning. At the same time, we cannot assign responsibility for all student failures to their teachers and, in turn, to their teacher preparation programs. Obviously, many influences on children and youth affect their interest in learning and the readiness with which they approach school experiences. No teacher influences students' learning in isolation.

Two decades ago, in a classic study of teacher characteristics, Ryans (1960) identified textbooks, prior learning, previous teachers, home influences, influence of peers, ability, study habits, and emotional makeup among factors that, in addition to the teacher, differentially affect students.

To hold that many factors influence learning is only to recognize reality; but to conclude that such complexity makes efforts to assess teaching in terms of learning unnecessary or unproductive is a serious mistake. We cannot afford the luxury of expending large amounts of time and money in training activities that have never been tested for effectiveness.

We should assume neither that all instructional efforts which fall short of perfection are ascribable to individual or institutional incompetence nor that good teachers and effective teacher preparation make little difference. Teaching has always required a capacity to live with partial success while continuing to aspire for the ideal.

Research on Teacher Effectiveness

McDonald (1976a) cited research suggesting that teacher influence in many circumstances may account for only about 25 percent of the variance in pupil achievement, approximately the same as the estimated effects of socio-economic status. He observed that "our expectations for teacher effects should be both more modest and more sanguine" and that frequent research findings of "no significant difference" result from looking for the impact of teachers in the total arena of student behavior rather than in the portion that may be properly assumed to be subject to teacher influence.

Recent studies by a number of researchers indicate that specific teacher behaviors in the classroom, combined with appropriate instructional content and classroom climate, are highly instrumental in promoting some types of learning as well as classroom order. Our review is intended only to suggest the promise of research on teaching for its improvement and for the design of teacher-preparation programs.

Thomas L. Good, a major figure in research on teacher effectiveness, asserted that a data base for the content of teacher education is developing, that it is now in the process of moving from a speculative base to a conceptual and empirical base, and that it is substantial enough to provide content and direction for teacher education. On the basis of process-product studies,

> classroom management, direct instructional principles, and information about teacher expectation effects would appear to be sensible parts of teacher education programs. . . . The balanced conclusion that teachers can make a difference in some areas but that it takes hard, sustained work (and still there will be some students who cannot be motivated) is a view that seems a more reasonable posture for teacher education programs. (1979a)

Good believes the most important result of teacher effectiveness research has been the development of concepts through which teachers can and "will necessarily have to interpret the form of potential applications in light of local conditions, distinct education values, etc." (1979a).

N. L. Gage (1978) proposed that we consider clusters of studies rather than single studies and test for significance in the combined results. Gage, director of Stanford University's Program on Teaching Effectiveness, illustrated his proposal by appraising results from studies of teacher behavior in four clusters: teacher indirectness and student achievement; teacher praise in relation to pupil attitudes; teacher acceptance of pupil ideals in relation to pupil achievement; and teacher criticism and disapproval and their impact on achievement. He concluded that:

> we do have some relationships between teacher behavior and pupil achievement and attitudes on which a scientific basis for the art of teaching may be erected....the path to increasing certainty becomes not the single excellent study, which is nonetheless weak in one or more respects, but the convergence of findings from many studies, which are also weak but in many different ways....Where the studies do not overlap in their flaws but do overlap in their implications, the research synthesizer can begin to build confidence in those implications. (Gage, 1978, p. 35)

Tentative conclusions supported by current research include:

1. Real effects may be expected from differences in teacher behaviors and other instructional variables (e.g., Stallings and Kaskowitz, 1974), but the effects that may be expected—and detected—within, say, a year's time are probably much more modest than formerly thought.
2. There apparently is no single effective instructional method or individual teacher behavior. To expect one isolated teacher behavior to show easily detectable effect on student learning is naive. Rather, teaching is a complex act and must be examined as constellations of behaviors and as behavior occurring in a larger context (e.g., Brophy & Evertson, 1978; Cruickshank, 1976; Dunkin & Biddle, 1974; Gage, 1979; Good, 1979a; McDonald, 1976a).
3. Effective teacher behavior varies according to the subject being taught (e.g., McDonald, 1976a, 1976b; McDonald & Elias, 1976; Soar & Soar, 1976; Tikunoff, Berliner, & Rist, 1975). The amount of positive teacher influence may vary according to subject area. Home environment may more strongly influence achievement in subjects such as reading and social studies than in science, mathematics, and foreign language (Coleman, 1975; Evertson, Anderson, & Brophy, 1978; McDonald, 1976b; Stallings, 1976). Berliner (1976) noted that teacher behavior has usually been studied in the subjects most strongly influenced by the home.

4. Effective teacher behavior varies according to such pupil characteristics as age and socioeconomic status (e.g., Brophy, 1976; Brophy & Evertson, 1974, 1976, 1978; McDonald, 1976; McDonald & Elias, 1976; Medley, 1979; Tikunoff, Berliner, & Rist, 1975) and the impact of teacher behaviors on learning may be greater for some types of students than for others. Gage (1979) concluded that the findings of research to date support both generality (that there are instructional methods and teacher behaviors effective regardless of subject, student characteristics, and so forth) and specificity (that there are methods and behaviors effective for specific subjects, types of learning, students, and so forth).

5. The stability of measures of teacher effectiveness and teacher behaviors is low or moderate from year to year (e.g., Berliner, 1976; Brophy, 1973, 1976; Shavelson & Atwood, 1977), but teachers who are low in effectiveness tend to remain low in effectiveness (Good, 1979b).

6. Individual teachers do make a difference; differences among teachers are substantial, and relatively effective and ineffective teachers can be identified for study (e.g., Berliner & Tikunoff, 1976; Brophy & Evertson, 1974; McDonald & Elias, 1976; Veldman & Brophy, 1973).

7. One area of teacher effectiveness research supports the folklore about classroom management—its importance and how to go about it—commonly found among teachers. However, both correlational and experimental studies are beginning to organize the amorphous term "classroom management" into principles by which the consequences of behaviors can be predicted and salient missing behaviors identified and developed (e.g., Brophy & Evertson, 1976, 1978; Good & Power, 1976; Kounin, 1970).

8. Differences among teachers in classroom management skills are detectable early in the school year, continue throughout the year, and predict levels of student attention and involvement later in the year (e.g., Anderson & Evertson, 1978).

9. The basic principles and specific skills of classroom management can be taught to teachers, and indications of how teachers best can be taught are accumulating (e.g., Berliner, 1978; Crawford & Stallings, 1978; Good, 1979a; Ponder & Doyle, 1977; Stayrook & Crawford, 1978).

10. A pattern of instruction being increasingly supported by research is called *direct instruction*. Employing direct instruction:

a teacher sets and articulates the learning goals, actively assesses student progress, and frequently makes class presentations illustrating how to do assigned work. Direct instruction does not occur when teachers do

not actively present the process or concept under study, when they fail
to supervise student seatwork actively, or if they do not hold students
accountable for the work. (Good, 1979b, p. 55)

A major dimension of direct instruction seems to be time—
the crucial time for gains in student achievement being that in
which students are actively engaged in instructional activities
(Fisher et al., 1978). This fact implies that instruction must be
challenging, interesting, and varied enough to keep students' attention; and, in turn, that teachers must be highly skilled in designing instruction, selecting materials, and motivating students.

Soar and Soar (1976) found that there appears to be an opti-
mum level for teacher directiveness. The common assumption
that "more is better" does not hold.

Direct instruction promotes a potentially repressive type of
teaching if it is understood simplistically and its principles applied
rigidly. Dunkin and Biddle (1974) have documented and analyzed
the ideological confusion of *coldness* and *directiveness* in past
research on teaching; effective teachers must understand the difference. Rosenshine (1979) noted that the relatively formal classroom indicated by the direct instruction pattern does not necessarily have to be humorless, cold, and rigid; and teachers in the
formal classroom do not necessarily have to be critical of the
child.

11. Teachers and teacher educators cannot ignore research showing
that classroom climate and affective behaviors are important (e.g.,
Tikunoff, Berliner, & Rist, 1975). Open approaches have been
found superior in promoting positive attitudes toward school and
teacher, independence, creativity, and curiosity (Peterson, 1979).
Stallings and Kaskowitz (1974; Stallings, 1976) found that open
classrooms promoted school attendance whereas direct academic
questions and large-group instruction correlated with increased
absences, and that children in more flexible classrooms scored
higher on a test of nonverbal problem-solving ability. Research
by Soar and Soar (1976, 1979) suggests that expressing positive
affect in the classroom is important, but may not be nearly so
important as not expressing negative affect.

12. Another major area that research identifies as influencing student
achievement is teacher expectations (Brophy & Evertson, 1976;
McDonald & Elias, 1976). Brophy (1976) noted that, although the
relationship between teachers' expectations and student achievement (the "self-fulfilling prophecy") was delineated by Rosenthal
and Jacobson in 1968,

until recently; teacher education programs and textbooks had little to say about how inappropriate expectations or attitudes can cause teachers to behave in self-defeating ways. Now a data base exists which grows regularly, indicating how teachers treat students when their expectations or attitudes interfere with optimal instruction. As these data become well known, problems of undesirable self-fulfilling prophecy effects should be minimized. (p. 31)

Brophy identified some of the negative teacher behaviors exhibited as:

providing low expectation students with more criticism and less praise, feedback, individualized attention; calling on them less frequently and being less willing to wait patiently for an answer if one is not given immediately; and refusing to allow them to even attempt work believed to be too hard for them. In short, self-fulfilling prophecies occur when teachers treat low expectation students by expecting less from them and teaching less to them.

Limitations of Research

While research on teacher effectiveness holds real promise for teacher education, teachers should recognize its limitations:

1. Researchers are still working to define and clarify the variables of teacher effectiveness (Berliner, 1976; Good, 1979a; Heath & Nielson, 1974; Kennedy & Bush, 1976). Bush, Kennedy, & Cruickshank (1977) provide a good example of work being undertaken to identify factors involved in variables as nebulous, but apparently important, as clarity of presentation.
2. The majority of research has been limited to basic skills development in reading and mathematics in grades one through five (Rosenshine, 1979). In a study of junior high school students, Evertson, Anderson, and Brophy (1978) found indications that indirect instruction may become more effective and feasible with older students, especially those of high ability.
3. The direct instruction model does not seem consonant with the goals of certain types of instruction, art and social studies for example. So far, most research has defined "student achievement" as "score on standardized achievement tests." Only the narrow goals reflected in such tests have been assessed to any extent. As Berliner noted, "off-the-shelf standardized tests make poor dependent variables for studies of teaching" because they lack content validity at the classroom level; correlate highly with standardized

intelligence tests; and are questionable when used with young, bilingual, or culturally different children (1976, p. 6).

Needed: A Broad Range of Teaching Skills

In a study of 27 primary grade teachers who had consistent patterns of student gains on standardized achievement tests over three years, Peck and Veldman (1973b) found relationships between the judgments of classroom observers and various psychological instruments that did not relate in turn to students' gains on achievement tests. The researchers suggested that the results pointed to another type of effective teaching. They concluded:

> ...beyond some moderate point, it almost looks as though those who get children to learn the mechanical, atomized knowledge and skills tapped by standardized achievement tests might unwittingly deter other kinds of learning, creating a subtly depressing, low risk-taking atmosphere that could conceivably keep children from learning to cope vigorously, self-reliantly, and happily with problems of learning and living.

Medley (1979) observed that most of the patterns of teacher characteristics and behaviors research has identified as bearing on student learning appear to be potentially modifiable by training. Teachers need to acquire a wide repertoire of skills and the ability to select according to context. Similarly, Brophy said:

> ...it is a fundamental misconception to equate effective teaching with the mastery and use of a few general approaches. Instead, it seems intuitively obvious (and data from our own studies and from many others support it) that effective teaching involves the orchestration of a very large number of relatively limited principles linking specific stimulus situations to teaching responses that differ in probable effectiveness. (1976, p. 34)

Teacher effectiveness research is not to the point where firm prescriptions for teachers may be drawn from it. Rather, it is essential that teacher education be conducted at a level more advanced than the simple application of technical principles, and in a context that permits practitioners to accept principles as hypotheses to be tested. This conception of the use of research is consistent with a professional rather than a technician view of teachers.

Summary

This limited sampling of recent research on teacher effectiveness lends support to the assertion that we now have enough pedagogical knowledge to justify significant reform and expansion of teacher preparation. Gage (1978), in considering applications of teacher effectiveness research to teacher-education programs, called for more work linking studies of desirable teacher behaviors with studies of preparation programs and their impact on the development of such behaviors.

Education is a profession, one that draws on the knowledge of many supporting disciplines and generates additional pedagogical knowledge. Effective teaching can be built on a scientific base, but as with other professions, teaching requires important components of judgment to adapt performance to situation. Elevating the level of teaching practice from the personal to the professional is vital to attaining genuine professional stature for teaching.

CURRICULAR COMPONENTS OF INITIAL TEACHER PREPARATION PROGRAMS

The education of teachers should be considered to begin with admission to college; it continues throughout their professional careers. Preservice education, inservice education, and continuing professional development are essential parts of a unified developmental process. Each makes an important contribution to the professional lives and performance of teachers; designing one in isolation from the others is likely to result in distortions of the career-long process. However, our discussion will confine itself to components of initial teacher-preparation programs: generic teaching domains; specific pedagogical learnings; general education; preprofessional education; academic specialization; and induction and field experiences. The section concludes with some observations about relationships of preservice preparation with inservice education and continuing professional development.

Generic Teaching Domains

Campus-based teacher-preparation programs must necessarily be generic in nature, directed toward preparing teachers to work effectively in a wide range of educational settings and to utilize a broad array of instructional skills in responding to the different learning styles of many children. To do otherwise is to make teachers technicians trained in a narrowly prescribed band of procedures, rather than practitioners educated to develop an understanding of the underlying principles for the performance skills. In this way, practice can be modified to meet changed circumstances. However, generic does not mean vague; it means that specific situations and examples are employed, principally to illuminate broader teaching concepts.

Common Skill Domains from the Helping Professions. In a study of human service or helping professions, Cole and Lacefield (1978) identified a series of process skill domains that representatives of professions such as nursing, social work, counseling, and teaching consider important:

1. Achieving, exhibiting, and maintaining competence in the academic content of the discipline or profession
2. Cogent and accurate verbal communications (semantics)
3. Making observations, constructing inferences, and distinguishing between the two
4. Using multiple theoretic-conceptual frameworks to observe and infer
5. Showing and maintaining respect and regard toward others, especially clients
6. Value clarification
7. General fluency and flexibility of thought, perception, and response.

Competency Clusters. In an effort to identify competencies that regular classroom teachers need if they are to serve students with handicaps and learning difficulties, Reynolds and a group of colleagues identified nine competency clusters representing a common body of practice for teachers:

1. *Curriculum:* Study of and firsthand experience with curriculum principles, guides, and structures from preschool through secondary levels; the means and procedures by which curriculum is developed, adopted, and changed; and practice in designing and modifying curriculum, especially to suit the individual needs of students.
2. *Teaching Basic Skills:* Instruction in teaching the skill areas; and supervised practical experience in simulated laboratory and field settings, including teaching of literacy skills, life-maintenance skills, and personal-development skills.
3. *Pupil and Class Management:* Proficiency in applied behavior analysis, group alerting, guiding transitions, materials arrangement, crisis intervention techniques, and group approaches to creating positive climate.
4. *Professional Interactions:* Opportunities for effective consultation and other forms of communication.
5. *Student-Student Relationships:* Ability to convey to students their responsibility for the social environment; to manage the social structures of classes by generating cooperative, mutually helpful behavior among students; to develop heterogeneously cooperative grouping procedures and peer and cross-age tutoring; and to teach students to use some of the basic counseling/guidance skills in relationships with other students.

6. *Exceptional Conditions:* Orientation to understanding exceptional children; school procedures for accommodating to children's special needs; the role of specialists who serve exceptional children; and hands-on experiences with the children and conferences with their parents.

7. *Conferral and Referral:* Training in how communities organize and conduct their agencies for social welfare, health, and education; systematic instruction in the roles and functions of (a) referral sources within the school structure and (b) agencies outside the schools that accept referrals; and firsthand experience in how both inschool and community agencies operate.

8. *Individualized Teaching:* Competence at the clinical level in assessing the individual student's educational needs and in adapting instruction to the individual. Starting from the first week of teacher preparation, trainees should be in the company of experienced teachers who expertly individualize education.

9. *Professional Values:* Much more detailed and powerful codes of ethical behavior, so that examples of acceptable behavior can be studied, and ambiguity and uncertainty minimized. School law, and the regulations that relate to it, should become part of preparation for all educators—for safeguarding pupils' rights, for self-protection, and for advocacy when new or revised laws are needed. (Adapted from summary in May-June 1979 issue of *TEACH: Teacher Education and Children with Handicaps*)

Thomas Ryan (1979) proposed six competency areas as a basis for teacher preparation and certification in Michigan: "Knowledge of self, knowledge of concept, knowledge of development and learning, ability to communicate, ability to manage instruction, ability to evaluate instruction."

Still another framework for identifying essential teaching skills, proposed by Ashton and Torrance (1977), included "observation, experimentation, communication, diagnosis, instructional design, and evaluation."

A Proposed Framework for the Generic Component. The framework of generic teaching domains we propose overlaps all of these proposals but is adapted principally from a manuscript by Smith (1980). The seven domains listed are not to be understood as courses but rather as parameters of knowledge and skill essential to the professional teacher and subject to treatment at many points in the curriculum.

1. *Observation:* "The ability to observe a phenomenon objectively is one of the primary marks of a professional in any field. In a field that involves relationships among human beings, objective observation is especially important. It is a safeguard against biases and

prejudices of all sorts—racial, class, socioeconomic, ideological, and personal'' (Smith, 1980).

2. *Diagnosis:* Analysis of student abilities, learning difficulties, environmental conditions, and programs of instruction (Smith, 1980).

3. *Instructional Design and Collaborative Planning:* Understanding of different types of learning, skill in defining objectives, and determining the sequence of instruction. Preparation of instructional programs, materials, and activities with recognition of the need to coordinate such efforts with colleagues.

4. *Instructional Management:* Managing space, time, resources, processes of teaching, student conduct:

With the possible exception of diagnosis, this is the domain in which more time must be devoted to training than any other. It is here that the prospective teacher must be disciplined in the skills of teaching and all the various aspects of classroom management. It is here that skills involved in such activities as lesson development, conduct of seat work, recitation, reinforcement, feedback, assignment making, and student accountability are to be developed. (Smith, 1980)

5. *Communication:* Communication skills are central to relating not only to students but also to colleagues, parents, and other community representatives. Communication demands a richness of experience that permits the representation of ideas in a variety of ways and with a sensitivity to the needs of others. It requires listening and reading skills as well as speaking and writing facility. Many of the concepts from counselor education are likely to support the development of skills of listening, interpreting, translating, and responding to students, parents, and professional associates.

6. *Evaluation:* Development of skills in the techniques of evaluating pupil progress and analyzing data related to diagnosis and planning of instruction. Also, development of skills in administering and interpreting standardized tests and designing valid, reliable measures of both formal and informal learning.

7. *Pedagogical Values:* This domain, like that of observation, permeates all of the other preparation categories:

The central task of teacher education is to provide teachers with a philosophy of education that will help them to think seriously and continuously about the purposes and consequences of what they do. This entails being aware of the value system of a particular educational environment as well as the effects of a personal value system on a school environment. (Howsam et al., 1976, p. 89)

The categories proposed by Smith did not include pedagogical values. In a letter to us, Smith suggested that too often the degree of our preoccupation with value questions is in direct proportion to our ignorance of the base of knowledge supporting effective teaching. Nonetheless, we include it as an important element of our proposal, because it can contribute not only to helping beginning teachers survive in the classroom, but also to developing a vision of what individuals and institutions might become.

Logical Operations in Teaching. Within the categories of instructional design and instructional management, some important teaching operations are common to teachers in every subject field and at every grade level—though, to be sure, in varying proportions. Broudy, Smith, and Burnett said that:

> Altogether one can distinguish some twelve different sorts of identifiable logical operations performed by teachers and pupils in the classroom:. . . [defining, explaining, assessing,] conditional inferring, classifying, comparing and contrasting, designating, reporting, stating, substituting, opining, and describing. (1964, pp. 118–119)

Unfortunately, the authors concluded that current programs of instruction often provide inadequately for improvement in these operations beyond a commonsense level.

Importance of Generic Approaches. Identifying common or generic competencies relevant to teaching in all subject areas and at all grade levels is important for a number of reasons. It encourages thinking about teaching less in a personal and particular sense and more in terms of broad common understandings. The teacher who views teaching in a common context with other professionals is more likely to learn from others and contribute to their professionalism. If the circle of shared knowledge must be kept small, encompassing only those who teach a particular content at a specified age level, teachers will not receive the reinforcement necessary for a strong profession.

We have observed that generic does not mean vague. Neither does it imply a narrowly prescriptive teacher-preparation program, nor is its consequence a rigid, standardized school curriculum. Teachers prepared in programs containing appropriate generic competency elements can communicate with colleagues more effectively, reinforce the efforts of other teachers, and make better use of the resources available for teacher preparation.

Teacher educators have sometimes been criticized for a rigid, monolithic view of teaching and teacher preparation. In reality, almost the reverse is the case. Despite similarities in course labels, individual teacher educators and institutions have been disposed to value their differences more than their similarities, on the grounds that such variations show responsiveness to unique teaching/learning conditions and a grassroots, democratic approach to curriculum development. Too frequently, however, variations among programs seem to result more from inadequate communication and fragmented approaches than from careful analysis.

Specific Pedagogical Learnings

Generic knowledge about teaching is only one dimension of the knowledge that plays a role in teacher preparation. Other knowledge is content-or subject-specific and varies according to the academic discipline under consideration. Still other pedagogical knowledge relates to age or grade level of the learner—early childhood, middle school, high school, adult. As a consequence, teacher preparation activities need to address teaching and learning skills unique to content areas and/or age or grade levels. Let us examine examples of content- and age-specific knowledge for teachers.

English/Language Arts Education. In the areas of diagnosis and evaluation, the prospective secondary English teacher needs generic instruction in constructing and evaluating classroom tests and in selecting, using, and interpreting commercial standardized tests; however, such instruction will not help much in evaluating students' progress in written composition. Composition activities can be neither designed nor evaluated by the techniques appropriate for, say, essay-type classroom test items; and, while there are commercial tests for predicting success in a composition course, no commercially available standardized test addresses students' ability to select a topic, match the topic to an approach, organize their thoughts, select and marshal detail, and communicate to an audience through writing (Braddock, 1976).

The secondary English teacher will have the task of evaluating and promoting a complex, highly variable skill that can be practiced with wide ranges of proficiency. Further, the strongly personal nature of written composition—the close connection between self and expression—means that the teacher's evaluative strategies will have serious consequences if they are inappropriate.

The English teacher can evaluate students' written compositions on four levels: assigning a grade, indicating faults, correcting faults, and teaching writing and thinking (Dusel, 1955). The first level—merely assigning a grade—can be accomplished by a teacher guided by nothing more than personal taste concerning what constitutes effective writing. This level of performance requires no subject-specific instruction for the prospective English teacher. The second and third levels—indicating faults and correcting faults—can be accomplished by a teacher who has learned the technical skills of an editor. The fourth level—the professional level at which evaluation serves to teach writing and thinking—requires the English teacher to know how to apply information about language development, the analysis of discourse, and composing processes (National Council of Teachers of English, 1976). Clearly, to achieve this level, the professional English teacher requires some sophisticated subject-specific instruction. The preparation program must make room for such instruction.

Early Childhood Education. We may illustrate the need for age-specific instruction for teachers by continuing the example of written composition. Children cannot read and write well enough for extended written composition activities until the late elementary grades; therefore, teachers in the early grades might assume that attention to composition should be delayed until children have the mechanical skills under control. In fact, young children have strong skills in oral composition; a variety of instructional techniques have been developed to expand these skills in oral self-expression (valuable in themselves and as a basis for later written expression) which can be used to promote acquisition of the mechanical skills. To employ the instructional techniques properly, teachers in the early grades also need a firm knowledge of the language acquisition and composing processes as these pertain to young children.

A Departure from the Usual Categories. We have deliberately avoided the usual treatment of the pedagogical components of initial teacher preparation in terms of foundations of education, general methods, special methods, and student teaching. Instead, these generic and specialized learnings could be addressed in appropriate courses; for example, a foundations component of pedagogical studies could illuminate the connections between the underlying disciplines and their application to educational practice. As Howsam et al. pointed out:

> The central weaknesses of foundational studies has been the tendency of many foundations professors to look at their fields as if they are full-blown disciplines, each with its own highly specialized conceptual framework, investigative procedures, and research methodologies.... The "discipline" approach is a retreat from what should be the basic purpose of all foundational studies in education: to provide interdisciplinary and conceptual illumination of the issues, problems, and procedures confronting contemporary educators everywhere so that more professional and humane public action might ensue. (1976, p. 87)

Rather than dealing with student teaching and prestudent teaching experiences independently, we have chosen to discuss early field experience, reality-based instructional techniques (simulation, microteaching, protocol materials), and student teaching in a later section entitled "Field-Oriented Activities and Induction into the Profession." We view induction into the practice of teaching as a process that should begin early in the professional sequence, expand in scope and complexity through student teaching and an internship, and culminate in full-term teaching, with provision for a year of follow-up supervision and consultation beyond the internship.

General Education

The general education of teachers should not differ from that of students in other fields "unless the differences represent extended opportunities for prospective teachers to explore the interrelationship of knowledge and their implications for teaching and learning" (Howsam et al., 1976, p. 82). Common faults of general-education programs are skimpy courses with overemphasis on taxonomy, nomenclature, and the use of apparatus—courses designed primarily as introductions to advanced study in the disciplines. Inadequacies of general studies are particularly damaging in the case of the prospective teacher, for elementary and secondary teachers are themselves teachers of general education. Consequently, if their own general education has been perfunctory or designed to meet advanced study objectives, the background they bring to their own teaching has suffered. An adequate general-education program should:

1. Contribute to personal development in areas such as physical and mental health, moral and aesthetic values, and creative expression;
2. Develop understanding and skills in communication and computation;
3. Promote an understanding of the natural and social environments;
4. Foster an understanding of the interrelationships of knowledge;
5. Represent a significant content learning experience.

Preprofessional Education

A major weakness of teacher preparation in comparison with other professions has been the absence of preprofessional studies in the disciplines that support education. Perhaps the most dominant of the underlying disciplines for teaching are psychology, sociology, cultural anthropology, and philosophy; but economics and political science are also relevant. Rather than the isolated introductory courses offered in general studies, prospective teachers need the opportunity to develop depth as well as breadth in the social and behavioral sciences.

Peters (1963) emphasized the importance of knowledge drawn from the supporting disciplines, as well as more direct pedagogical knowledge: "Education, like medicine, is a profession, not a discipline. . . . It can only be an effective one if it draws on the disciplines which lean on its problems" (pp. 21–22). Scheffler (1965) underscored the point, urging that we avoid isolating ourselves from "attempts to formulate principles relevant to our work, no matter what their disciplinary labels," and suggesting instead that we encourage linkages between the social and behavioral sciences and the concerns of schools and teaching (p. 61).

If we seriously believe that teachers are professionals rather than technicians, we must help them understand the theoretical bases for professional practice. Such understanding will in part depend on a strong program of preprofessional studies.

Academic Specialization

The dichotomy in teaching between content and method has always been a contrived one, for every effective teacher must possess knowledge of the subject matter to be taught as well as pedagogical knowledge and skills. However, the standard college curriculum. is wholly unsuited for direct transmission to students in the public schools. Smith, Cohen, and Pearl described the problem:

> To go from the disciplines to the content of instruction involves a tremendous burden of translation. A teacher must sift out what is directly relevant to his work even for the purposes of his own interpretive background. Only in part can the content of the disciplines be adapted to the child's level of knowledge and experience. . . . The teacher should know the content he is to teach as well as that of the disciplines from which his instructional subject matter may be taken. The first is necessary for teaching anything at all. The second supplies a depth of knowledge essential to the teacher's feeling of intellectual security and his ability to handle instructional content with greater understanding. . . .
>
> The failure of academic faculties to realize what they teach in the discipline-oriented courses is not the complete subject matter preparation of the teacher is one obstacle to the development of a more adequate program. Another obstacle is the failure of the pedagogical faculties to define their own role in the teacher's subject matter preparation. Perhaps the most serious result of these failures is the inadequate preparation of the teacher in the subject matter which he will actually teach. Often he cannot follow its roots very far into the disciplines or handle it skillfully in teaching. And he is frequently unable to see its significance in the life of his pupils. This situation is due to the fact that courses in the content of instruction have been taught either by academic instructors who have little knowledge of children, youths, and the curriculum of the public school, or by members of pedagogical departments who may know a great deal about children but little about the disciplines. (1969, p. 122)

For the beginning teacher, subject matter in the academic specialization should be considered in terms of (a) the content of the disciplines that contribute to the particular teaching field, (b) the content of instruction— that is, the subject matter judged appropriate for teaching to pupils, and (c) knowledge about knowledge—the elements of subject matter, its logical structure, uses, modes of inquiry, and ways in which information is manip-ulated and its dependability determined. While the traditional dominance of the liberal arts disciplines in higher education has supported a large role for the academic majors in teacher-education programs, we need to reexamine this component as well as the pedagogical elements. Collaboration between colleges of education and the academic departments is necessary to facili-tate efforts to learn what prospective teachers find most useful about their academic specialization courses (Epstein, 1973).

Field-Oriented Activities and Induction into the Profession

Teacher educators have long recognized that prospective teachers need a more graduated transition from their college studies to full status as class-room teachers. The provisions for job induction in teaching are meager and relatively unstructured compared to those of other professions, and even compared to those of the skilled trades. The person goes almost directly from being a student to being a teacher expected to perform the full profes-sional role (Lortie, 1975, p. 59). A large part of the anxiety of beginning teachers can be attributed to this abrupt transition.

Student teaching has, of course, provided the future teacher with something of an induction to teaching, and most teachers consider it the most valuable and relevant part of their preparation to teach (Ryan, Kleine, & Krasno, 1972). However, the limitations of student teaching are well known. It is often too brief and too narrow an exposure, and its quality depends too much on the specific situation which is beyond the control of the training institution. Because cooperating teachers typically receive no reduction in workload, most of their influence on student teachers lies in presenting a model to be imitated. Student teachers enter the cooperating teacher's already established instructional situation and gradually merge with it; about the time they have some clear sense of personal deficiencies, problems, and unanswered questions, the experience is over. Thus, begin-ning teachers have been made aware of some problems, but alone face the task of solving them.

In many institutions, recent changes in programs have provided a more appropriate background for the student-teaching experience. In our institution, for example, planned field experiences providing observational and tutorial opportunities precede student teaching. Nearly every under-graduate course has a field component designed to supply examples of con-ceptual knowledge as reflected in the real world of the classroom.

Microteaching, Simulation, and Protocol Materials. In the past 10 to 15 years, teacher education has acquired some excellent instructional tech-niques to supplement field experience in bridging the gap between the col-lege classroom and the public classroom—for example, microteaching, simulation techniques, and protocol materials.

Microteaching is a highly controlled, scaled-down teaching experience. The teacher conducts a short lesson with, usually, four or five students, in order to practice a specific teaching skill. The teacher receives immediate feedback (often with the assistance of a videotape recording of the lesson) and, ideally, attempts to improve that performance in a second teaching experience. Microteaching offers the prospective teacher a psychologically safe and manageable situation in which to concentrate on practicing specific teaching skills with continuous diagnostic feedback. The efficacy of microteaching as an instructional technique has been well documented (Allen & Eve, 1968; Allen & Ryan, 1969; Borg, 1969; Bush, 1966).

Simulation is "the creation of realistic experiences to be played out by participants in order to provide them with lifelike problem-solving experiences related to their present or future work" (Cruickshank, 1968). For example, prospective teachers might be presented a written or filmed instance of a common, but critical, decision that teachers have to make; they would analyze the problem to identify relevant, irrelevant, and missing information; forces impinging on the problem situation; alternative and "best" courses of action for the teacher; and probable consequences. The efficacy of simulation in giving teacher-education students a sense of being involved in realistic and beneficial activities also has been documented (Cruickshank, 1968).

Protocol materials are reproductions (such as print, film, audiotape) of behaviors that illustrate concepts of teaching and learning. Their primary purpose is to teach the prospective teacher to observe and interpret human behavior in terms appropriate to pedagogy (Gee & Berliner, 1974). For example, rather than simply learning about the concepts of positive reinforcement and negative reinforcement, the future teacher might view a film of a teacher approving and disapproving student behavior and the consequences such actions have on subsequent student behaviors. The use of the film, unlike field experience, guarantees that clear instances of the important concepts will occur, that the prospective teacher will see those instances and have attention directed to them, and that there will be time to think about and to analyze what has occurred—perhaps even time to see the film again. Research indicates that well-designed protocol materials are highly effective in promoting acquisition of pedagogical concepts and that teacher-education students view them favorably. Although protocol materials are not intended to modify teachers' classroom behavior directly, there is a little evidence that they may do so incidentally (Gliessman & Pugh, 1978).

These three techniques may be called *reality-based education* for teachers, in that they bring real problems of classroom, school, and community to the teacher-education classroom. The neophyte does not have to deal with all of the bewildering complexities of teaching at once. Unlike field experience, these techniques ensure that the future teacher will have a uniform and complete exposure to a range of experiences. However, they are expensive compared to the traditional textbook-lecture-written test format of undergraduate education that is the standard by which teacher education is funded. The extra expenses in materials—films, videotape equipment, specially prepared written materials—are obvious. Less obvious are the expenses in personnel and time. Having students actually learn, practice, and demonstrate a teaching skill through microteaching takes a much longer time and much more individual attention from the instructor than having them read about and respond to test items about the same skill. Observing contrasted examples of concepts takes longer than memorizing definitions of the same concept. Applying knowledge by drawing up a concrete, detailed plan to individualize instruction for a hypothetical class of thirty students takes longer than simply acquiring the knowledge without applying it.

In short, a teacher-education program will require more time if it is (a) based on the realities of the classroom, (b) designed to ensure that graduates have actually demonstrated proficiency in specific skills before entering their classrooms, and (c) designed to make the transition to the classroom a gradual process. Unfortunately, a recent study of preservice teacher education (*The State of Teacher Education 1977*) indicated that microteaching and simulation are now being used much less as instructional techniques, probably because they are expensive and declining enrollments have forced teacher-education institutions to trim programs.

Beginning Teacher Needs. Incorporating early planned field experiences and reality-based instructional techniques in initial teacher-preparation programs encourages reexamination of the role and nature of the student-teaching experience. Early field experiences in conjunction with other professional courses, plus a year-long teaching internship, suggest shortening the student-teaching experience, dividing that experience among several grade levels and/or community settings, and changing the placement of student teaching in the preservice curriculum.

Numerous studies of beginning teacher concerns emphasize their need for help on the job and their sense of isolation from the preparing institution. Accreditation visits by the National Council for Accreditation of Teacher Education disclose a common shortcoming among institutions: the lack of systematic follow-up for maintaining contact with recent graduates and for modifying programs in light of beginning teacher needs.

We propose that a full-year paid internship be added to five years of initial teacher preparation to permit the development of both pedagogical skills in applying conceptual knowledge and a sound conceptual base of knowledge. We further recommend that during the first year of full-time regular teaching following the internship, school systems and colleges and universities join in providing assistance to new teachers on a systematic basis.

With Smith and Orlosky, we believe the preservice-preparation program does not qualify a graduate for admission to full status as a teacher, but rather for an internship in the schools. The preservice program must necessarily be generic; however, the test of this preparation lies in the individual's capacity to apply generic learning in specific community and school settings and with particular children. Developing such application skills and evaluating the candidates' ability to apply them effectively are the major functions of the induction/internship year. The public schools have a major role in accepting the products of campus-based teacher-education programs as interns and sharing responsibility for developing them into competent beginning teachers.

We concur with Smith and Orlosky that, after graduation from the university, interns should be residents in training and that certification as teachers should be contingent upon successful completion of an internship and on the recommendation of the authorities under whom the internship was served. Until then, individuals should be certified only as interns on the recommendation of the preparing institution (Smith & Orlosky, 1975, p. 172).

Thomas Ryan's discussion of a clinical year compresses the internship and follow-up supervision into the first year of full-time employment:

> Employment carries with it the responsibility to apply knowledge and skills to perform a particular role in a specific setting. Thus the transition from participant in a preparation program to employment as a teacher is often accompanied by difficulties of adjustment. Traditionally these difficulties are recognized by the imposition of a probationary period of three years prior to the award of tenure and continuing certification. The system assumes the need for special support during the transition period, but support is often inadequate. There is a clear and pressing need to provide organized support for newly employed teachers.
>
> Thus, a *clinical year is proposed during which first-year teachers attempting to apply knowledge and skill in a specific role in a specific setting would receive systematic support.* This role-specific support would be provided through a coordinated effort involving local eduation agencies, institutions of higher education, and the State Department of Education. (1979, p. 4)

Follow-up of Recent Graduates. The importance of assistance to new teachers was emphasized in recent testimony before Congress. Pat Weiler, director of the Teacher Center Resource Exchange, American Federation of Teachers, proposed that a new section be added to Teacher Corps legislation to provide funds for support for beginning teachers. The funds would be used for released time for consultation, work with experienced teachers in the teacher center, and observation in classrooms managed by successful teachers (Weiler, 1979).

We would also recommend calling for financial support to higher-education institutions to permit continuing supervision and consultation with beginning teachers. Federal funding has long supported such opportunities in vocational education. At the University of Kentucky, for example, the workloads of vocational educators permit them to spend full days in the classroom of recent graduates as well as to offer coursework after the regular school in field locations convenient to groups of graduates.

At the University of Kentucky, we have developed another mechanism for follow-up of first-year teachers in special education:

> Fifty-seven students. . . received from their student teaching supervisor a blank cassette tape that carried these instructions, "This is an S.O.S. tape. I'll tape an answer and send it back to you." Graduates who were near enough to do so were also invited to make a telephone call or to come in and talk with their former supervisor if they needed assistance. Those who were teaching in other states were invited to write for help if they preferred not to use their tapes.

> Of the sixty-four follow-up contacts that were made, twelve were the S.O.S. audio cassettes. Questions raised were analyzed by the professor and a response was recorded on another cassette and mailed back to the teacher. Every effort was made to make the response practical and specific. The response emphasized helping the teacher recall concepts that were taught and apply them to on-the-job situations. Each S.O.S. problem was a specific instance of a general rule. (Morsink, Blackhurst, & Williams, 1979)

Relationship with Inservice Education and Continuing Professional Development

We should make it clear that we are not proposing to replace inservice education and continuing professional development with a longer initial preparation program. Rather, we advocate removing remedial content from them and thereby freeing them for their legitimate purposes.

Although many educators use the terms *inservice education* and *continuing professional development* interchangeably, we differentiate between them to support a concept of career-long teacher education that reponds to the needs of the individual teacher, of the employing school districts, and of the teaching profession. With Smith and Orlosky (1975), we view inservice education as any training of school personnel to prepare them to satisfy a need of the school system. The skills and concepts comprising the substance of the training program are determined by deficiencies in the instructional, administrative and support services of the school. [Continuing professional development,] in contrast, consists of experiences and studies to satisfy the personal needs of the school personnel. Its character is determined not by the deficiencies of the system, but by the interest of each individual in his own personal and professional development and career advancement.

Thus, continuing professional development serves the professional teacher-scholar, who possesses a high level of teaching proficiency; the ability to supervise and coordinate the activities of professional and paraprofessional associates; and the ability to assume leadership roles in school, community, and profession (Howsam et al., 1976, p. 103).

Issues Arising from Confusion of Functions. Some important issues in teacher education result from a confusion of the objectives for preservice education, inservice education, and continuing professional development. Because preservice programs have not accepted the goal of developing professional competencies in teacher candidates to a level of professional practice that guarantees the safety of the pupil/client, we have diverted inservice education from its proper concentration on helping teachers respond to particular needs of their employing school system, and are trying to use it to correct deficiencies in their preservice preparation.

Many colleges and universities, pressured by declining enrollments and budgetary limitations, have neglected their major responsibilities—the initial preparation and continuing professional development of teachers—by approving for graduate degrees a collection of situation-specific inservice education experiences. As Arnold et al. (1977, p. 55) pointed out:

> School systems should not expect formal graduate degree programs to substitute for their own critical assessment of faculty competencies for tenure and salary decisions; neither should institutions of higher education or teacher organizations assume that employer-based programs of inservice education can meet the broad obligations of career development for teachers. Confusing the particular functions of preservice preparation, inservice education, and continuing professional development can only weaken the effectiveness of each.

If we can design and implement a comprehensive system of teacher education with properly delineated responsibilities for preservice preparation, inservice education, and continuing professional development, we can assure a safe level of beginning competence; improve the responsiveness of the teaching staff to school system needs; and recognize and support the career-long personal and professional interests of individual teachers.

A Complex Task

Our discussion has emphasized the need to expand the time and resources allotted to initial teacher preparation and a possible framework for the curricular elements of external programs. We do not imagine that our proposed six-year program could be implemented easily or in one step; nor that increased time alone will be sufficient to place teacher education on a fully professional basis. Rather, we believe the practitioner's need for safe practice with clients is the beginning point for all decisions about preparation programs, including time and curriculum.

Before considering extended preparation programs, teacher-education institutions must decide whether to eliminate or compress any content in present programs. They must weed out obsolete content; they must distinguish the necessary reiteration of concepts for expansion, refinement, and application from the unnecessary duplications. Material appropriate to all programs must be located in core courses; whenever possible, material appropriate to several programs should be included in common courses or taught through schedule-blocking, self-instruction, or other efficient methods.

An extended program should not simply allot more time to do the same job, or tack a body of miscellany onto an existing four-year program. Rather, all components should comprise a logical, effective sequence; and the program or any part of it should be discarded if ineffective.

Other Elements Influencing the Quality of Teacher Preparation. The content and structure of initial teacher education programs, while central to the preparation of competent professionals, are just two elements in a complex system. Among other elements that interact are:

1. Selection and admission criteria for teacher education (Arnold et al., 1977);
2. Performance standards for students in teacher education programs and for graduation from those programs (Arnold et al., 1977);
3. Preparation and qualifications of the teacher-education faculty;
4. The reward system within the higher education institution;
5. The cooperation of area school systems in the field components of the program;
6. Education legislation and certification policies.

ISSUES RELATING TO EXTENDING INITIAL TEACHER PREPARATION

Four-year programs of teacher education do not now prepare graduates adequately to begin the practice of teaching. However, we believe that the current base of knowledge will permit significant improvement, provided adequate time and resources are made available for the task. Many questions remain to be considered and resolved:

1. Should teacher education become a graduate-level program, with admission coming only after successful completion of a baccalaureate program that includes certain specified pre-education courses in the underlying disciplines? Does intermixing general liberal education and the professional studies benefit or detract from either?

2. Does the complexity of the task and the need for ensuring an apropriate level of safe practice require five years of preparation? Five years plus an internship? Six years plus an internship? Some other alternative?

3. What impact would extending initial programs of teacher preparation have on minority and low-income students? Would the added personal expense to teacher candidates (in actual costs of extended schooling and in deferment of full-employment salaries) reduce the numbers of minority and poor entering teaching at a time when we have been attempting to expand their involvement?

4. How much variation in the content and structure of initial teacher preparation is desirable?

5. What is the most appropriate blend of campus-based and field-based experience in initial preparation? What role should microteaching and simulation experiences have in the process?

6. Can the proposed substantial expansion of the field component be funded within the framework of higher-education budgets, or will it be necessary to develop state-supported funding for school systems that assume significant roles in teacher preparation?

7. How important is it that the teacher-education unit be viewed as a professional school rather than an academic department or college? Should a professional degree (comparable to the MD or JD) rather than the present academic degree be awarded at the conclusion of initial preparation?

8. Does the proposal to extend initial teacher preparation threaten the continued participation of liberat-arts colleges in teacher education? Does it imply new kinds of collaborative relationships among institutions? Is it realistic to expect public and private in-

stitutions to coordinate program components with other institutions?

9. What changes in teacher certification are implied by extensions of initial preparation? Does the assumption that initial preparation should bring teachers to a fully professional level reduce or eliminate the case for provisional certification or for periodic certificate renewal? What role should teaching colleagues play in certificate extension or renewal?

10. Would the extension of initial teacher preparation and the consequent need for substantial enhancement of teacher salaries renew the interest in differentiated staffing and the need for training programs for aides or paraprofessionals?

11. What use should be made of competency tests for teachers? Should extended preparation programs be assessed partly or wholly by competency tests developed outside of the preparing institution? What qualifications predictive of successful teaching should candidates for admission to teacher education display? What distinguishes these traits from those assumed to be training objectives of the initial preparation program?

12. What system of governance is appropriate to such an extended program of initial preparation and to the related roles for inservice education and continuing professional development?

CONCLUSIONS

Teachers need to know, to do, and to be. They need conceptual knowledge to explain the relationships between events, actions, and things; but beyond "knowing about," teachers need to "know how." An appropriate blend of knowing the principles underlying good teaching and possessing the skills for implementing those principles is essential. But "knowing how" is in turn subject to the qualification "how well?" "Knowing how to do something is one thing, knowing how to do it well is...another, and doing it brilliantly is still a third" (Scheffler, 1965, pp. 95–96). Our training programs must enable *all* teachers to "do it well" while encouraging many teachers to "do it brilliantly."

Beyond the demands of knowledge and skill is the ultimate expectation that teachers become models or mentors for those they instruct. They must exemplify in their behavior the qualities they seek to engender in others. This expectation is nowhere more legitimate than in the process of teacher preparation.

Preparing competent professionals demands time and resources well beyond those now available. For this reason we urge the profession to design and implement an extended program of initial preparation so that further training to overcome deficits is not an inevitable and immediate obligation of beginning teachers. Although five years of campus-based, field-oriented preparation followed by a year of supervised internship will be expensive in time and other resources, we stress that the social and individual costs of failing to provide high-quality teacher preparation are far greater.

REFERENCES

AACTE Task Force on Profiles of Excellence. (1982, February). *Educating a Profession: Profile of a Beginning Teacher.* Washington, DC: American Association of Colleges for Teacher Education.

AACTE Task Force Report on Extended Programs. (1982, February). Washington, DC: American Association of Colleges for Teacher Education.

Adams, Ronald D. (1979). Western Kentucky Follow-Up Evaluation of Teacher Education Graduates. In Shirley M. Hord and Gene H. Hall (Eds.), *Teacher Education Program Evaluation and Follow-Up Studies: A Collection of Current Efforts.* Austin, TX: University of Texas Research and Development Center for Teacher Education.

Allen, Dwight W. (Ed.) (1967). *Micro-Teaching: A Description.* Stanford, CA: Stanford University.

Allen, Dwight W., & Eve, Arthur W. (1968, December). Microteaching. *Theory Into Practice, 7*(5), 181–85.

Allen, Dwight W., & Ryan, Kevin. (1969). *Micro-Teaching.* Reading, MA: Addison-Wesley.

Anderson, L., & Evertson, C. (1968). *Classroom Organization at the Beginning of School: Two Case Studies* (Report No. 6003). Austin, TX. (ERIC Document No.: ED 166 193).

Anderson, L., & Scott, C. (1978, May-June). The Relationship Among Teaching Methods, Student Characteristics, and Student Involvement in Learning. *Journal of Teacher Education 29*(3): 52–57.

Arnold, Daniel S., Denemark, George W., Nelli, Elizabeth, Robinson, Andrew, & Sagan, Edgar L. (1977). *Quality Control in Teacher Education: Some Policy Issues.* Washington, DC: American Association of Colleges for Teacher Education and ERIC Clearinghouse on Teacher Education.

Arnold, Daniel S., & Wilson, Angene. (1976). *Beyond Panting Lizards to a Fifth Year.* Lexington, KY: University of Kentucky College of Education.

Ashton, Patricia, & Torrance, E. Paul. (1977, May). Educational Psychology: The Crux of Interdisciplinary Field-Based Approach to Teacher Education. *Teacher College Record, 78*(4), 437–45.

Bell, Daniel. (1966). *The Reforming of General Education.* New York: Columbia University Press.

Bell, T. H. (1979, April). Can We Establish a More Explicitly Defined Discipline of Teacher Education in Academe? Paper presented at the Conference on Excellence, Salt Lake City, Utah.

Berliner, David C. (1976). Impediments to the Study of Teacher Effectiveness *Journal of Teacher Education, 27*(1), 5–13.

Berliner, David D. (1978, March). Changing Academic Learning Time: Clinical Interventions in Four Classrooms. Paper presented at the American Educational Research Association, Toronto, Canada.

Berliner, David C., & Tikunoff, W. The California Beginning Teacher Evaluation Study: Overview of the Ethnographic Study. *Journal of Teacher Education 27,* 24–30.

Borg, Walter. (1969). Videotape Feedback and Microteaching in a Teacher Training Model. *Journal of Experimental Education 37,* 9–16.

Borich, Gary, & Fenton, Kathleen. (1977). *The Appraisal of Teaching: Concepts and Process.* Reading, MA: Addison-Wesley.

Boyer, Ernest. (1982, January). Teaching in America. First Annual President's Lecture. New Haven, CT: Yale University.

Braddock, Richard. (1976). Evaluation of Writing Tests. In: Alfred H. Grommon, (Ed.), *Reviews of Selected Published Tests in English.* Urbana, IL: National Council of Teachers of English.

Brophy, Jere E. (1973, Summer). Stability of Teacher Effectiveness. *American Educational Research Journal, 10,* 245–52.

Brophy, Jere E. (1976, Spring). Reflections on Research in Elementary Schools. *Journal of Teacher Education, 27*(1), 31–34.

Brophy, Jere E., & Evertson, Carolyn M. (1974). *Process-Product Correlations in the Texas Teacher Effectiveness Study—Final Report* (Report No. 74-4). Austin, TX: University of Texas Research and Development Center for Teacher Education.

Brophy, Jere E., & Evertson, Carolyn M. (1975). *Teacher Education, Teacher Effectiveness, and Developmental Psychology* (Report No. 75-15). Austin, TX: University of Texas Research and Development Center for Teacher Education.

Brophy, Jere E., & Evertson, Carolyn M. (1976). *Learning from Teaching: A Developmental Perspective.* Boston, MA: Allyn & Bacon.

Brophy, Jere E., & Evertson, Carolyn M. (1978). Context Variables in Teaching. *Educational Psychologist, 12*(3), 310–16.

Broudy, Harry S. (1956, January). Teaching—Craft or Profession. *Educational Forum, 20,* 175–84.

Broudy, Harry S., Smith, Othanel B., & Burnett, Joe R. (1964). *Democracy and Excellence in American Secondary Education.* Chicago: IL: Rand McNally.

Bush, Andrew J., Kennedy, John J., & Cruickshank, Donald P. (1977, March/April). An Empirical Investigation of Teacher Clarity. *Journal of Teacher Education, 28*(2), 53–57.

Bush, Robert N. (1966, July). Microteaching: Controlled Practice in the Training of Teachers. *Communication, 48,* 201–207.

Clark, David L., & Marker, Gerald. (1975). The Institutionalization of Teacher Education. In Kevin Ryan (Ed.), *Teacher Education: Seventy-Fourth Yearbook of the National Society for the Study of Education, Part II.* Chicago, IL: University of Chicago Press.

Cogan, Morris L. (1975). Current Issues in the Education of Teachers. In Kevin Ryan (Ed.), *Teacher Education: Seventy-Fourth Yearbook of the National*

Society for the Study of Education, Part II. Chicago, IL: University of Chicago Press.

Cole, Henry, & Lacefield, Warren. (1978). Skill Domains Critical to the Helping Professions. *Personnel and Guidance Journal, 57*(2), 115–23.

Coleman, James S. (1975). Methods and Results in the IEA Studies of Effects of School on Learning. *Review of Educational Research, 45,* 355–86.

Committee on Secondary Education. (1980, March). *Proposed Guidelines for the Professional Component of the Undergraduate Program Leading to the Provisional High School Certificate.* A Report presented to The Kentucky Council on Teacher Education and Certification. Frankfort, KY: Kentucky State Department of Education.

Corrigan, Dean. (1982, February). Quality in Teaching and Teacher Education. Paper presented at Annual Meeting of the American Association of Colleges for Teacher Education, Houston, Texas.

Crawford, J., & Stallings, J. (1978). Experimental Effects of Inservice Teacher Training Derived from Process-Product Correlations in the Primary Grades. Stanford, CA: Stanford University Center for Educational Research.

Cremin, Lawrence A. (1978). The Education of the Educating Professions. In *The Knowledge Base for the Preparation of Educational Personnel, Yearbook 1978.* Proceedings of the 30th Annual Meeting, American Association of College for Teacher Education. ERIC Document No. ED 148 829

Cronbach, Lee J., & Snow, Richard E. (1977). *Aptitudes and Instructional Methods: A Handbook for Research on Interactions.* New York: Irvington Publishers.

Cruickshank, Donald R. (1968, December). Simulation. *Theory Into Practice, 7*(5), 190–193.

Cruickshank, Donald R. (1974, Winter). The Protocol Movement: An Example of Efforts To Wed Theory to Practice in Teacher Education. *Journal of Teacher Education, 25*(4), 300–11.

Cruickshank, Donald R. (1976, Spring). Synthesis of Selected Recent Research on Teacher Effects. *Journal of Teacher Education, 27*(1), 57–60.

Cruickshank, Donald R., Kennedy, J. J., & Myers, B. (1974, December). Perceived Problems of Secondary School Teachers. *Journal of Educational Research, 68,* 154–59.

Denmark, George W. (1971, May). Performance: Teaching and Learning. *California Elementary Administrator, 34*(4), 21–23.

Denmark, George, & Nelli, Elizabeth. (1980, October). Emerging Patterns of Initial Preparation for Teachers: Generic Teaching Domains. Paper presented at Conference on OPERATION PROTEACH, Report No. 2. Gainesville, FL: College of Education, University of Florida.

Dunkin, M. J., & Biddle, B. J. (1974). *The Study of Teaching.* New York: Holt, Rinehart, and Winston.

Dusel, William J. (1955, October). Determining an Efficient Teaching Load in English. *Illinois English Bulletin.* Cited in Dwight L. Burton, Kenneth L. Donelson, Bryant Fillion, and Beverly Haley, (1975). *Teaching English Today.* Boston, MA: Houghton Mifflin Company.

Edelfelt, Roy. (1980, October). Redesigning Teacher Education. Paper presented at Conference on OPERATION PROTEACH, Report No. 2. Gainesville, FL:

College of Education, University of Florida.

The Education of Teachers: Some Reflections. (1982). The Proceedings of the Second Annual Colloquium on Teaching and Learning. Birmingham, AL: School of Education, University of Alabama in Birmingham.

Epstein, Leon D. (1973). Liberal Arts Perspective. In Donald J. McCarty and associates, *New Perspectives on Teacher Education.* San Francisco, CA: Jossey-Bass.

Evertson, Carolyn M., Anderson, Linda M., & Brophy, Jere E. (1978). Process-Outcome Relationships in the Texas Junior High School Study: Compendium. Paper presented at the Annual Meeting of the American Educational Research Association, Toronto, Canada.

Fisher, Charles, Cahen, Leonard S., Filby, Nicola N., Marliave, Richard, & Berliner, David C. (1978). *Teaching Behaviors, Academic Learning Time, and Student Achievement: Final Report of Phase III-B, Beginning Teacher Evaluation Study.* San Francisco, CA: California State Commission for Teaccher Preparation and Licensing, Far West Laboratory for Educational Research and Development.

Gage, Nathaniel Lees. (1978). *The Scientific Basis of the Art of Teaching.* NY: Teachers College Press.

Gage, Nathaniel Lees. (1978). The Generality of Dimensions of Teaching. In Penelope L. Peterson and Herbert J. Walberg, *Research on Teaching: Concepts, Findings, and Implications,* Berkeley, CA: McCutchen.

Gee, J., & Berliner, D. G. (1974). An Abstract of "Protocols: A New Dimension in Teacher Education." In A. Schmeider, *Literature Searches of Major Issues.* ERIC Document No.: ED 090 144

Gideonse, Hendrik. (1982, February). The Necessary Revolution in Teacher Education. Paper presented at Annual Meeting of the American Association of Colleges for Teacher Education, Houston, Texas.

Gliessman, David, & Pugh, Richard C. (1978, November/December). Research on the Rationale, Design, and Effectiveness of Protocol Materials. *Journal of Teacher Education, 29*(6), 87–91.

Good, Thomas L. (1979a). Research on Teaching. Paper presented at conference, Exploring Issues in Teacher Education: Questions for Future Research, University of Texas, Austin.

Good, Thomas L. (1976). Teacher Effectiveness in the Elementary School. *Journal of Teacher Education, 30*(2), 52–64.

Good, T., & Power, C. (1976). Designing Successful Classroom Environments for Different Types of Students. *Journal of Curriculum Studies, 8,* 1–16.

Gorton, R. A. (1973, January). Comments on Research—The Beginning Teacher. *NASSP Bulletin, 369,* 100–108.

Haberman, Martin, & Stinnett, T. M. (1973). *Teacher Education and the New Profession of Teaching.* Berkeley, CA: McCutchan.

Harvey, Wayne, chairman. (1979). *Study of the Professional Preparation Component for The Provisional High School Certificate.* Lexington, KY: Kentucky Council on Teacher Education and Certification Sub-Committee.

Hawkins, David. (1976). Liberal Education: A Modest Polemic. In Ed Rose (Ed.), *Forms and Formulations of Education.* Lincoln, NE: Study Commission on Undergraduate Education and the Education of Teachers, University of Nebraska.

Heath, Robert W., & Nielson, Mark A. (1974). The Research Basis for Performance-Based Teacher Education. *Review of Educational Research, 44,* 463–84.

Hermanowicz, Henry J. (1966). The Pluralistic World of Beginning Teachers. In *The Real World of the Beginning Teacher.* Report of the 19th National TEPS Conference. Washington, DC: National Education Association.

Hodenfield, G. K., & Stinnett, T. M. (1961). *The Education of Teachers.* Englewood Cliffs, NJ: Prentice-Hall.

Howsam, Robert B. (1979). The Semi-Profession Assumption. Paper presented to the Forum of Educational Organization leaders, Arlington, Virginia.

Howsam, Robert. (1981, November). The Trouble with Teacher Preparation. *Educational Leadership, 39*(2), 144–147.

Howsam, Robert B., Corrigan, Dean C., Denemark, George W., & Nash, Robert J. (1976). *Educating a Profession.* Report of the AACTE Bicentennial Commission on Education for the Profession of Teaching. Washington, DC: American Association of Colleges for Teacher Education.

Ingersoll, G. M. (1976, Summer). Assessing Inservice Training Needs Through Teacher Responses. *Journal of Teacher Education, 27,* 169–73.

Jersild, Arthur T. (1966). Behold the Beginner. In *The Real World of the Beginning Teacher.* Report of the 19th National TEPS Conference, Washington, DC: National Education Association.

Kennedy, John J., & Bush, Andrew J. (1976, Spring). Overcoming Some Impediments, *Journal of Teacher Education, 27*(1), 14–17.

Kennedy, J. J., Cruickshank, D. R., & Myers, B. (1976, January). Problems of Beginning Secondary Teachers in Relation to School Location. *Journal of Educational Research, 69,* 167–72.

Kounin, J. (1970). *Discipline and Group Management in Classrooms.* NY: Holt, Rinehart, and Winston.

Ladd, Edward T. (1966). Interpretation and Perspectives. In *The Real World of the Beginning Teacher.* Report of the 19th National TEPS Conference. Washington, DC: National Education Association.

Lindsey, Margaret. (1973). Curricular Developments. In Donald J. McCarty (Ed.), *New Perspectives in Teacher Education.* San Francisco, CA: Jossey-Bass.

Lortie, Dan C. (1975). *Schoolteacher: A Sociological Study.* Chicago, IL: University of Chicago Press.

McDonald, Frederick J. (1976a). Report on Phase II of Beginning Teacher Evaluation Study. *Journal of Teacher Education, 27*(1), 39–42.

McDonald, Frederick J. (1976b). The Effects of Teaching Performance on Pupil Learning. *Journal of Teacher Education, 27*(4), 317–19.

McDonald, F. J., and Elias, P. (1976). The Effects of Teaching Performance on Pupil Learning. Beginning Teacher Evaluation Study, Phase II, 1973–1974, Final Report: Vol. I. Princeton, NJ: Educational Testing Service. ERIC Document No. ED 127 364.

Mackey, James A., Glenn, Allen D., & Lewis, Darrell R. (1977, July). The Effectiveness of Teacher Education. *Peabody Journal of Education, 54*(4), 231–238.

Medley, Donald M. (1979). The Effectiveness of Teachers. In Penelope L. Peterson and Herbert J. Walberg, *Research on Teaching: Concepts, Findings, and Implications.* Berkeley, CA: McCutchan.

Monahan, William G. (1977, December). Some Straight-Talk About Teacher Preparation. *Educational Leadership, 35,* 202–204.

Morsink, Catherine V., Blackhurst, A. Edward, & Williams, Sharon. (1979, March). Follow-up Support to Beginning LD Teachers. *Journal of Learning Disabilities, 12,* 150–54.

National Council of Teachers of English (NCTE). (1976). *A Statement on the Preparation of Teachers of English and the Language Arts.* Urbana, IL: NCTE.

The National Support Systems Project. (1980). *A Common Body of Practice for Teachers: The Challenge of Public Law 94-142 to Teacher Education.* Washington, DC: American Association of Colleges for Teacher Education.

Nelli, Elizabeth. (1981, Nov.–Dec.). Program Redesign in Teacher Preparation. *Journal of Teacher Education, 32*(6), 39–42.

Peck, Robert F., & Veldman, D. J. (1973a). Effects of Teacher Characteristics on Cognitive and Affective Gains of Pupils. Austin, TX: University of Texas Research and Development Center for Teacher Education.

Peck, Robert F., & Veldman, D. J. (1973b). Personal Characteristics Associated with Effective Teaching. Austin, TX: University of Texas Research and Development Center for Teacher Education.

Peters, R. S. (1963). Comments (on a paper by John Walton). In John Walton and James L. Kuethe (Eds.), *The Discipline of Education.* Madison, WI: University of Wisconsin Press.

Peterson, Penelope L. (1979). Direct Instruction Reconsidered. In Penelope L. Peterson and Herbert J. Walberg. *Research in Teaching: Concepts, Findings, and Implications.* Berkeley, CA: McCutchan.

Pigge, Fred L. (1978, July/August). Teacher Competencies: Need, Proficiency, and Where Proficiency Was Developed. *Journal of Teacher Education, 29,* 70–76.

Ponder, Gerald, & Doyle, Walter. (1977, April). Teacher Practicality and Curriculum Change: An Ecological Analysis. Paper presented at annual meeting of American Education Research Association.

Reynolds, Maynard. (1978, November/December). Basic Issues in Restructuring Teacher Education. *Journal of Teacher Education, 29*(6), 25–29.

Robinson, Sharon. (1981, May). Preparation for Teaching: Making It Relevant. Paper presented at the CTF/NEA/WCOTP North American Conference, Philadelphia, PA.

Rosenshine, B. (1979). Content, Time, and Direct Instruction. In Penelope L. Peterson and Herbert J. Walberg, *Research on Teaching: Concepts, Findings, and Implications.* Berkeley, CA: McCutchan.

Rosenshine, B. (1976, Spring). Recent Research on Teaching Behaviors and Student Achievement. *Journal of Teacher Education 27*(1): 61–64.

Rosenthal, Robert, & Jacobson, L. (1968). *Pygmalion in the Classroom: Teacher Expectation and Pupils' Intellectual Development.* NY: Holt, Rinehart, and Winston.

Ryan, K., Kleine, P., & Krasno, R. (1972). Preservice Preparation—Too Little for Too Many. In *Realities and Revolution in Teacher Education.* Report #6 of the Commission on Public School Personnel Policy in Ohio. Cleveland, OH: Greater Cleveland Associated Foundation.

Ryan, Thomas F. (1979). A Conceptual Framework for Teacher Preparation and Professional Development in Michigan. Unpublished manuscript, Western Michigan University.

Ryans, D. C. (1960). *Characteristics of Teachers: Their Description, Comparison, and Appraisal.* Washington, DC: American Council on Education.

Scannell, Dale P., & Guenther, John E. "The Development of an Extended Program." *Journal of Teacher Education, 32* (1), 7-12; Jan.-Feb. 1981.

Scheffler, Israel. (1963). In John Walton and James L. Kuethe (Eds.), *The Discipline of Education.* Madison, WI: University of Wisconsin Press.

Scheffler, Israel. (1965). *Conditions of Knowledge: An Introduction to Epistemology and Education.* Chicago, IL: Scott-Foresman.

Schlechty, Phillip C., & Turnbull, Ann P. (1978, November/December). Bureaucracy of Professionalism: Implications of P. L. 94-142. *Journal of Teacher Education, 29*(6), 34–36.

Shavelson, Richard, & Atwood, Nancy. (1977). Generalizability of Measures of the Teaching Process. In Gary Borich and Kathleen Fenton, *The Appraisal of Teaching: Concepts and Process.* Reading, MA: Addison-Wesley.

Smith, B. Othanel. (1976). On the Content of Teacher Education. Paper presented at the Conference on Research in Teacher Effects, University of Texas, Austin.

Smith, B. Othanel. (1980). *A Design for a School of Pedagogy.* Washington, DC: U.S. Department of Education.

Smith, B. Othanel, Cohen, Saul B., & Pearl, Arthur. (1969). *Teachers for the Real World.* Washington, DC: American Association of Colleges for Teacher Education.

Smith, B. Othanel, & Orlosky, Donald. (1975). *Socialization and Schooling: The Basics of Reform.* Bloomington, IN: Phi Delta Kappa.

Snyder, Harry M., & Ruggles, David P. (1979, April). Is It Time for a Fifth Year for Teacher Education? *Issues in Education: Educator's Service Newsletter* (Western Kentucky University College of Education), *5*(1).

Soar, Robert S., & Soar, Ruth M. (1976, Fall). An Attempt To Identify Measures of Teacher Effectiveness from Four Studies. *Journal of Teacher Education, 27* (3), 261.

Soar, Robert S., & Soar, Ruth M. (1979). Emotional Climate and Management. In Penelope L. Peterson and Herbert J. Walberg, *Research in Teaching: Concepts, Findings, and Implications.* Berkeley, CA: McCutchan.

Stallings, Jane A. (1976, Spring). How Instructional Processes Relate to Child Outcomes in a National Study of Follow Through. *Journal of Teacher Education, 27*(1), 43–47.

Stallings, Jane, & Kaskowitz, David. (1974). *Follow-Through Classroom Observation Evaluation, 1972–1973.* Office of Education Contract, OEC-0-8522480-4633 (100).

The State of Teacher Education 1977. (1977). Lewin and Associates, Inc., National Center for Education Statistics. A Summary of the National Survey of the Preservice Preparation of Teachers. Washington, DC: National Center for Education Statistics.

Stayrook, N., & Crawford, J. (1978). An Experiment on Teacher Effectiveness and Parent-Assisted Instruction in the Third Grade: The Observational Data. Stanford, CA: Stanford University School of Education, Center for Educational Research at Stanford. ERIC Document No. ED 160-648.

Stinnett, T. M. (1974). *A Manual on Standards Affecting School Personnel in the*

United States. Washington, DC: ERIC Document No.: ED 097-335.

Teacher Education Conference Board. (1981). *The Effective Teacher.* Albany, NY: Teacher Education Conference Board.

Tikunoff, W., Berliner, D., & Rist, R. (1975). An Ethnographic Study of the Beginning Teacher Education Study Known Sample, Technical Report No. 75-10 5, Special Study A. San Francisco, CA: Far West Laboratory for Educational Research and Development.

Turner, Richard L. (1975). An Overview of Research in Teacher Education. In *Teacher Education: Seventy-Fourth Yearbook of the National Society for the Study of Education, Part II.* Chicago, IL: University of Chicago Press.

Veldman, Donald J., & Brophy, Jere E. (1973). Measuring Teacher Effects on Pupil Achievement. Paper presented at symposium of annual meeting of American Educational Research Association.

Weiler, Pat. (1979, May 25). Testimony for American Federation of Teachers before the U.S. House of Representatives, Subcommittee on Postsecondary Education, for Reauthorization of Higher Education Act, Title V. Detroit, MI.

Weisenstein, Greg R., & Meredith D. Gall. (1978, November/December). Adapting Teacher Education To Include Mainstreaming: Deans' Grants Projects. *Journal of Teacher Education, 29* (6), 22–24.

What Competencies Do Regular Classroom Teachers Need? (1979, May/June). *TEACH: Teacher Education and Children with Handicaps, 1* (3), 3.

Woellner, Elizabeth H. (1977–1978). *Requirements for Certification for Elementary Schools, Secondary Schools, Junior Colleges.* 42nd edition. Chicago, IL: University of Chicago Press.

Author Index

Italic page numbers indicate bibliographic citations.

Subject Index

U

Uncertainty, learned, 40–45
Understanding. *See* Knowledge
University
    preparation of teachers at, 1–8
    service of teacher educator to, 138–139

V

Values, 80–81, 224–225
Videotapes to assess perceptual skills, 84–85

View of classroom life, 37–39
Vocational choice, 155, 158

W

Weiler, L., 180